NEW CASEBOOKS

POETRY

WILLIAM BLAKE Edited by David Punter
CHAUCER Edited by Valerie Allen
COLERIDGE, KEATS AND SHELLEY Edited by Peter J. Kitson
JOHN DONNE Edited by Andrew Mousley
SEAMUS HEANEY Michael Allen
PHILIP LARKIN Edited by Stephen Regan
VICTORIAN WOMEN POETS Edited by Joseph Bristow
WORDSWORTH Edited by John Williams
PARADISE LOST Edited by William Zunder

NOVELS AND PROSE

AUSTEN: *Emma* Edited by David Monaghan
AUSTEN: *Mansfield Park* and *Persuasion* Judy Simons
AUSTEN: *Sense and Sensibility* and *Pride and Prejudice* Edited by Robert Clark
CHARLOTTE BRONTË: *Jane Eyre* Edited by Heather Glen
CHARLOTTE BRONTË: *Villette* Edited by Pauline Nestor
EMILY BRONTË: *Wuthering Heights* Edited by Patsy Stoneman
WILKIE COLLINS   Edited by Lyn Pykett
JOSEPH CONRAD Edited by Elaine Jordan
DICKENS: *Bleak House* Edited by Jeremy Tambling
DICKENS: *David Copperfield* and *Hard Times* Edited by John Peck
DICKENS: *Great Expectations* Edited by Roger Sell
ELIOT: *Middlemarch* Edited by John Peck
E.M. FORSTER Edited by Jeremy Tambling
HARDY: *Jude the Obscure* Edited by Penny Boumelha
HARDY: *Tess of the D'Urbervilles* Edited by Peter Widdowson
JAMES: *Turn of the Screw* and *What Maisie Knew* Edited by Neil Cornwell
LAWRENCE: *Sons and Lovers* Edited by Rick Rylance
TONI MORRISON Edited by Linden Peach
GEORGE ORWELL Edited by Byran Loughrey
SHELLEY: *Frankenstein* Edited by Fred Botting
STOKER: *Dracula* Edited by Glennis Byron
STERNE: *Tristram Shandy* Melvyn New
WOOLF: *Mrs Dalloway* and *To the Lighthouse* Edited by Su Reid

DRAMA

BECKETT: *Waiting for Godot* and *Endgame* Edited by Steven Connor
APHRA BEHN Edited by Janet Todd
SHAKESPEARE: *Antony and Cleopatra* Edited by John Drakakis
SHAKESPEARE: *Hamlet* Edited by Martin Coyle
SHAKESPEARE: *King Lear* Edited by Kiernan Ryan

SHAKESPEARE: *Macbeth* Edited by Alan Sinfield
SHAKESPEARE: *The Merchant of Venice* Edited by Martin Coyle
SHAKESPEARE: *A Midsummer Night's Dream* Edited by Richard Dutton
SHAKESPEARE: *The Tempest* Edited by R. S. White
SHAKESPEARE: *Twelfth Night* Edited by R. S. White
SHAKESPEARE ON FILM Edited by Robert Shaughnessy
SHAKESPEARE'S HISTORY PLAYS Edited by Graham Holderness
SHAKESPEARE'S TRAGEDIES Edited by Susan Zimmerman

GENERAL THEMES

FEMINIST THEATRE AND THEORY Edited by Helene Keyssar
POST-COLONIAL LITERATURES Edited by Michael Parker

New Casebooks Series
Series Standing Order
ISBN 0–333–71702–3 hardcover
ISBN 0–333–69345–0 paperback
(outside North America only)

You can receive future titles in this series as they are published by placing a standing order. Please contact your bookseller or, in case of difficulty, write to us at the address below with your name and address, the title of the series and the ISBN quoted above.

Customer Services Department, Macmillan Distribution Ltd
Houndmills, Basingstoke, Hampshire RG21 6XS, England

New Casebooks

SHAKESPEARE'S HISTORY PLAYS: *RICHARD II* to *HENRY V*

WILLIAM SHAKESPEARE

EDITED BY GRAHAM HOLDERNESS

First published 1992 by
MACMILLAN PRESS LTD
Houndmills, Basingstoke, Hampshire RG21 6XS
and London
Companies and representatives
throughout the world

ISBN 0–333–54901–5 hardcover
ISBN 0–333–54902–3 paperback

A catalogue record for this book is available
from the British Library.

This book is printed on paper suitable for recycling and
made from fully managed and sustained forest sources.

10   9   8   7   6   5   4
03   02   01   00   99

Printed in Hong Kong

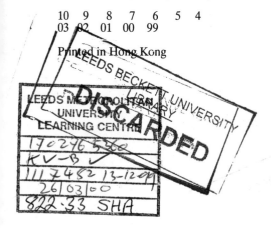

Contents

Acknowledgements

The editor and publishers wish to thank the following for permission to use copyright material:

Linda Bamber, extracts from *Comic Women, Tragic Men: A Study of Gender and Genre in Shakespeare* (1982), by permission of Stanford University Press;

Catherine Belsey, extracts from 'Making Histories Then and Now: Shakespeare from *Richard II* to *Henry IV*' in Francis Barker, Peter Hulme and Margaret Iverson (eds), *The Uses of History: Marxism, Postmodernism and the Renaissance* (1991), by permission of Manchester University Press;

James L. Calderwood, extracts from *Metadrama in Shakespeare's Henriad* (1979), by permission of University of California Press. Copyright © 1979 The Regents of the University of California;

Derek Cohen, extract, '*Henry IV*: Carnival and History' from *Shakespearean Motives* (1988), by permission of Macmillan Ltd and St. Martin's Press, Inc.;

Jonathan Dollimore and Alan Sinfield, for extracts from 'History and Ideology: the Instance of *Henry V*' in John Drakakis (ed.), *Alternative Shakespeares* (1985), Methuen and Co., by permission of Routledge;

Graham Holderness, extracts from *Shakespeare's History* (1985), Gill and Macmillan, by permission of the author;

Coppélia Kahn, extracts from *Man's Estate: Masculine Identity in Shakespeare* (1981), by permission of University of California Press. Copyright © 1981 The Regents of the University of California;

Robert S. Knapp, extracts from *Shakespeare: The Theatre and the Book* (1989), by permission of Princeton University Press;

Robert Ornstein, extracts from *A Kingdom for a Stage: The Achievement of Shakespeare's History Plays* (1972), Harvard University Press, by permission of the author and Arden Press, Cleveland, Ohio;

Annabel Patterson, extracts from *Shakespeare and the Popular Voice* (1989), by permission of Basil Blackwell Ltd;

Leonard Tennenhouse, extracts from 'Rituals of State: History and the Elizabethan Strategies of Power' from *Power on Display* (1986) Methuen and Co., by permission of Routledge.

Every effort has been made to trace all the copyright holders but if any have been inadvertently overlooked the publishers will be pleased to make the necessary arrangement at the first opportunity.

General Editors' Preface

The purpose of this new series of Casebooks is to reveal some of the ways in which contemporary criticism has changed our understanding of commonly studied texts and writers and, indeed, of the nature of criticism itself. Central to the series is a concern with modern critical theory and its effect on current approaches to the study of literature. Each New Casebook editor has been asked to select a sequence of essays which will introduce the reader to the new critical approaches to the text or texts being discussed in the volume and also illuminate the rich interchange between critical theory and critical practice that characterises so much current writing about literature.

The series itself, of course, grows out of the original Casebook series edited by A. E. Dyson. The original volumes provide readers with a range of critical opinions extending from the first reception of a work through to the criticism of the twentieth century. By contrast, the focus of the New Casebooks is on modern critical thinking and practice, with the volumes seeking to reflect both the controversy and the excitement of current criticism. Because much of this criticism is difficult and often employs an unfamiliar critical language, editors have been asked to give the reader as much help as they feel is appropriate, but without simplifying the essays or the issues they raise.

The project of New Casebooks, then, is to bring together in an illuminating way those critics who best illustrate the ways in which contemporary criticism has established new methods of analysing texts and who have reinvigorated the important debate about how we 'read' literature. The hope is, of course, that New Casebooks will not only open up this debate to a wider audience, but will also encourage students to extend their own ideas, and think afresh about their responses to the texts they are studying.

John Peck and Martin Coyle
University of Wales, Cardiff

Introduction

GRAHAM HOLDERNESS

Virtually all modern critical accounts of Shakespeare's historical drama, including the various types of theoretically informed and 'poststructuralist' criticism – New Historicism, poststructuralism, feminism, cultural materialism – represented in this anthology, take their bearings from E. M. W. Tillyard's *Shakespeare's History Plays*, published in 1944.[1] That continual orientation back towards so early a source of interpretation is an unusual critical relationship, particularly given that Tillyard's work, together with other related studies of Shakespeare and of the history plays deriving from that same period, are so firmly rooted in precisely the kinds of conservative, nationalistic and authoritarian ideology contemporary criticism has sought comprehensively and systematically to challenge. In Tillyard's study the sequence of plays from *Richard II* to *Henry V* were constituted as a central chapter in the great nationalistic 'epic' of England (an American critic subsequently even found a name for this epic narrative – the *Henriad*[2]). The plays are interpreted as a linked and integrated series, revealing a broad and complex panorama of national life, unified and balanced into a coherent aesthetic 'order' mirroring the political order of the Elizabethan state. The central action of the plays is the education of a prince, the perfect ruler, Henry V, who is shown learning the wisdom of experience, undergoing trials of chivalry and morality, and achieving a perfect balance of character as a preliminary to establishing a perfectly balanced state. The plays were presented by Tillyard as operating between public and private dimensions, linking the formation of a perfect monarch to the unification of England as an ideal kingdom. Tillyard's

1

study thus reproduces the plays as parables of political order, or as what some of the critics represented here would prefer to call strategies of legitimation, cultural forms by means of which the dominant ideology of the Tudor state validated its own moral and political power, through the voluntary intervention and commitment of a loyal and talented subject, Shakespeare.

The general case made by Tillyard was that the historical ideas informing Shakespeare's plays were to be located within a world-view dominated by the heritage of medieval Christianity. In this philosophical (or rather metaphysical) system the state or 'body politic' was not considered merely sociologically, as a particular form of civil organisation, but metaphysically, as one of the functions of a universal order, created and supervised by God, and governed directly by divine providence. In this hierarchical model of universal relations human beings occupied an intermediate position with God and the angels above, and the animal and plant kingdoms below. The structure of a well-ordered state was a microcosm of the hierarchical cosmos, containing within itself (as it was in turn contained within) a 'chain of being', stretching from the monarch at the head, through the various gradations of social rank down to the lower orders. The ruler of a body politic possessed power which reflected, but was also subject to, that of God; a king therefore ruled by divine right. The natural condition of a state, like the natural condition of the cosmos, was 'order', defined primarily in terms of the maintenance of this rigid hierarchy. Since the state was a function of the divine order, any rupturing of this pattern must to contemporary witnesses have appeared not as legitimate social change, but as disorder or 'chaos', a disruption of a divine and natural order incurring the inevitable displeasure of God. The extreme forms of such disruption, such as the deposition of a legitimate king and the usurpation of a throne (the action of *Richard II*), would constitute a gross violation of order, inevitably punished by the vengeance of God, working through the machinery of providence.

This account of Elizabethan intellectual and cultural history as the dominance of a single unified philosophical system was initially developed by Tillyard in *The Elizabethan World Picture* (1943),[3] and then subsequently applied specifically to the functioning of the political state within the universal order in *Shakespeare's History Plays*. Here the whole sequence of Shakespeare's English chronicle dramas becomes a grand illustration of the operation of divine providence in human affairs, with the deposition and murder of Richard II initiating a disruption of the universal order, a century of social chaos and civil war, the eventual punishment of those responsible and their descendants by the exercise of divine wrath – a process ended only by the 'succession' of Henry VII, the first Tudor monarch, to the English throne. The plays are read as offering a unified historical narrative expressing a politically and morally orthodox monarchist philosophy of history, in which the Tudor dynasty is celebrated as a divinely sanctioned legitimate regime, automatically identifiable with political stability and the good of the commonwealth. This ideology is in Tillyard's argument derived from a system already developed by the great Tudor historical writers, particularly Edward Halle in his *Union of the Noble and Illustrious Houses of Lancaster and York* (1548), and was continually hammered into the popular consciousness by various forms of loyalist political discourse, notably the homilies against rebellion and disobedience appointed to be read in churches.[4]

Tillyard's version of the history plays as loyal celebrations of Tudor power, functioning within the context of a general ideology in which that power was conceived as an element of an inclusive natural order, became a strong and powerful critical position dominating discussion of the plays for many years. Essentially similar approaches to these plays were put forward in the 1940s by Lily B. Campbell and by G. Wilson Knight.[5] They were then promulgated more widely to different publics by J. Dover Wilson, through the popular revised 'complete works' the *New Shakespeare* (1953), and through his influential study *The Fortunes of Falstaff* (1964); and by critics of the *Scrutiny* movement such as D. A. Traversi in *Shakespeare from 'Richard II' to 'Henry V'* (1957), and (with a more independent perspective) L. C. Knights.[6]

Constitutive to the release and formation of modern critical possibilities was the interrogation of this authoritarian critical stance. Gradually and from a range of different perspectives, critical, scholarly and historical, other writers demonstrated that these early critics had constructed their model of Elizabethan culture from a narrow and highly selective range of sources, drawing the ideological framework they described from works of contemporary government propaganda and Tudor apology, or arbitrarily stripping loyalist and orthodox details from sources (such as Holinshed's *Chronicles of England, Scotland and Ireland* [1577, 2nd edition 1587][7] which, when examined more comprehensively, delivered much more complex and interesting accounts of the history they were reconstructing.

Where Tillyard emphasised Shakespeare's indebtedness to Edward Halle, regarded as the most orthodox of the contemporary historians, later critics proposed a more significant reliance on Holinshed, or a more eclectic frequentation of a wider range of sources reflecting many different political and ideological perspectives. Where Tillyard asserted that the Machiavellian school of historical research and political science had no impact whatsoever on English culture, later critics found in Shakespeare's plays a secular and ironic investigation of the processes of political change curiously akin to the understanding of Machiavelli.

It is not that the ideology Tillyard described did not exist, nor even that it was not, as he affirms, a dominant ideology. The key questions raised by post-Tillyard criticism of the history plays pertained to the status of this ideology within Elizabethan culture and society, and to its relationship with the historical drama. Was this Christian and politically apologetic 'Tudor myth' really a universal mode of understanding the world in the later sixteenth century? And is it the case that Shakespeare's plays embody and express that myth, thus forming a constitutive element (to shift into more modern terminology) of the cultural apparatus of Tudor state propaganda?

Being in essence a historical interpretation of literature, Tillyard's work was in turn reliant on the picture of Elizabethan society to be found in the pages of particular historians, notably Trevelyan's *History of England*.[8] This dependence of literary criticism on historical scholarship naturally entailed a vulnerability to change in that discipline as well as shifts within the methodologies of literary criticism itself, and to the general ideological shifts influencing all intellectual activity, which as it happens were in this period (at the end of the Second World War) enormous and far-reaching. Subsequent to the work of pre-war historians, historical scholarship researched more deeply into the cultural and ideological context of Tudor and Elizabethan England, and demonstrated that Tillyard's 'Elizabethan world-picture', powerful and influential though it may have been, was only one dimension of Renaissance ideology: an official, orthodox, conservative world-view, imposed and preached by church and state through executive government, legislation and the voices of an organic establishment intelligentsia. Not every Elizabethan could have accepted the state's official explanation of things: there were within the culture intellectual divisions over matters of religion, politics, law, ethics; there were Catholics and Protestants and Puritans, monarchists and republicans, believers in the divine right of kings and defenders of the common law and the rights of the subject. In the Tillyardian view political thought in the 1590s was dominated by an almost superstitious belief in the significance of the political settlement of 1485 when, over a century before Shakespeare's history plays were composed, the civil wars (the 'Wars of the Roses') were ended by the accession of the first Tudor monarch, Henry VII. Yet only 50 years subsequent to the production of these plays, the entire kingdom of Britain was divided by a Civil War of much greater consequence, in the course of which the people found it legally and morally possible to execute the king and declare a republic. The killing of kings, by secret murder or open battle, was virtually a national sport in the fourteenth and fifteenth centuries (Richard II, Henry VI, Richard III all died violently at the hands of their powerful rivals): but the execution of Charles I by decision of the people in their representative assembly, parliament, was a strikingly new form of 'deposition', indicating a new constitutional situation quite different from the traditional late-medieval pattern of aristocratic competition and baronial struggle. Acrimonious debates foreshadowing the bitter ideological divisions of the mid-seventeenth century were already to be heard in the early parliaments of James I, who succeeded Elizabeth in 1603 – and indeed even earlier, albeit in a muted and coded form, in the later years of Elizabeth's own reign. It would be difficult indeed to explain how Tillyard's unified organic society of the 1590s could have collapsed so quickly and easily into the most extreme form of political crisis.

The critique of Tillyard and his school involved more, however, than combating his historical interpretation of Elizabethan culture and politics. It was necessary also to engage with the ideological inflection of Tillyard's own intervention of 1944, and to situate his critical views within the ideological crisis of British nationalism as the war drew to a close, and as the imperialism built on British nationalism entered its last, terminal phase. One of the key features of contemporary theoretically informed criticism is its loss of faith in the traditional values of objectivity in criticism and disinterestedness in the critic. At some distance both from the events of the 1940s and from their historical repercussions and persuasive rhetorical strategies, it became possible to recognise that Tillyard, Wilson Knight and Dover Wilson all found in Shakespeare's history plays a ruling ideology of order because that is precisely what they wanted to find. Their real ideological commitment (suppressed and implicit in Tillyard, frequently overt and declamatory in Wilson Knight and Dover Wilson) was only indirectly to the order of a vanished historical state, and directly to the political and ideological problems of Britain in the late 1930s and 1940s. The Elizabethans, Tillyard asserted, believed implicitly in 'order', hated the idea of 'disorder', and had no use for a philosophy such as Machiavelli's which proposed disorder, rather than order, as the natural condition of existence.

> Such a way of thinking was abhorrent to the Elizabethans (as indeed it always has been and is now to the majority) who preferred to think of order as the norm to which disorder, though lamentably common, was yet the exception.[9]

The parenthesis quietly affirms a continuity between the conservatism of the Elizabethans and the instinctive conservatism of the modern-day 'majority'. Yet the single most obvious shift in post-war (post-Depression, post-Empire, post-Hiroshima, post-Holocaust) culture was an immediate preference for systems of thought offering a principle of 'disorder' rather than a metaphysic of 'order' as the most convincing explanation of the universe. Unsurprisingly, within a decade or so after Tillyard, critics were beginning to find in Shakespeare's political vision a distinct strain of Machiavellian scepticism. Tillyard's traditional patriotism must already have seemed distinctly old-fashioned to the generation who returned from the war to vote in a Labour government in the election of 1945.

Nonetheless, Tillyard's study remains the critical text which above all others framed and shaped the subsequent and continuing debate over the history plays largely because, as Alan Sinfield and Jonathan Dollimore have pointed out,[10] Tillyard positioned the plays firmly within a context in which the terms history, historical evidence, historiography, must be regarded as indispensable theoretical factors in the activity of interpretation. Tillyard's approach was based on a 'historicist' methodology quite distinct from the traditional forms of 'literary history' that preceded him. Literary history presented the history of literature as an independent realm of art and thought, a sequence of great writers producing major works which then constituted the literary 'tradition'. Historicist approaches such as those of G. W. F. Hegel (1770–1831) or Thomas Carlyle (1795–1881) substituted a broader, more inclusive totality of cultural development, in the form of a concept of 'history' of which literature was an essential component. Here 'literature' became identified as the 'voice' or 'spirit' of an age or a society. Tillyard's work embodied a Hegelian analysis of literature as the expression of a common spirit of the age. In some ways Tillyard's study must be acknowledged as revolutionary (just as Marx acknowledged the revolutionary significance of Hegel[11]), since both the critical orthodoxy it established and the counter-currents it provoked assume the historical as a basic premise, and therefore open up the debate for some of the characteristic concerns of contemporary criticism.

Tillyard's thesis was in its cultural moment radical and controversial, and it was opposed almost immediately by critical positions which looked backward to other traditional certainties, as well as forward to more recent critical interventions. What Tillyard was proposing was a particular relationship between the writer and (what we would now call) ideology, which proved quite unacceptable to critics committed to a more traditional notion of art as free from the constrictions of ideology or the determinants of history. Such critics as Irving Ribner in *The English History Play in the Age of Shakespeare* and A. P. Rossiter in some influential lectures delivered in the 1950s and published in *Angel with Horns*[12] accepted the historicism of Tillyard's position, but denied his contention that Shakespeare held and expressed the orthodox thought of his time. Such an affirmation of ideological complicity with a dominant system of thought challenged the traditional post-romantic concept of the writer as a free imagination, liberal of sympathy and pluralist in ideas. Ribner, for example, proposed that the ideological 'frame' into which Tillyard located Shakespeare was far too narrow for his myriad-minded genius:

> What Tillyard says of Shakespeare is largely true, but by limiting the goals of the serious history play within the narrow framework of Halle's particular view, he compressed the wide range of Elizabethan historical drama into entirely too narrow a compass. There were other schools of historiography in Elizabethan England. The providential history of Halle, in fact, represents a tradition which, when Shakespeare was writing, was already in decline.[13]

Employing the same metaphor of Tillyard's historicist thesis as a 'frame', Rossiter argued that Shakespeare's particular genius consisted in a refusal to work within the parameters of ideological orthodoxy: the 'frame' of Tudor historical thought is always in Shakespeare's work qualified and questioned by a supreme intelligence playing freely around the underlying issues.

The essay chosen to open this volume, extracted from Robert Ornstein's *A Kingdom for a Stage*,[14] exemplifies this line of opposition to Tillyard, displaying a characteristic double movement: restoring the status of the author as a free and independent witness to the historical processes and ideas addressed in his work; and insisting on a more rigorous and complex historical methodology on the part of the critic. At the outset Ornstein insists on the originality of Shakespeare's formal artistry in developing, virtually single-handed, the genre of the Elizabethan history play. Ornstein defends his apologetics for the author's originality by observing that most (post-Tillyard) criticism of the history plays continually reaffirms the doctrine of the dramatist's ideological orthodoxy. This view is here countered by the notion of the 'artist' as a 'libertarian' in thought and sympathy, rather than a conservative ideologue perennially 'mindful of authority'.[15] This particular line of argument, though clearly arguing for a 'progressive' against a 'conservative' position (Ornstein actually distinguishes between a 'right wing' of Shakespeare criticism, as exemplified by Tillyard, and the contrary, oppositional possibility of a 'left wing' or 'Falstaffian' approach) is actually in some senses defending traditional values against modern historicism. Where Tillyard weighed the historical significance of the plays, Ornstein insists that the ultimate standard of judgement to be used for the interpretation of an art such as the historical drama is 'the aesthetic' rather than the historical.

At the same time Ornstein looks forward to the preoccupations of contemporary criticism by urging consideration of the complexities of Elizabethan historical thought, and indeed of Renaissance ideology (though that is not one of his terms) in general. An approach prepared to acknowledge the 'diversity, contradictions, shadings' in Elizabethan ideology should produce an image of the age more fitting the self-evident complexity of the plays themselves. Lastly, Ornstein insists that literature should not be seen as a passive reflector of social attitudes and ideas: the kind of writing we now separate off from other kinds of writing as 'literature' was in the Renaissance a positive and creative force amid the intellectual currents shaping the thought of the age.

Throughout his essay Ornstein emphasises the intellectual independence of both the writer and his audience: despite censorship and other forms of ideological coercion, Elizabethan dramatists and theatregoers had minds of their own. Shakespeare's *Richard II* appears in Tillyard's study as a parable of Tudor historical orthodoxy, demonstrating the horrors entailed and the punishments incurred by regicide. Yet, as Ornstein points out, this was not at all the most common view of Richard II in moral and historical writing of the time; and the only historical evidence we have as to contemporary ideological interpretation of the play – the commissioning of a performance by supporters of the Earl of Essex on the eve of his abortive rebellion – suggests that the play might have been understood as subversive rather than loyalist in its presentation of rebellion and deposition.[16]

Ornstein's historical argument takes the positions of Ribner and Rossiter a stage further. Both Tillyard and Lily B. Campbell claimed that Shakespeare's historical vision was identical to that of Edward Halle, which in turn reflected the orthodox Tudor political position of the homilies against disobedience and rebellion. Ornstein questions all the terms of this proposed ideological relationship, arguing that Halle's position was not that attributed to him by Tillyard and Campbell; that Shakespeare's historical dramas seem closer to the more empiricist historical writing of Holinshed; and that in any case the dramatist used a wide range of sources, with widely differing ideological origins and political inflections. The Shakespeare that emerges from Ornstein's pages is neither that of Tillyard, nor yet that of contemporary poststructuralist criticism. His Shakespeare is no loyal apologist for the Tudor state; but neither has he yet become any of the 'Shakespeares' of modern criticism – the anonymous decentred subject and 'dead' author, the patriarchal bard, the operator of ideological forms whose writing betrays contradiction even as it seeks to compose unity. Surveying the process of history with the imaginative liberty and ideological independence of the 'artist', Shakespeare discovered at work an altogether more Machiavellian process, in which 'politics is the art of accommodation and survival'. Like the modern intellectual, Shakespeare emerges from these pages in the guise of a free and independent citizen of the republic of letters: 'Shakespeare was not content', Ornstein affirms, 'to serve as the spokesman for an official version of history in the tetralogies.'[17]

Ornstein's book appeared in 1972. In the course of the 1970s and 1980s a whole range of new critical approaches to Shakespeare's history plays emerged, capable of a much more comprehensive and systematic exposure and demystification of the ideological character of Tillyard's thesis. Prominent among them was a 'new historicism' which offered to reconstitute the chronicle plays in different and politically oppositional ways. 'New Historicism', a critical movement originating in America and strongly influenced by the work of the radical historian and psychological theorist Michel Foucault, and the Marxist theoretician Louis Althusser,[18] started from the same point as Tillyard, with a will to grasp the relationships between literature and the larger cultural totality of 'history'. Where the old historicism relied on a basically empiricist form of historical research, confident in its capacity to excavate and define the events of the past, New Historicism drew on poststructuralist theory, and accepted 'history' only as a contemporary activity of narrating or representing the past. It follows from this that New Historicism dismisses the claims of traditional scholarship to objectivity and disinterestedness: historians reconstruct the past in the light of their own ideological preoccupations and constraints. New Historicism rejects the conception of unified historical periods (such as the 'England of Elizabeth'), replacing what it regards as a propagandist myth by the alternative notion of different, contradictory and discontinuous 'histories' experienced by the various groups within a society; so the history of the Elizabethan aristocracy is not the same as that of the Elizabethan peasantry, and the history of women cannot be subsumed into the history of men. Lastly, for New Historicism there can be no privileging of 'literature' as an ahistorical body of achievement standing out from a historical 'background'. All writing is equally historical, and occupies its own foreground. The texts conventionally designated as 'literature' need therefore to be read in relation to other texts not so prioritised.

These theoretical principles produced an entirely different historical method from that employed by Tillyard. New Historicism began to examine Renaissance drama as a functional 'discourse' in which the ideological conflicts and material power-struggles of the age would be fought out in more or less overt forms. If history is always a contemporary narrative, then what Tillyard saw as the intellectual spirit of an age becomes merely that story the Tudor government wished to have told about its own rise to power and continuing dominance; and it becomes legitimate for a modern critic to refashion that story otherwise, to disclose a different range of meanings and values. If the notion of historical totality needs to be replaced by the alternative concept of a fragmentary and discontinuous series of historical differences, then the drama should be able to speak of diverse and contradictory ideologies. If the kinds of writing traditionally separated off as 'literature' need to be restored to their intertextual relations with other kinds of writing, then new methods of inquiry and explication become appropriate.

These methods can be exemplified in the work of New Historicist critics such as Louis Montrose, Jonathan Goldberg and Stephen Orgel,[19] which shows the Elizabethan literary and dramatic genres and forms acting out the ideological discourse of the time, representing and reproducing the power of the monarchy, and indirectly or symptomatically giving voice to currents of political and ideological opposition. They can be seen at their most characteristic in the work of the founder of New Historicism, Stephen Greenblatt.[20] Greenblatt's method takes its starting-point from an interdisciplinary convergence of literary and historical methodologies. The traditionally constitutive structures of literary understanding – the author, the canon, the organic text – are deconstructed, and the dramatic texts returned to the historical culture from which they emanated. The traditionally indispensable techniques of literary investigation – verbal analysis, qualitative identification, evaluation – are largely abandoned in favour of an intertextual juxtapositioning of authorised literary works with the products of 'non-literary' discourses. Thus in an influential essay on the history plays[21] Greenblatt read the second tetralogy in relation to Thomas Harriot's *A Brief and True Report of the New Found Land of Virginia* (1588), in order to demonstrate that both the drama and the contemporary political document embody the same ideological structure.

Throughout Greenblatt's essays other plays and other texts, together with contemporary beliefs and cultural customs, social practices and institutional structures, are continually thrown into an exciting and liberating interplay of discourses, as the critic traces the continuous flow and circulation of ideological forms and political interventions throughout the complex body of Renaissance society. The isolation of Shakespeare as deified author, and the strict perimeters of demarcation between Shakespearean texts and other forms of writing, are convincingly broken down, and Renaissance culture opened up to new methods of literary and historical analysis. The ultimate objective of that analysis is the sphere of the political: through verbal and structural investigation of a range of rhetorical strategies, the critic discloses the conditions of cultural, ideological and political power, and the dramatic texts become sites for the negotiation and authorisation, interrogation and subversion, containment and recuperation of the forms of Renaissance power.

Thus literature can be seen to enact a type of political discourse. Yet wherever in New Historicist readings literature seems to voice subversive or alternative attitudes or emotions, these are always contained within the dominant ideology: the provocation, challenging and defeat of subversion is in fact one of the means by which a dominant ideology secures its power. In the critical extract here reproduced (essay 2), which exemplifies this approach, Leonard Tennenhouse relates the chronicle plays of the 1590s to other genres such as the court masque, and finds in both a common ideological structure: the idealisation of state authority. In Shakespeare's history plays, he argues, power is shown to descend not lineally, through blood and legal inheritance, but discontinuously, through power-struggles. Political power is seen to depend not on legitimacy but on legitimation, on the capacity of the contender to seize and appropriate the signs of authority: 'Power is an inversion of legitimate authority which gains possession, as such, of the means of self-legitimation . . .'.[22] Figures of carnival, forms of inversion and misrule, play an important role in these structures, since authority needs to define itself as order against oppositional energies that can be designated as 'disorder'. Henry V's mis-spent youth as the unruly Prince Hal bestows on him the oppositional character of a contender, a power of challenge to legitimacy; but the conflict enacted in the plays between authority and misrule serves to clarify rather than to interrogate the distinction between legitimate and illegitimate powers.

The methods employed by 'old' and 'new' historicisms could hardly be more distinct. For Tillyard, order and misrule were simply real forces present in the moral and political world of Elizabethan England. Shakespeare's achievement was to designate and distinguish them as ethical categories, and to articulate a model of their appropriate relationship. Tennenhouse regards the plays as constituent elements of a cultural formation in which state power was producing the images of its own legitimacy, and provoking the oppositional energies against which it could define its own licit authority. Here the critic's own political evaluation of the plays is committed to an oppositional exposure of such strategies of legitimation. Old and new historicisms, however, despite their obvious antagonisms, appear to be in agreement that the relationship between dominant and subversive ideologies within the plays is implicitly an orthodox or conservative one. Tennenhouse acknowledges, in a qualification unthinkable by Tillyard, that this view of the plays as loyal expression of a dominant ideology is not the only possible interpretation: 'By examining how he includes recalcitrant materials and dramatises their suppression under the pressure of official strategies of idealisation, we could identify such a subversive Shakespeare.'[23] In general, however, American New Historicism has not concerned itself with this 'subversive Shakespeare', preferring to reproduce a model of historical culture in which dissent is always already suppressed, subversion always previously contained, and opposition always strategically anticipated, controlled and defeated. This particular political interpretation of the past, in which struggle, resistance, contradiction serve only to reproduce and confirm the power of a dominant state apparatus and a hegemonic ideology, implies in the present a form of political quietism, in which there is a clear role for the intellectual, but no acknowledgement of any other agency of democratic or progressive change.[24] This characteristic of New Historicism has in the past decade become a target for the more politically engaged forms of poststructuralist criticism such as British cultural materialism, represented here by the work of Catherine Belsey, Jonathan Dollimore and Alan Sinfield, and particularly by feminism.

Feminist criticism is a clear example of the way in which, in contemporary criticism, a politics of culture operates in more or less direct relationship with a committed politics of social and economic action. Feminist criticism is recognisably an element in the general effort to assert a feminist consciousness or theory into culture and society. Feminist criticism is overtly political in the sense that it declares its ideological purposes openly, and makes no attempt to disguise the links between feminist writing and women's organisation and struggle. Beginning with oppositional re-readings and re-interpretations of literary texts, feminism has gone on, together with other forms of poststructuralist criticism, to require of its readers a radical critique of the whole concept of 'literature', and of the institutions which support literature as a cultural activity. For feminists these institutions are male-dominated, both in terms of the actual power in the hands of the men who run them, and in terms of the 'patriarchal' ideologies the institutions presuppose and foster. The feminist intellectual who identifies such 'patriarchal' ideologies in Renaissance literature is not only writing about a history marked by masculine dominance and the subjection of women; she is also writing out of a cultural situation in which contemporary structures of oppression and institutionalised inequality bear directly upon her. Her utterance is therefore inevitably polemical, tendentious, political.

The fact that feminist criticism is linked with a 'political' movement should not be taken to indicate that there is anything like party
unity or ideological unanimity among the various practitioners: and
there are within feminist studies of Shakespeare a range of interpretive approaches and theoretical positions. Feminist critics have re-
read Shakespeare's texts with a new kind of attention to the female
characters in the plays, producing what is termed an 'images of
women' criticism. This approach has been used to argue that the
presentation of women in Shakespeare is generally positive and
supportive, even proto-feminist;[25] and also that the plays represent
women negatively, within a framework of patriarchal ideology.[26]
Other feminist work has drawn on the social history of women,
marriage and the family in the Renaissance, debating the role of
Shakespeare's drama within a process of general change.[27] Much
American feminist criticism has based its explorations in psycho-
analytical theories of gender and sexuality, interpreting the texts as
paradigms of masculine anxiety and female subjection. Some of the
most advanced and difficult feminist work has developed along this
line, synthesising psychoanalysis with deconstructionist studies in
language.[28]

Two of the pioneers of feminist Shakespeare criticism, Linda
Bamber and Coppélia Kahn, in their respective discussions of the
history plays (essays 3 and 4), offered interestingly divergent accounts of the relations between femininity, masculinity and history in
the second tetralogy. For Bamber, there can be no dialectical relation
here between femininity and history, since history is a grand narrative of male achievement, a 'masculine-historical struggle for power',
a 'military-political adventure', which specifically denies any significant space to 'feminine Otherness'.[29] Those contrasting images of
apparently powerful and aggressive women – such as Joan of Arc or
Queen Margaret – which can be found in the earlier historical cycle
Henry VI – Richard III, do not resolve this problem, since they may
more appropriately be considered as male impersonators who unsex
themselves in order to ape the violence and cruelty of men: though
they participate in history, they do not participate in history *as
women*.

Bamber therefore posits 'a female principle apart from history', a
positive image of feminine Otherness which can issue, albeit from a
position of acknowledged impotence, a challenge to the priorities of
masculine *his*tory. Richard's Queen Isabel is described for example
as 'queen of an alternative realm' in which the female principle is

'fully differentiated from the masculine Self'; and it is only as such that the imagery of woman can hope to assimilate any degree of power: 'Only as the Other are women in Shakespeare consistently the equals of men. Only in opposition to the hero and the world of men, only as representatives of alternative experience do the women characters matter to Shakespeare's drama as much as the men.'[30] Since the genre of the historical drama could not contain a full expansion of this female principle, which would subvert its very *raison d'être*, feminine Otherness has to wait for the genre of tragedy to provide it with an occupiable space. The relationship between 'femininity' and 'history' is thus constructed in Linda Bamber's argument as a binary opposition of mutually incompatible contraries.

In this early feminist polemic can be found the origins of that enduring sense of incompatibility between the Renaissance history play and the priorities of feminist analysis, which has deflected such critics from that dramatic genre, and which has its theoretical counterpart in current disagreements between feminism and other new theoretical perspectives such as New Historicism and cultural materialism.[31] If indeed the kind of historiographical vision produced by such drama effectively expels the female as a significant dramatic presence, then the much more pronounced interest displayed by feminist criticism in tragedy, comedy and romance would be strategically intelligible.

Coppélia Kahn's treatment of the history plays in her book *Man's Estate* (1981) discovers an alternative to this resigned acknowledgement of female occlusion: she is not primarily concerned with the representation of women, but rather with dramatic explorations of masculine ideology: 'the patriarchal world of Shakespeare's history plays is emphatically masculine. Its few women are relatively insignificant, and a man's identity is determined by his relationship to his father, son or brother'. Kahn's theoretical approach thus enables a direct address to the dramatised historical context as a patriarchal structure, the ideological site of a crisis of masculine identity. In this approach there is no irreconcilable split between masculine and feminine principles: Kahn is able to delineate effectively Richard II's attempts to assume a maternal sovereignty over his kingdom, or Falstaff's appropriation of female potentialities, his 'curiously feminine sensual abundance'.[32] The methodology employed is claimed as both 'psychoanalytic' and 'historical': but in practice the former approach is far more constitutive than the latter: both family relationships and problems of identity tend to be seen as independent of history, gravitating towards the immanent structure of a psychological archetype.

The methodologies employed here by both Bamber and Kahn have an important place in the historical development of feminist Shakespeare criticism. On the other hand their approaches have been criticised by other feminist critics who have consistently resisted any divorce between feminist theory and historical knowledge – especially Catherine Belsey, Kate McKluskie, Lisa Jardine and Juliet Dusinberre.[33] Their proposed application of a 'materialist feminism' is perhaps potentially capable of resolving some of the theoretical problems implicit in the earlier feminist initiatives of Bamber and Kahn.

Robert Knapp's essay on 'Shakespearean Authority' (essay 5) is more eclectic in its theoretical methodologies than any of the work surveyed so far. Though drawing extensively on advanced theoretical work in psychoanalysis, semiotics and poststructuralism, Knapp is concerned to synthesise these perspectives with more traditional forms of literary and theatrical history, and to secure an adjustment between new theoretical initiatives and the critical achievement of some intellectuals who (in, for example, studies of narrative, rhetoric and genre) anticipated many of the directions taken by modern literary theory. Where much new work in criticism and theory emphasises sharp divergences between Renaissance culture and the 'modern (or post-modern) condition' of the critic,[34] Knapp's basic approach starts from the premise that our modern uncertainties and ambivalences about such matters as the truth or artifice of fictional representation, the opacity or transparency of language, the power of performance or the illusion of theatricality, were much in evidence within the cultural discourses from which Shakespeare's plays emerged. Drawing on the kinds of political, economic and social history which depict the late sixteenth/early seventeenth centuries as a period of transition, in which such central cultural-political issues as the authority of the monarch, the unity of society, the theatrical representation of the body, and the semiotic value of writing, underwent large-scale change, Knapp finds the historical legacy of Renaissance culture answering readily to poststructuralist preoccupations and methods.

The achievement of the Elizabethan drama, Knapp argues, was partially dependent on a prior establishing of generic codes: that is, the emergence of distinct forms or patterns of literary and theatrical narrative such as tragedy and comedy. At the same time the drama specialised in mixing or confusing these generic modes, and producing new syntheses – such as historical drama, which is often linked with tragedy (plays were often called 'tragicall histories'), and romance, which can mix the elements of both tragedy and comedy. This generic diversity does not, for Knapp, indicate any kind of cultural naïvety on the part of a sixteenth-century dramatist like Shakespeare: on the contrary, it is defined as a form of 'authority', by means of which the drama could simultaneously invoke and subvert common assumptions, certainties, beliefs and ideological convictions. This formal plurality enabled the Renaissance theatre to force, on its stages and in its plays, a systematic confrontation and articulation of opposites – 'presence and absence', 'word and deed', 'text and other'. Knapp's general case is thus that the characteristics attributed to literature by poststructuralist criticism – the establishing of ideological certainties accompanied by a continual challenging and subversion, the invocation of binary oppositions which are simultaneously deconstructed, the power of language to embody meaning and imitate reality in a 'presence' which is then revealed as a slipping, fugitive, not-quite-there, perpetually deferred 'absence' – were in any case characteristics of Renaissance theatrical writing – 'the defining essence of drama'.[35] Knapp diverges from some of his theoretical mentors by insisting that such a fluid, plural, semiotically unstable cultural form was produced by the exercise of a cultural authority on the part of the writer. A deconstructionist critic would want to locate these features of literature not in the intentions of the author, or in the calculated organisation of the text, but in the nature of language, and in the theoretical liberty of the reader. Knapp, however, restores the power of the author as producer of the plural text: it is the author whose formal choices and decisions resulted in a drama of radical 'indecidability': 'I want to claim that Shakespeare's management of the three (or four) Elizabethan genres displays the logically different possibilities of preserving a real – and therefore wounding – indecidability within these variously named but similar antinomies that have governed my discussion – theatre and book, symbol and function, cognitive and performative, non-natural and natural, metaphor and metonym, word and deed.'[36]

The second tetralogy begins, in Knapp's reading, with the historical conflict over the king's 'two bodies'[37] – was the king a single, unitary presence whose body formed part of the divine power of kingship; or was it rather possible to divide the royal 'body natural', the character of a particular king or queen, from the immortal body of the royal state or 'crown'? The former would suggest that the king is untouchable, since an injury to him would damage the metaphysical fabric of the monarchy itself. The latter would suggest, taken to its logical conclusion, that a 'bad' king could be removed from the royal office by deposition or destruction of his natural body, without harming the royalty of the state; and that that royalty could then be restored by the insertion into the body politic of another 'natural body', another king. *Richard II* begins also, however, in this reading, with another conflict, that between two types of authority. In keeping with his absolutist conviction of his own power, Richard occupies a symbolic order in which sovereignty is embodied in 'names, forms and ceremony'; Bolingbroke on the other hand represents the possibility of a material authority based in force, 'an authority enacted, empowered, and embodied'.[38] Each of these contenders for authority, however, in practice represents a self-contradictory position. Richard uses his powers of language, his right to name and to stage rituals, irresponsibly and in order to distort the reality of political practice. Bolingbroke cannot rest content simply with the power of naked force, but must claim the right to manipulate Richard's language of symbolic order. In doing so, Bolingbroke discloses the self-contradiction underlying a power that arbitrarily names itself as legitimate: 'no more for Bullingbrook than for Richard does the power to change names and forms confer the power to create a stable reality' ('Bullingbrook' is the spelling of 'Bolingbroke' found in Elizabethan texts).[39]

Knapp's initial reading of *Richard II* thus exemplifies his method. In the basic, constitutive conflict of the play Knapp finds a confrontation of antinomies precisely similar to those regarded by poststructuralist criticism as characteristic of literary discourse. Does a ceremonial display of power prove the possession of legitimate authority? Does the capacity to seize power entitle a contender to appropriate legitimate authority? Does theatrical representation offer the spectator a guaranteed reality, or a misleading illusion? Do the signs of a literary text embody meaning and presence, or tantalise the reader with a perpetually deferred realisation, a haunting 'absence'? In Knapp's method of analysis, the language of politics and the politics of language become interchangeable terms: 'Shakespeare's kings live in the dangerous middle ground between mimesis and figuration, between being the player king and being the specular consequence of some figural pressure or procedure.'[40] For these dramatised monarchs, as for contemporary literary theory, there is radical uncertainty as to whether people use language or are used by it; whether thought is free or the product of ideology; whether signification is governed by the will and intention of a speaker, or by the operation of a structure which lies beyond the speaker and is susceptible to no individual's control.

One of the roots of contemporary theoretically informed criticism is Marxist political philosophy, from which modern literary and cultural studies have to some extent derived their concern with ideology, with social and economic history, with the state, with problems of power and resistance, struggle and oppression. In its purest (many would say rather its 'crudest') form Marxism is a political science entailing a political commitment: a philosophy that requires an unswerving dedication to the destruction of the capitalist state and economy, and the establishing, if necessary by violent means, of a proletarian communist state. In practice Marxism has never represented a single ideology or a single party: there have been many types of 'Marxist' political organisation, and very different types of society have emerged from 'Marxist' political action. Marxism is today associated particularly with the communist regimes of Eastern Europe, authoritarian states that have recently turned away from centralised communist structures, not without enormous difficulties, but to the evident relief of their peoples. In intellectual terms, however, Marxism has exercised a powerful and complex influence, capable of considerable development and transformation. In Britain in the late 1960s and 1970s many intellectuals working in literary and cultural studies would have called themselves Marxists, and were involved in Marxist political organisations. Now Marxism is less a political creed than a philosophy, a sociology, and a method of cultural analysis. In American intellectual circles this has been more generally the case all along, as Stephen Greenblatt has observed:

> It is possible in the United States to describe oneself and to be perceived as a Marxist literary critic without believing in the class struggle as the principal motor force in history; without believing in the theory of surplus value; without believing in the determining power of economic base over ideological superstructure; without believing in the inevitability, let alone the imminence, of capitalism's collapse.[41]

It is more difficult from this side of the Atlantic, where Marxist political science and Marxist cultural theory have much stronger and more visible intellectual roots, to accept as 'Marxism' an intellectual position emptied of all the principal tenets of Marxist philosophy. In contemporary British criticism Marxism is more likely to be acknowledged – along with poststructuralism or deconstruction, feminism and psychoanalysis – as a seminal influence, and the Marxist element in cultural work likely to be more clearly in evidence. It is possible that this difference is more apparent than real, and is due rather to the strongly overt anti-communism of American culture, which probably makes it professionally more difficult there for an intellectual to acknowledge the Marxist inheritance.[42] The work of Leonard Tennenhouse, with its rigorous analysis of power-relations and ideological contradiction in Renaissance society, displays the traces of its Marxist antecedents with relative clarity; and some degree of Marxist permeation can be detected even in so refined a scholarly discourse as that of Robert Knapp. It is nonetheless clear that as we approach, in the later stages of this volume, the work of Belsey, Holderness, Dollimore and Sinfield, that British 'cultural materialism' (the title itself derived directly from Raymond Williams[43], but ultimately from Marx's 'historical' or 'dialectical materialism') is more evidently and openly Marxist than its American counterpart New Historicism.

One of the key contemporary debates in political philosophy is that between Marxism and theories of 'post-modernism'. One of Marxism's acknowledged intellectual achievements was that of exposing and demystifying some of the great ideological illusions by which human societies justify their structures of oppression and inequality. Marxism exposes the liberal idea of progress, the pretensions of religion, the masking of economic exploitation as a 'natural' condition, the disguising of capitalism's violence as 'orderly' and 'peaceful'. Post-modern theory, particularly in the work of Jean-François Lyotard,[44] takes this process a stage further, to a point where Marxism itself is exposed along with progress, religion, nature, as yet another grand illusion constructed and sustained in the interests of arbitrary political power. Lyotard identifies all these ideologies as 'grand narratives' which are in themselves inevitably oppressive, since they conceal the real diversity, contradiction, difference of social and cultural experience. Where Marxist historicism conceives of 'history' as a real process of development with measurable laws, with an identifiable origin and a projected outcome, 'history', for Lyotard, is a fiction designed to confer a spurious unity on a complex process of discontinuous and differential development.

Catherine Belsey's work[45] is characterised by a synthesis of Marx-ism, poststructuralism, British social history and feminism. In the essay published here (essay 6) she revalues the work of Tillyard in the light of post-modern theory. 'History' has in the past been conceived in empiricist and historicist terms, as 'what actually happened', fact as opposed to fiction. Post-modernism renders such confidence in the objective reality of the past impossible. The kind of historicism represented by Tillyard, which acknowledged the historical as part of a national cultural life signified by the notion of 'English history', is usually thought of as an assertion of nationalistic confidence. Belsey proposes that Tillyard's historical myth should be regarded rather as an expression of growing anxiety about the crisis of the post-modern world, in which the optimism behind the enlightenment values of liberal capitalism – progress, equality, political liberty – began to seem newly empty. She traces an early consciousness of this epistemological scepticism in the theoretical work of Ferdinand de Saussure,[46] the founder of structuralist linguistics; locates its defining crisis in the immediate aftermath of the Second World War; and identifies its emergence into full theoretical consciousness in post-modernism. Belsey thus traces a distinct line from Saussure to Lyotard, with *The Postmodern Condition* introduced as the logical culmination of a century's work, dethroning the last of the metanarrative signifiers, History. After Lyotard, there can be no belief in a single historical trajectory.

Most Marxist cultural theorists[47] demonstrate considerable unease at this wholesale disposal of the certainties of history. Belsey, however, finds it possible to accommodate a revised Marxism to the theoretical subversions of post-modernism. Marx's theory of the 'modes of production', which offered a model of social development as a periodic sequence of economic systems, each destroying its predecessor, with the ultimately inevitable overthrow of capitalism by socialism, is now visible as a myth, one of the fictitious metanarratives exploded by Lyotard. Belsey welcomes this revision of Marxism, arguing that Marx's theory of the 'relations of production', a method of analysing dispositions of economic and political power within a social formation, is far more important for contemporary cultural and political theory. Lyotard defined the essence of the post-modern condition as a general 'resistance to metanarratives', a turning away from grand master-narratives and towards what he called *petit récits*, partial and fragmentary constructions of specific experience with no global, totalising aspiration to tell the whole story, or to speak for all. Belsey finds such an inflection towards *petit récits* in the work of Marx himself, and in New Historicism. The methods of New Historicism are identified as characteristically post-modern: arbitrary, self-consciously fragmentary explorations into history which discover no grand narratives, no heroic quests, only voyages of ruthless conquest and suppression. At the same time, Belsey argues, New Historicism, in common with other aspects of post-modern theory, tends towards a different but equally unsatis-factory kind of unity – it is all surface, it fails to acknowledge contradiction, it leaves no room for political intervention. This for Belsey shows New Historicism working in a contrary direction to the emphases of Lyotard, who calls for an acknowledgement of differ-ence and contradiction which New Historicism denies.

Shakespeare's second tetralogy can be read in a way that makes it answer to these theoretical problems. The plays present a particular historical 'metanarrative', but then reveal this to be a fiction or myth, and dwell instead on *petit récits* of subversion, reversal, fragmenta-tion. Shakespeare's history plays are about history in the same way as post-modern thought is about history.

The essays on individual plays collected in the later part of this volume, though all clearly operating within the same theoretical parameters as the preceding general discussions of the second tetra-logy as a whole, are chosen more to represent a range of possible approaches than to exemplify distinct theoretical positions. The critics featured here tend not to orientate their work by means of strategic references to leading theoreticians from past and present – Marx, Freud, Althusser, Foucault, Lyotard – but rather to employ an eclectic range of methods derived from Marxism, social history, textual studies, anthropology, linguistics, as well as poststructuralism.

James L. Calderwood's essay on *Richard II* (essay 7) is part of a larger body of work concerned with the concept of 'metadrama' in Shakespeare. 'Metadrama' alludes to the self-reflexive aspects of a dramatic text, those formal properties that make a text capable of interrogating itself. In common with much poststructuralist criti-cism, Calderwood's primary concern is with language, not as a referential system pointing towards a world of things beyond itself, nor as a system of communication bearing the message of an objec-tive reality, but in terms of its internal structures and operations. 'Instead of regarding language as a means towards political ends, I would find Shakespeare solving problems of language by means of politics.'[48] The central plot of *Richard II* for this language-centred analysis is not the fall of a king or the rise of a usurper, but an action Calderwood calls 'the fall of speech'. Richard's language is 'sacramental', expressing and embodying his own imaginative conviction of his divine right. In this form of speech the relationship between word and thing, or between name and person, is not associative or metaphorical but literal: the name 'King Richard' constitutes within this language-system an inalienable right to sovereignty and power. The sacramental quality of Richard's speech ties his existence to both nature and God, to a world in which words and their referents assume an indissoluble unity, and in which God is an invisible third partner in all the king's utterances. Bolingbroke by contrast employs a language in which the third partner is not God but material force. While Richard claims the name of power without the material means of power, Bolingbroke is content to deploy force without a name. Calderwood sees the action of the play as depicting a 'debasement of kingship', enacted by 'the secularising of language, the surrender of a sacramental language to a utilitarian one in which the relations between words and things is arbitrary, unsure and ephemeral'.[49]

Calderwood's method thus internalises what is normally understood as an action taking place in some dimension of historical 'reality' (whether that of historical evidence or of historiography, Elizabethan chronicle or Tudor myth) to the medium of language as an all-encompassing, independent realm. So, too, is the author internalised into this linguistic action: Calderwood proposes a relationship of analogy between Richard's sacramental language of metaphysical unity, and the writer's investment in a poetic language capable of realising that quality of undivided, prelapsarian experience. The 'fall of speech' is thus something that happens within the art of the writer as well as within the experience of the fallen king and his conqueror. Once the historical action of the play has divided its poetic language into the irreconcilable contraries that lie between Richard's speech of 'divinely guaranteed truth', and Bolingbroke's reductive utilitarian language of 'ubiquitous lies', the possibility of restoring language and history to their original unity becomes ever more remote. The kingship of Henry IV is a 'lie', lacking any sanction of sacramental speech; his son enters the drama in the guise of a corresponding 'lie', his pretence of prodigality and misrule, although his ambition is to restore value and meaning to both kingship and language. As Henry V, Hal secures his power not by restoring the sacramental language of sovereignty, but by establishing the dominion of 'rhetoric, the language of conquest', which suppresses both value and meaning as it triumphs over opposition. The fall of language enacted in the play constitutes an irreversible defeat for Shakespeare the dramatist, whose verbal achievement has no more endurance than Henry's brief reign.

Calderwood's method, though derived from American linguistics[50] rather than from French structuralism, displays some of the characteristic preoccupations of poststructuralist linguistic theory and criticism: 'It is the purpose of the play to drive a wedge between words and their meanings, between the world order and the word order, between the king and the man who is king, between names and metaphors.'[51]

Derek Cohen's approach to *Henry IV, Part I* (essay 8) draws on a body of criticism, both old and new, which applies to the interpretation of drama perspectives derived from anthropology. An anthropological concern with such matters as primitive belief, ritual, magic and myth, is different from both a 'history of ideas' perspective, which would afford a place to such mythical conceptions as elements in a general world-view, and from psychoanalytic interpretations, based in the theories of Freud or Jung, in which myths figure as psychological archetypes. Anthropology is rather concerned, synchronically and sociologically, with belief systems, ritual practices, mythical narratives, as structural elements of a particular culture. For a true anthropological reading, the interpretation of drama is not simply a matter of identifying ritual or mythic content within narratives: but rather of recognising drama as a form of ritual in its own right. 'Theatrical' and 'performance' studies of drama tend to attach much more importance to forms of ritual and ceremony, to the symbolic use of mask and costume, to notions of transformation through the adoption of certain stylised modes of gesture and speech, than more literary approaches which foreground character, narrative, language, representation.

An anthropological reading of *Henry IV, Part I* makes available to analysis a subtext of primitive blood-ritual and sacrificial violence, which enters into negotiation with the more pragmatic dimensions of politics and history. Characters may appear to be motivated by conventional concepts such as 'honour' and 'loyalty'; but they are in reality moved by deeper and more ancient impulses. Cohen shows that the central action of the play – the rivalry between the Prince and Henry Hotspur – can be understood as an action of ritual sacrifice, in which the heroic figure of Hotspur is ceremonially slaughtered by the Prince in an exercise of what René Girard calls 'good violence'.[52] The 'mythical encounter' of the two protagonists is prepared for by Hal's elaborate ceremonial oath-taking before his father (III.ii.124–59), in which he constitutes himself not only as a putative hero, but also as a sacerdotal figure dressed in a priestly symbolic costume, a 'bloody mask' and a 'garment all of blood', preparing to cleanse the body politic by formal blood-sacrifice. In killing Hotspur ritually (sacrificing a godlike hero), rather than pragmatically (eliminating an enemy of the state) Hal is able to confirm and then appropriate Hotspur's heroic qualities, strengthening both his own claim to sovereignty and the authority of the monarchy he is to inherit.

Cohen's argument further depends on a notion of drama *as* ritual: 'the mere fact of silent observation of a ceremony (social, religious, theatrical) compels one into a posture of collusion.'[53] In drama conceived as theatrical representation or fictional mimesis, transformation is temporary and provisional: a woman can disguise herself as a man, but will eventually reveal herself again as woman; a prince may pretend to be a wastrel, but will revert ultimately to his innate princeliness. In ritual (as for example in a rite of passage from boyhood to manhood) the change effected is real and irreversible. Most discussions of Elizabethan drama assume the theatrical medium to have been a sophisticated, secularised cultural form in which ritual is merely staged, symbolic language perceived as representation rather than reality. Cohen argues for the contrary view that a play like *Henry IV, Part I* could function as ritual, compelling the spectator into a 'collusion' with the transformative powers of symbolic language and ritual gesture. In this respect an anthropological reading can deliver a view of the play very close to New Historicist interpretation: in the one perspective, collusion is demanded by the power of symbolic ritual; in the other, ideological complicity is secured by the structural containment of subversion.

My own essay on Falstaff (essay 9) also draws on anthropological theories, though with a somewhat different emphasis. In this account drama is not conceived as ritual, a cultural form requiring collusion from its observers; but as an active and energetic interplay of conflicting impulses capable both of representing and exposing the conditions of ideological unanimity and social harmony. The work of Mikhail Bakhtin is used to provide an explanatory model for ritualised forms of social protest, resistance and subversion: carnival, the organised social provocation and containment of those forces which threaten order and stability. Where earlier writers (such as, for example, C. L. Barber in *Shakespeare's Festive Comedy*, 1959) tended to acknowledge carnival simply as a safety valve for anarchic energy, a necessary release of disruptive impulses calculated to restore and maintain social equilibrium, Bakhtin argued that carnival was also a form of popular resistance, the prototype of a demotic culture. Although contained within the licensed perimeters of an allowed public space, a holiday or festival, carnival could express genuine popular values, such as freedom and equality, and genuine popular aspirations, such as collective unanimity and universal abundance. My essay proposes that the *Henry IV* plays establish, through the figure of Falstaff, exactly such an opposition between the popular and ruling-class uses of carnival. From the point of view of established power, in this case the Lancastrian state, carnival has the function of safety valve: a disorganised form of opposition which ultimately endorses the authority of the state. From the alternative point of view afforded to the audience by the plebian discourse of Falstaff, and by the capacity of the drama to foreground the play of ideological contradictions in language and action, carnival appears rather as an anti-authoritarian affirmation of alternative values.

Bakhtin shows that throughout the medieval and early Renaissance periods, where carnival forms held a tenacious place throughout culture and the arts, the dominant image of carnival was the human body, as in Falstaff huge in substance and gross in appetite, symbol of collective energy and vitality; and the dominant form was that of the grotesque, a parodic and subversive discourse which expressed the unstable, irrepressible, infinite energies of the people. With the development of capitalist society, this volatile image of the collective body was reduced to the nuclear, self-enclosed 'bourgeois ego'; and the grotesque style disciplined to neo-classical harmony, proportion and decorum. My essay demonstrates a range of correspondences between Shakespeare's dramatic structure and Bakhtin's theory. Falstaff clearly is the grotesque body, symbol of collective aspiration and pleasure. Falstaff's fate in critical interpretation precisely parallels the fate of the grotesque body in cultural history: just as carnival was subdued by authority, so an authoritarian critical tradition has systematically suppressed the subversive content of Falstaff's dramatic and theatrical presence. This argument does not of course account for all critical responses to Falstaff; on the contrary, there is another strong tradition, deriving ultimately from the Romantic movement, which validates the values endorsed by Falstaff at the expense of authority, discipline and repression. It may be salutary to recall this 'sentimental' perspective when reading accounts which seem too easily to identify Falstaff with a voice of subversive protest; after all, getting drunk and rearranging the furniture is not to accomplish a social revolution.

The two essays included here on *Henry V* represent contributions to very recent debates about the historicity of Shakespeare's history plays. Annabel Patterson's essay (10), drawn from her book *Shakespeare and the Popular Voice* (1989), though clearly conscious of New Historicism, is in a sense a reworking of more traditional historicist approaches. Where New Historicism tends to avoid obvious, commonsense historical analogies, preferring to intertextualise forms of writing which seem widely divergent from one another, Patterson returns to a more straightforward relation between text and history, linking drama with contemporary historical event, class-relations at both socio-historical and cultural levels, and historiography. Her historical concerns include the immediate historical context of the play's production, with particular reference to the emerging contest for popularity between the Queen and the Earl of Essex; the nature and status of historical writing (i.e. the formal writing of history) within the same period; and the significance of retrospective references within the drama to periods of the historical past, such as ancient Rome. All these preoccupations have, of course, formed the substance of many other approaches to the plays, right back to Tillyard's. Patterson's most illuminating emphasis is her bringing into the equation a question not often addressed within historical studies, that of bibliography – the material history of a dramatic text's production and circulation through the specific cultural conditions of its genesis.

Textual bibliography has since the eighteenth century been dominated by a single approach: the belief that editorial responsibility consists of establishing, from the many variant and divergent texts of a particular play that may be available, the 'best' possible text of a play, a conception usually defined as that which would best reproduce the author's intentions, or would approximate most closely to the author's 'manuscript'. The Renaissance texts are normally hierarchised into 'good' and 'bad' texts, the former expressive of authorial integrity, the latter 'corrupted' by theatrical practice, unscrupulous actors and illiterate printers. Modern texts of Shakespeare's plays are thus compilations of readings from different Elizabethan texts, often with emendations, act and scene divisions, stage directions which do not appear in the original texts at all, but were interpolated by eighteenth-century editors. Scholars are now beginning to recognise that the existence of variant original texts, hitherto obscured by the traditional procedures of editors in search of the one true text, is a highly significant body of evidence bearing on literary and theatrical practices of the Renaissance. One effect of a focus on textual iterability is to return these cultural productions to the complex determinants of a material history, winning them away from the ahistorical status of transcendent art bestowed on them by the dominant procedures of textual editing and circulation.

Patterson considers not one text or play of *Henry V*, but two: that preserved in the First Folio of 1623, and the alternative version published in 1600 as *The Chronicle History of Henry the fifth* (the 'First Quarto').[54] Patterson sees the latter text, long relegated to the inferior and corrupt status of 'bad Quarto', as having an illuminating relationship with the political conflicts of the period 1599–1601. The absence from the Quarto text of much material that appears in the Folio, including all the Choruses, makes this *Henry V* a much more straightforward, unambiguous patriotic play, a drama which would seem in its ideological orthodoxy and political loyalty to answer quite readily to the interpretive stresses of Tillyard's analysis of Elizabethan culture. The longer version in the Folio text is a much more ambivalent production, offering a liberal and even possibly dangerous range of political comment on the immediate historical situation of its production. Above all, the Chorus prefatory to Act IV, which makes a coded reference to Essex's Irish campaign, problematises the text in ways that link it to the contradictory stresses of contemporary history. The first Quarto text here appears as a printed version deliberately adapted to pull it back from the incendiary political conflicts into which the fuller version, for whatever reason, seems to have intervened. Patterson's major achievement is to bring bibliography into the environment of historical debate, and to propose that variant texts should not be measured one against the other by aesthetic criteria, but should be seen as the diversified testimonies of an active history: 'We need', she argues 'to resituate both Quarto and Folio in their larger, mutual relationship to persons, events and cultural practices.'[55]

The second contribution on *Henry V*, 'History and Ideology' by Jonathan Dollimore and Alan Sinfield (essay 11), represents British cultural-materialist criticism, a form of Marxist criticism that has developed in close relation to New Historicism, poststructuralism, feminism and semiotics.[56] Though concerned, as Annabel Patterson is concerned, with situating the play into an immediate contemporary history that is in turn to some degree accessible by empiricist methods of inquiry, the approach of Dollimore and Sinfield is distinguished by the insistence on a theoretical exposition of history and a theoretical analysis of the relations between history and drama. The latter methodology appears notably in the shape of a formal Marxist analysis of ideology, defined as a body of 'those beliefs, practices and institutions which work to legitimate the social order'.[57] Dollimore and Sinfield are careful to offer a complex account of ideology, substantially different from the cruder Marxist categories of an earlier philosophical context (see above, pp. 19–20). Ideology, like the state, is characterised by internal contradiction and conflict: only by engaging with and negotiating contradiction can ideology hope to offer apparent resolutions of social conflict, giving the state an appearance of natural and divinely ordained unity. But as ideology confronts the contradictions it exists to occlude, it cannot help but exhibit those contradictions, foregrounding them in ways that render possible resistance and counter-analysis. *Henry V*, for example, addresses the idea that a war of foreign conquest is the most effective way of uniting an internally divided state: but in order to address this ideology the play finds it necessary both to represent the means by which such unity may be achieved, and to present the very contradictions the occlusion or suppression of which must predetermine the achievement of unity. Hence the play dwells as much on the obstructiveness of those conditions impeding unity as it does on the possibilities for attaining unity. In this way Dollimore and Sinfield propose a new relation between text and history, via the mediations of ideology: 'the play is fascinating precisely to the extent that it is implicated in and can be read to disclose both the struggles of its own historical moment and their ideological representation.'[58]

The work of Dollimore and Sinfield makes possible a broad general distinction between American 'New Historicism' and British radical criticism, at which I have already hinted (see above, pp. 19–20). New Historicism intersects at many points with the procedures of radical critics concerned with the 'political' investigation of Renaissance culture. On the other hand, there are important differences between American New Historicism and British cultural materialism, differences that are now becoming more clearly visible than they were a mere few years ago. Cultural materialism is much more concerned to engage with contemporary cultural practice, where

New Historicism confines its focus of attention to the past; cultural materialism can be overtly, even stridently polemical about its political implications, where New Historicism tends to efface them. Cultural materialism partly derives its theory and method from the kind of cultural criticism exemplified by Raymond Williams, and through that inheritance stretches its roots into the British tradition of Marxist cultural analysis, and thence into the wider movement for socialist education and emancipation; New Historicism has no sense of a corresponding political legacy, and takes its intellectual bearings directly from 'poststructuralist' theoretical and philosophical models. American 'political' critics seem to think of their ideology as having been formed in the environment of 1960s campus radicalism – in 'the political crucible of the 1960s'[59] – where their British counterparts are at least as likely to derive their ideological formation from the welfare state of the post-war Labour reconstruction, a real though temporary period of socialist achievement.[60] Dollimore and Sinfield suggest, in the conclusion to their essay, such a distinction between their methodology and those of (say) Greenblatt and Tennenhouse: '*Henry V* can be read to reveal not only the strategies of power but also the anxieties informing both them and their ideological representation.'[61] It is through the analysis of such 'anxieties' that historical drama becomes more than what Tillyard, long before such terminology entered literary criticism, claimed it to be: an 'ideological state apparatus' loyally sanctioning the hegemonic ideology and the dominant power. The terms of the debate remain the same, it could be argued, though their configuration has experienced radical movement. In fact it is only through such movement that the terms we now assume as given were made visible at all.

NOTES

1. E. M. W. Tillyard, *Shakespeare's History Plays* (London, 1944).

2. See Alvin B. Kernan, '*The Henriad*: Shakespeare's Major History Plays', in *Modern Shakespeare Criticism*, ed. Alvin B. Kernan (New York, 1970), pp. 245–75.

3. E. M. W. Tillyard, *The Elizabethan World Picture* (London, 1943).

4. *Certain Homilies Appointed to be read in Churches in the time of Queen Elizabeth* (London, 1908); and see Tillyard, *Elizabethan World Picture*, pp. 18 and 108.

5. Lily B. Campbell, *Shakespeare's Histories* (San Marino, California, 1947), and G. Wilson Knight, *The Olive and the Sword* (Oxford, 1944).

6. J. Dover Wilson, *The Fortunes of Falstaff* (Cambridge, 1964), and D. A. Traversi, *Shakespeare from 'Richard II' to 'Henry V'* (London, 1957). The *New Shakespeare* edition, by Arthur Quiller-Couch and John Dover Wilson, was published in 1926, and then in revised form in 1953. *Scrutiny* was an influential literary journal, edited by F. R. Leavis, published between 1932 and 1953, which carried many of L. C. Knights's essays on Shakespeare.

7. Raphael Holinshed, *Chronicles of England, Scotland and Ireland* (London, 1577, 2nd edition 1587, facsimile reprint New York, 1965).

8. J. M. Trevelyan, *History of England* (London, 1926).

9. Tillyard, *Shakespeare's History Plays*, p. 21.

10. Jonathan Dollimore and Alan Sinfield, 'History and Ideology: the instance of *Henry V*', in *Alternative Shakespeares*, ed. John Drakakis (London, 1985), pp. 208–10 (passage omitted from the extract included in this volume as the final essay).

11. See Karl Marx, *Critique of Hegel's Philosophy of Right*, in Karl Marx and Frederick Engels, *Collected Works*, vol. 2 (London, 1975).

12. Irving Ribner, *The English History Play in the Age of Shakespeare* (Princeton, 1957); A. P. Rossiter, *Angel with Horns and Other Shakespeare Lectures*, ed. Graham Storey (London, 1961).

13. Ribner, *English History Play*, p. 12.

14. Robert Ornstein, *A Kingdom for a Stage* (Cambridge, Mass., 1972).

15. See below, p. 39.

16. For the relations between *Richard II* and the Essex rebellion, see Annabel Patterson, pp. 173–7 below, and Graham Holderness, *Shakespeare's History* (Dublin, 1985), pp. 141–4; and *Shakespeare Recycled: The Making of Historical Drama* (Hemel Hempstead, 1992), pp. 83–94.

17. See below, p. 46.

18. Formative works include Michel Foucault, *The Archaeology of Knowledge* (London, 1972), *Language, Counter-memory, Practice*, ed. Donald Bouchard (Oxford, 1977), and *Power/Knowledge*, ed. Colin Gordon (Brighton, 1980); Louis Althusser, *For Marx* (*Pour Marx*, Paris, 1966), trans. Ben Brewster (Harmondsworth, 1969).

19. See Louis Adrian Montrose, 'Renaissance Literary Studies and the Subject of History', *English Literary Renaissance*, 16 (1986), 5–12, and 'Of Gentlemen and Shepherds: the Politics of Elizabethan Pastoral Form', *English Literary History*, 50:3 (1983), 415–59; Jonathan Goldberg, *James I and the Politics of Literature: Jonson, Shakespeare, Donne and*

their Contemporaries (Baltimore, 1983), and 'Shakespearean Inscriptions: the Voicing of Power', in *Shakespeare and the Question of Theory*, ed. Patricia Parker and Geoffrey Hartman (New York and London, 1985); Stephen Orgel, *The Illusion of Power: political theatre in the English Renaissance* (Berkeley, 1975).

20. See Stephen Greenblatt, *Shakespearean Negotiations* (Oxford, 1988), and *Learning to Curse* (London, 1990).

21. 'Invisible Bullets', in Alan Sinfield and Jonathan Dollimore (eds), *Political Shakespeare* (Manchester, 1985), pp. 18–47.

22. See below, p. 60.

23. Leonard Tennenhouse, *Power on Display* (London, 1986), p. 125.

24. See below, pp. 29–30.

25. See for example Irene Dash, *Wooing, Wedding and Power* (New York, 1981), and Marianne Novy, *Love's Argument: Gender Relations in Shakespeare* (Chapel Hill, Indiana and London, 1984).

26. See, for example, Kathleen McKluskie, 'The Patriarchal Bard: feminist criticism and Shakespeare (*King Lear* and *Measure for Measure*)', in Sinfield and Dollimore, *Political Shakespeare*, pp. 88–108; Peter Erickson, *Patriarchal Structures in Shakespeare's Drama* (Berkeley and London, 1985).

27. See Juliet Dusinberre, *Shakespeare and the Nature of Women* (London, 1975); Kathleen McKluskie, *Renaissance Dramatists* (Hemel Hempstead, 1989); Lisa Jardine, *Still Harping on Daughters: Women and Drama in the Age of Shakespeare* (Brighton, 1983); Catherine Belsey, *The Subject of Tragedy: Identity and Difference in Renaissance Drama* (London, 1985).

28. For representative samples of work by Julia Kristeva, Hélène Cixous and Luce Irigaray, see *New French Feminisms*, ed. Elaine Marks and Isabelle de Courtivron (Brighton, 1981).

29. See below, pp. 64, 66.

30. See below, p. 66.

31. See, for example, Carol Thomas Neeley, 'Constructing the Subject: Feminist Practice and the New Renaissance Discourses', *English Literary Renaissance*, 18 (1988).

32. See below, p. 79.

33. See *The Matter of Difference: Materialist Feminist Criticism of Shakespeare*, ed. Valerie Wayne (Hemel Hempstead, 1991).

34. See below, p. 88.

35. See below, p. 87.

36. See below, p. 88.

37. Derived from E. H. Kantorowicz, *The King's Two Bodies* (Princeton, 1957).

38. See below, p. 89.

39. See below, p. 90.

40. See below, p. 99.

41. Greenblatt, *Learning to Curse*, p. 3.

42. See Walter Cohen, 'Political criticism of Shakespeare', and Don E. Wayne, 'Power, politics and the Shakespearean text: recent criticism in England and the United States', in *Shakespeare Reproduced*, ed. Jean E. Howard and Marion F. O'Connor (London, 1987).

43. See Jonathan Dollimore, 'Shakespeare, Cultural Materialism and the New Historicism', Dollimore and Sinfield, *Political Shakespeare*, p. 2.

44. Jean-François Lyotard, *The Postmodern Condition: A Report on Knowledge* (*La Condition postmoderne*, Paris, 1979), trans. Geoff Bennington and Brian Massumi (Manchester, 1984).

45. Catherine Belsey, *The Subject of Tragedy* (London, 1985), *Critical Practice* (London, 1980) and *John Milton: Language, Gender, Power* (Oxford, 1988).

46. Ferdinand de Saussure, *Course in General Linguistics*, trans. Wade Baskin (London, 1974). See also Terence Hawkes, *Structuralism and Semiotics* (London, 1977) for an introduction to Saussure's work and influence.

47. Frederic Jameson, 'Postmodernism, or the Cultural Logic of Late Capitalism', *New Left Review*, 146 (1984), 53–92, and 'Postmodernism and Consumer Society', in *Postmodern Culture*, ed. Hal Foster (London, 1985); Terry Eagleton, 'Capitalism, Modernism and Postmodernism', *New Left Review*, 152 (1985), 60–73.

48. James L. Calderwood, *Metadrama in Shakespeare's 'Henriad'* (Berkeley, 1979), p. 4.

49. See below, p. 122.

50. Calderwood refers to Ludwig Wittgenstein's *Philosophical Investigations*, which 'holds that language has no single essence' (Calderwood, *Metadrama in Shakespeare's Henriad*, 1979, p. 213), and to the work of American linguist Benjamin Whorf, who argued that 'the structure of our thought and perception is radically determined by the structure of our language . . . constitutive of reality for us' (p. 27n.).

51. See below, p. 125.

52. See below, p. 147.

53. See below, p. 138.

54. Hitherto the Quartos and other variant texts have been virtually inaccessible except in facsimile and variorum editions. Harvester-Wheatsheaf will be publishing, under the series title *Shakespearean Originals*, new editions of some Quarto texts, including *The Cronicle Historie of Henry the Fift*, ed. Graham Holderness and Bryan Loughrey (Hemel Hempstead, 1992).

55. See below, p. 171.

56. This relationship can be seen in critical anthologies such as *Political Shakespeare*, ed. Dollimore and Sinfield, and *Alternative Shakespeares*, ed. John Drakakis (London, 1985).

57. See below, p. 182.

58. See below, p. 195.

59. Don E. Wayne, 'Power, politics and the Shakespearean text: recent criticism in England and the United States', in *Shakespeare Reproduced*, p. 56.

60. Alan Sinfield has recently offered an analysis of this formative period in *Literature, Politics and Culture in Postwar Britain* (Oxford, 1989).

61. See below, p. 197.

1

The Artist as Historian

ROBERT ORNSTEIN

Shakespeare had not only to create a suitable dramatic form for the History Play but he had also to recreate that form again and again as his vision of politics and history deepened. . . . So different, in fact, are the History Plays from one another that it is difficult to generalise about their subject matter, much less about their dramatic and poetic qualities. If I lay too much stress on what is original and individual in the History Plays, it is because recent scholarship has so often declared them conventional in form and substance and traditionally staid in their political and moral attitudes. We are asked to believe that the Shakespeare who blazed the path in tragedy for Chapman, Tourneur, Webster, Beaumont and Fletcher, Middleton, and Ford was content to follow the lead of the plodding didacticists who supposedly created the genre of the History Play, and like them dedicate his art to moralistic and propagandistic purposes. The pity of this scholarly insistence on the conventionality of the History Plays is that it threatens to turn living works of theatre into dramatic fossils or repositories of quaint and dusty ideas.[1] Instead of bridging the gulf of the centuries, the historical approach to the History Plays seems to widen it by identifying Shakespeare's mind and art with a past that viewed through the lens of scholarship appears more remote than ever before. . . .

No doubt the History Plays were more topical in their concerns than Shakespeare's other drama. They were also uniquely 'public' plays in that they dealt with the political anxieties and patriotic enthusiasms, the shared memories and aspirations which make a people conscious of their oneness and destiny as a nation. Necessarily, therefore, Shakespeare was constrained in these plays by Chron-icle 'fact' and by accepted opinion. He could no more think of making Richard III a Yorkist Hamlet than he could deny Henry V his praise as a conquering hero. But if one does not expect Shakespeare to be emancipated in his political attitudes or recklessly heterodox in his interpretations of history – an Elizabethan revisionist or debunker of eminent Plantagenets – neither does one expect him to step for-ward in the History Plays as the laureate of Tudor royalism. One could imagine him in a time of national peril dedicating one or two plays to what he thought were necessary patriotic purposes. Can we believe, however, that he dedicated nine plays – the weightier part of all the drama he wrote before *Hamlet* – to the claims of orthodoxy? And can we imagine that a dramatic form as prescribed and conven-tional as the History Play is made to seem allowed scope for the artistic development which made him capable of plays like *Hamlet* and *King Lear*?

The scholarly insistence on the orthodoxy of the History Plays would be more tolerable if it were tinged with some regret that the Soul of the Age lent his great art to doctrinaire purposes. But instead of regret, there seems to be pleasure in the scholarly discovery of the orthodoxy of this character's thought and the 'correctness' of that character's acts.[2] If there is a left and right wing in the criticism of Shakespeare, one libertarian (or Falstaffian) in sympathies, the other conservative and mindful of the need for authority and discipline, then the party of the right (and of Prince Hal) seems entrenched in the scholarship on the History Plays. Rather than complain of the bias of particular scholars, however, I would point out the inherent bias of the historical method toward what is conventional and ortho-dox in Elizabethan culture, because any search for the 'norms' of Elizabethan thought must lead to a consensus of truisms and pieties. In sketching the main contours of Elizabethan thought, scholarship often smooths out the jagged edges and wrinkles of individual opin-ion. It does not maintain that all Elizabethans were typical, but it often creates the impression that there were only two categories of Renaissance thought and art – the orthodox and the deviant – and it seems to insist that we place Shakespeare on one side of the angels or another.

. . . But the heart of the matter is something else again: an implicit refusal by historical scholarship to grant that the ultimate standard for the interpretation of art is aesthetic. Insisting on the primacy of Shakespeare's didactic intention, scholarship would have us believe that the interpretation of the History Plays does not depend on sensitivity to nuances of language and characterisation or awareness of Shakespeare's poetic and dramatic methods; it depends instead on the appropriate annotation of the doctrine of the plays. . . . Convinced that the 'Elizabethan response' which he postulates is the authentic one, the literary scholar assures us that if we were Elizabethan enough in our attitudes, we would have no difficulty in interpreting Shakespeare correctly. If, for instance, we recognised that York's stance in *Richard II* is impeccably orthodox, we would not think his eagerness to have his only son executed unconscionable or, as it seems in the play, somewhat comic.[3]

It is doubtful, however, that a modern audience can be so tutored by scholarship as to become for a time royalist enough to admire the orthodoxy of York's behaviour in the last act of *Richard II*. And it is doubtful that even the most dedicated students of literature can teach themselves to look at the History Plays through Elizabethan eyes. . . . A case in point is the scene in *Henry IV Part I* (II.iv), where Hal, aided by Poins, plays a joke on Francis, the drawer. Perhaps it is wrong to be slightly pained by the callousness of Hal's treatment of Francis, but if we are pained, at least we are responding immediately and honestly to the lines which Shakespeare wrote and to a human situation which we can understand because we have experienced or witnessed its analogue in our own lives. We recognise Hal's boredom in the tavern, and his condescension to those who are his inferiors. We recognise, too, the pleasure which he takes in playing cat-and-mouse games with other people – with Poins, Falstaff and the Lord Chief Justice in *Henry IV Part II*, and with the English traitors and the French Princess Katherine in *Henry V*. Arguing that 'we must not judge Shakespeare by standards of twentieth-century humanitarianism', Tillyard would have us believe that Elizabethan audiences (in which apprentices far outnumbered princes) would not have been troubled at all by Hal's conduct because they thought the Francises of the world hardly human.[4] If we accept this dubious generalisation about Shakespeare's contemporaries, however, we do not respond 'properly' to Shakespeare's representation of life; what we respond to is a learned admonition against modern sentimentality which saves Hal's ideality by degrading Shakespeare's humanity and cheapening his art. If Tillyard is correct, the Francis episode is not a fascinating revelation of Hal's personality; it is an irrelevant and purposeless bit of low humour, which exposes Shakespeare's 'Elizabethan' snobbery and coarseness.

Because we do not have the same social attitudes and political assumptions as Shakespeare's audience, it is possible that our responses to his plays are, by Elizabethan standards, somewhat distorted. Too accustomed perhaps to the security of stable political institutions, we may be more tolerant of aberration than were Elizabethans, and we may be inclined to sentimentalise characters like Falstaff whom Shakespeare thought of as threats to order and morality. If this is so, we must hope that the experience of great literature will enlarge our perspective and make us conscious of what is sentimental or romantic in our valuations. To be educated in this way, however, we must have the shock of artistic recognition; we must be convinced by the compelling truth of the artistic portrayal of life. We cannot simply be scolded about our ignorance and assured that if we had an Elizabethan view of serving boys, we too would enjoy the sport of baiting Francis. It is worth noting that Poins, Hal's assistant in the game, who is as coarse and common in his outlook as any Elizabethan one would ever want to meet, seems to lack the proper Elizabethan outlook, because he does not get the joke of baiting Francis and asks Hal the point of it.[5]

The appeal to Elizabethan attitudes is frequent enough in the literature on the History Plays for us to wonder why it should be easier to predict the responses of Shakespeare's audience than to interpret his artistic intentions from the thousands of lines which embody them. If we grant that there was in Shakespeare's England a community of shared values and beliefs which scholarship can cautiously describe, we must grant too that a wide range of individual and group attitudes must have existed in his society, which knew more than its share of religious and political turmoil and social and economic change. When we consider how reluctant we would be to generalise about the attitudes of our contemporaries – or to define the beliefs of our next-door neighbours, for that matter – we must be astonished at the confidence with which scholars characterise Elizabethan convictions. Perhaps the Elizabethans seem simpler and more transparent than do our contemporaries, because we know less about the diversity, contradictions, shadings and facets of their beliefs – or because these nuances are not apparent in the documents and treatises which we consider the repositories of Elizabethan 'thought'. In any event, Shakespeare's contemporaries sometimes appear in scholarly portraits as a fundamentally naïve and credulous folk, who managed to create a highly sophisticated civilisation and great monuments of art while retaining emotional enthusiasms and stock responses.

More unfortunate still is the curiously Philistine blueprint for Elizabethan culture sometimes implicit in the scholarship that looks always outside the realm of literature to explain and annotate literary ideas. Such an approach creates the impression that Elizabethan poets and dramatists made no significant contribution to the thought of their age, that they found their moral values in sermons and took their psychology from treatises on the humours, their political ideas from the Tudor and Elizabethan Homilies. What an approach to the era of Shakespeare, Marlowe, Spenser, Jonson and Donne! One cannot imagine Sir Philip Sidney, who eloquently argued that literature may be more philosophical than philosophy and more historical than history, agreeing that the light of artistic intelligence was wholly reflected in his time and not particularly bright. Nor can one imagine the Elizabethan dramatists considering themselves 'blessed fellows' (as Hal contemptuously describes Poins) 'to think the way everybody thinks'. If not particularly intellectual, the dramatists were shrewd observers of their contemporary scene, and if they were not clever enough to invent political myths, they were clear-sighted enough to discern the contradictions and expediencies of Tudor royalism.

. . . We can determine what sixteenth-century historians, politicians and artists thought about the historical figures who appear in Shakespeare's plays. We can also assume that Shakespeare was aware of the dangers of portraying these figures and of treating political issues in heterodox ways. Government officials alert to subversive ideas censored and banned dramatic texts and performances, and on various occasions they haled forth the playwrights and actors to be tried for their slanderous or profane libels. But though the fear of censorship, official reprisals and imprisonment probably dampened rebellious spirits, and though the playwrights and actors were dependent on royal patronage and support, they were not as easily intimidated as the government would have liked. And just as the dramatists were relatively free and sometimes satiric spirits, so too Elizabethan theatregoers had minds of their own, and were no doubt not all of one mind about any performance or any play. What plays and what characters of Shakespeare they loved, we know, even as we know which plays of Jonson they booed. How they interpreted the History Plays, we do not know – or, more correctly, what we know about Elizabethan responses to *Richard II* seems to contradict the chief assumptions of recent scholarship. Embodied in *Richard II*, we are told, is the orthodox view that the deposition of Richard was a heinous sin that brought down on England God's wrath and the curse of civil war.[6] Yet on the eve of Essex's rebellion, his adherents paid a bonus to Shakespeare's company to play *Richard II*, presumably in hope that it would stir the audience to sympathy for the uprising. Quite possibly Essex's followers were so blinded by their fanaticism that they lost sight of the orthodoxy of *Richard II*, but if so they were not the only ones, because we know of Elizabeth's bitter remark about the popularity of the play – a bitterness founded in the knowledge that her enemies identified her and her favourites with Richard and his circle of flatterers.[7]

One can not speak with certainty of Shakespeare's view of Richard II; one can hope only to interpret *Richard II* thoughtfully and sensitively. But one can state with some certainty that the supposedly orthodox view of Richard II, which can be found in Holinshed's Chronicles, is not the view of most Tudor and Elizabethan writers who deal with his character and reign. The anonymous author of *Woodstock* (c. 1592), a play which Shakespeare apparently used for *Richard II*, depicts the youthful Richard as thoroughly despicable and corrupt, and he portrays the barons who rebel against Richard as patriotic defenders of the commonweal.[8] The authors of *The Mirror for Magistrates* (1559) proclaim the sinfulness of rebellion, but they do not exclaim against Richard's deposition. Described in the *Mirror* as a vicious, lecherous, predatory 'Kyng that ruled all by lust, / That forced not of vertue, ryght, or lawe', Richard is treated not as a martyred king but as a tyrant whose fate may serve as a warning to lawless monarchs:

> Thus lawles life, to lawles deth ey drawes.
> Wherefore byd Kynges be rulde and rule by right,
> Who wurketh his wil, and shunneth wisedomes sawes,
> In flateries clawes, and shames foule pawes shal light.[9]

Tudor and Elizabethan Chroniclers are less vehement in their condemnation of Richard, but without exception they detail his personal vices and his political rapacity and disregard of law.[10] Knowing that Richard was often cited by sixteenth-century writers as an example of royal lawlessness and incompetence, we can understand why the *Homily against Disobedience and wilful Rebellion* (1574) takes John, not Richard, as its example of English royalty betrayed by disloyal subjects – why Catholic polemicists cited the deposition of Richard in justifying disobedience to tyrants[11] – and why Essex's party wished to have *Richard II* performed on the eve of their uprising.

To understand how an uncharacteristic view of Richard II came to be regarded by scholars as the 'orthodox' Elizabethan view we have to retrace the steps by which the Tudor myth of history became prominent in the scholarly interpretation of the History Plays. As early as 1913, the distinguished historian C. L. Kingsford had pointed out the extent to which Hall's narrative of the reign of Henry VI was 'mere Tudor fiction based on Yorkist misinterpretation' of the characters of Margaret, Suffolk and Humphrey.[12] Kingsford noted that Hall's Chronicle (1548) 'was intended as a glorification of the House of Tudor' and that Hall grasped the pattern of fifteenth-century English history which 'appears also in the continuous cycle of Shakespeare's histories. The downfall of Richard II, the glories of Henry V, the long struggle of Lancaster and York ending in the happy union of the rival houses, were all stages in the preparation for a greater Age.[13] When some decades later literary scholars confirmed Shakespeare's use of Hall's Chronicle for the plays of the first tetralogy, they went further than Kingsford in identifying Shakespeare's view of history with Hall's.[14] Where Kingsford saw Hall as an ardent supporter of the Tudors, Lily B. Campbell in her book on the History Plays makes him out to be a propagandist whose 'chronicle was undoubtedly written to serve the political purposes of Henry VIII, being directed to teaching political lessons in general and one imperative lesson in particular, the destruction that follows rebellion and civil dissension in a realm'.[15] Implicitly identifying the political lessons of Hall's Chronicle with those of the Tudor Homilies, Professor Campbell makes Hall seem a spokesman for Tudor orthodoxy, and she asserts that 'each of the Shakespeare histories serves a special purpose in elucidating a political problem of Elizabeth's day and in bringing to bear upon this problem the accepted political philosophy of the Tudors'.[16] More sweeping still is Tillyard's claim that the picture of English history in the tetralogies is based on the Tudor myth which Hall promulgated in his Chronicle and which supposedly moralises the calamity of the War of the Roses in the following way:

> Over against Richard [II]'s inability is set Henry IV's crime, first in usurping the throne and secondly in allowing Richard to be killed against his oath. God punished Henry by making his reign unquiet but postponed full vengeance till a later generation, for Henry (like Ahab) humbled himself. But Henry was none the less a usurper and this was a fact universally accepted by the Elizabethans. Hall notes the immediate

jealousy of the house of York when Richard was deposed. Henry V by his politic wisdom and his piety postpones the day of reckoning. He learns from the example of past history and chooses good counsellors; he banishes his evil companions; he does his best to expiate his father's sin by having Richard reburied in Westminster. But his wisdom does not stretch to detecting the danger from the House of York. With Henry VI the curse is realised and in the dreaded form of a child being king – 'woe to the nation whose king is a child'.[17]

Because Tillyard's exposition of the Tudor myth seems to explain the form and comprehend the substance of Shakespeare's tetralogies, it has had an enormous influence on the criticism of the History Plays.[18] . . . There is very good reason to doubt that Shakespeare wrote his tetralogies to set forth what Tillyard calls the Tudor myth of history. There is reason also to question whether the view of history which Tillyard sets forth as the Tudor myth was in fact the Tudor myth and can be attributed as such to Hall. Certainly Hall was familiar with this moralistic interpretation of the past and refers to it in his Chronicle, but he never acknowledges it as his own. . . .

Like most Henrician writers, Hall dwells on the horrors of civil war, and on the unnaturalness of dissension, strife and factionalism in England. He does not, however, propagandise for the Tudor doctrine of obedience; he never postulates the sacredness of royal authority, nor does he exclaim against the sin of rebellion. His central theme is announced in his opening paragraph:

> What mischief hath insurged in realmes by intestine devision, what depopulacion hath ensued in countries by civill discension, what destestable murder hath been committed in citees by separate faccions, and what calamitee hath ensued in famous regions by domestical discord and unnaturall controversy . . .[19]

For Hall, England's tragedy was the result of the emulous pride and rivalry of the houses of Lancaster and York, whom he compares to the Guelphs and Ghibellines. He does not preach the doctrine of non-resistance nor does he anathematise those who take arms against anointed majesty. Pleading for patriotic devotion to the commonweal, he celebrates the unity and the peace which the Tudors restored to a ravaged England. . . . Hall's great theme – the Tudor theme – was reconciliation, not retribution. He regards the English, not as sinners who had to be redeemed, but as a chosen people who had to wander in the desert of civil strife before they were led to their nationhood by the Tudors. When one turns the pages of Holinshed, who begins his account of English history with its legendary beginnings, one has a vivid sense of the conflicts and disorders that plagued so much of England's past. One knows from Holinshed that the reign of Richard II was tumultuous from its start, and that long before Mowbray and Bolingbroke quarrelled, Richard was engaged in a bitter struggle for power with his closest kin and most powerful subjects. . . .

If Shakespeare's interest in history had been shallow and opportunistic, if he had turned to the Chronicles merely to find plot materials and had been willing to accept without question the judgements of his sources, he would have found all he needed to write his History Plays in a single Chronicle as comprehensive as Holinshed's. Yet he used Hall as his primary source for the first tetralogy, and, in addition to Holinshed, read Stowe, Foxe, the *Mirror for Magistrates*, a host of lesser Chronicles and historical accounts, plays and poems. One could reasonably conclude that a man who consulted so many source materials and who wrote nine or ten plays about English history and three about Roman history had a very deep and serious interest in the past. But so persistent is the idea of the unintellectual Shakespeare that scholars would rather conjure up the ghost of vanished ur-texts than accept the probability that he read widely in history and thought critically and independently about it. Dover Wilson, for example, suggests that *Richard II* is based upon materials gathered from half a dozen English and French historical sources, but he would have us believe that this research was done by some unknown dramatist whose lost play Shakespeare revised.[20] (If Shakespeare had had Jonson's foresight, he would also have documented his historical scholarship with footnotes.) When one compares Shakespeare's plays with their source materials, one sees that, far from exploiting the merely sensational or theatrical possibilities of history, Shakespeare again and again deepens characterisations and illuminates political issues – again and again his vision of the past is more penetrating and acute than that of the Chroniclers. Yet it is astonishing how often scholars will fasten on minor confusions of names or muddles of fact in the History Plays as evidence of Shakespeare's indifference to historical truth.[21] . . .

Can we believe that Shakespeare was so shallow in his assessment of the temper of his countrymen, and so fearful of the threat of incipient anarchy, that he wrote play after play to persuade his audiences of the need for order and obedience? If we may judge from his characterisations of common men in the History Plays, he knew that his fellow Englishmen were neither giddy nor eager for change.

He may even have suspected that as a people the English were far more conservative than were their Tudor monarchs, who came to power by armed rebellion, who changed the established religion, radically altered the Church, dissolved the monastic orders, and centralised political power under the throne – all the while proclaiming that whatever is is right. When, as in sixteenth-century England, the government becomes revolutionary, it is likely that those who rebel are conservatives who resort to arms in attempts to restore traditional ways of life.[22] Actually, the Tudor regimes were threatened, not by ideologists who proclaimed from afar the right of rebellion, but by disgruntled aristocrats at home and by impoverished peasants in outlying counties who clung fiercely to the Old Faith. The Catholic earls who led the Northern Rebellion did not proclaim the right of rebellion. They swore that they took arms against those who 'abused the queen', and that their goal was to restore 'ancient customs and liberties'.[23] Shakespeare, I think, understood that men do not easily shrug off the habit of obedience, nor do they easily renounce time-honoured oaths of allegiance and fealty. All men – and rebels not the least – consider treason abhorrent, but there are occasions when ambition irresistibly beckons or when men think themselves so terribly wronged or threatened that they must take arms to defend the right and reform the regime. Marching against the King, they act and speak like the rebels in *Richard II*, who challenge law and appeal to ancient traditions. Ready to stoop to true authority, they are also ready, however, to contest violently the legitimacy of the authority which oppresses them. As is so often apparent in the Chronicles, rebels come not as rebels but as patriots, saviours, and restorers of order, determined to protect their monarch from his evil counsellors if they have to dethrone him to do so. And if, as will happen, they depose him, they very quickly discover that he never belonged on the throne to begin with.[24]

Because the Tudor claim to the throne was not unquestionable, and because opportunists and enemies of the regime often used the pretence of restoring the true inheritor to the throne, a trace of the blood royal and a connection to the throne proved fatal to many gentlemen and women in Henrician days. But the plots and the attempted coups on behalf of this pretender or that failed because Englishmen were not inclined to risk their lives and England's peace for the sake of a subtly argued genealogy. Knowing his countrymen, Shakespeare does not suggest that men chose sides in the War of the

Roses according to their beliefs in de facto authority or legitimacy. They took sides because of their feudal attachments, because of the appeal of family honour and pride, or as they were prompted by ambition, greed, patriotism or revenge. In the sixteenth century as in earlier times Englishmen were willing enough to support the existing government so long as conditions were reasonably tolerable. They preferred to suffer the political evils they knew than to risk the unknown terrors of civil war. I doubt, however, that the Tudor doctrine of de facto political authority inspired fierce loyalty to the regime, for men (as Shakespeare realised) will not eagerly sacrifice their lives to preserve the existing regime, when they know that they will be able, in good conscience, to support the rebels if they succeed.[25] Despite Tudor efforts to make rebellion unthinkable, men did think about it, and the wittiest of them understood that in rebellion, as in most human enterprises, nothing succeeds like success. A successful rebel, John Harington shrewdly observed, is no rebel at all: 'Treason doth never prosper; what's the reason? / For if it prosper, none dare call it treason'. This cynical epigram is not the gospel according to Machiavelli – it represents good, though maliciously phrased, Tudor theology: God defends the right of whoever wins.

Hardly cynical in his portrayal of human behaviour, Shakespeare nevertheless records in the History Plays the ease with which men turn their coats and alter their allegiances and yet remain men of conscience. He allows us to savour the irony of ingenious political rationalisations, but he is not quick to brand equivocations of loyalty hypocrisy. He knows that politics is the art of accommodation and survival, and he knows too that because political theoreticians invoke metaphysical absolutes it is difficult for them to adjust to changing circumstances without seeming to abandon their principles. At various times during the sixteenth century, for example, the radical Protestant and Catholic positions on obedience to kings turned about face. The zealous reformers who in Henrician days promulgated the Lutheran doctrine of obedience to princes, preached the right of resistance during Mary's reign, and with the accession of Elizabeth once again vehemently insisted on the religious duty of non-resistance to kings. But as the century wore on and Elizabeth refused to prosecute the cause of total Reformation, the Puritan faction became again an opposition party, and half a century later Puritan revolutionaries used the arguments of the Marian exiles to justify the execution of Charles.[26] When the official religious policy of the Tudor monarchs bent and twisted and reversed itself, it was impossible for men of religious zeal to walk a straight and narrow path. . . .

A master of theatrical spectacle, Shakespeare could appreciate the need for spectacle in politics, for the ceremonies which make all the world a stage for the mystery of power. He could also appreciate the mythopeic genius of the Tudors, who traced their descent to legendary kings and who consciously imitated the splendour of Plantagenet rule in their courtly pomp and stately progresses. When Henry VII had ascended the throne as a saviour-bridegroom whose marriage to the Yorkist princess Elizabeth reunited the royal houses of England, Elizabeth presented herself to the nation as the bride of England – as the Virgin Queen who loved her people so well that she would accept no other husband. Aware that all successful leaders create their personal mythologies, Shakespeare does not hesitate to grant the Lancastrian kings the political instincts of the Tudors. Where the Chronicles tell of a Prince Hal whose youth was misspent but who put on a new man when crowned, Shakespeare depicts a prince who deliberately fashions the legend of his prodigality and miraculous reformation, even as his father had artfully made himself seem a man of destiny who obeyed heaven's will in becoming King.

If we ask, 'Did Shakespeare believe in the myth of Tudor deliverance from the tyranny of Richard III?' the answer must be, 'Yes, even as Americans believe in the myth of their deliverance from the tyranny of George III'. For the sense of the past is almost always touched by mythic memories, and without epic legends of heroism and sacrifice a nation's history lacks meaning and form. But I do not think that Shakespeare was content to serve as the spokesman for an official version of history in the tetralogies. Rather he makes the memory of Agincourt and the memory of Bosworth the polarities of a personal mythic interpretation of England's history. The triumph at Agincourt epitomises the heroic impulse of a people beginning to embark again on the adventure of empire. The victory at Bosworth recalls the hope of reconciliation and brotherhood among Englishmen that was still unfulfilled at the close of the sixteenth century and that would grow more remote in the seventeenth century as political and religious antagonisms intensified.

From Robert Ornstein, *A Kingdom for a Stage: The Achievement of Shakespeare's History Plays* (Cambridge, Mass., 1972), pp. 10–20, 22, 25, 27–31.

NOTES

['The Artist as Historian', a sustained and considered critique of various positions derived from Tillyard, is drawn from the introductory chapter to Robert Ornstein's book. The chapter has been cut for the purposes of this volume. Ed.]

1. Insisting that the History Plays reveal Shakespeare's 'official self', E. M. W. Tillyard remarks also that the 'political doctrines of the History Plays fascinate partly because they are remote and queer', *Shakespeare's History Plays* (New York, 1946), p. 146.

2. The triumphant discovery of orthodoxy is evident in Tillyard's *Shakespeare's History Plays*, and to a lesser degree, in Irving Ribner's *The English History Play in the Age of Shakespeare* (Princeton, 1957) and M. M. Reese, *The Cease of Majesty: A Study of Shakespeare's History Plays* (London, 1961). Lily B. Campbell also insists upon Shakespeare's orthodoxy in *Shakespeare's Histories: Mirrors of Elizabethan Policy* (San Marino, 1947). At its worst, this approach has some of the characteristics of a security investigation and clearance. In his chapter on 'The English Chronicle Plays', for example, Tillyard informs us that Marlowe in *Edward II* 'shows no sense of national responsibility' though he uses 'two current political orthodoxies'; he notes further that 'On the matters of civil war and obedience to the king, the author of *Woodstock* is ample, explicit and suitably orthodox', a curious view of a play which applauds armed rebellion against a corrupt monarch. See *History Plays*, pp. 108–9, 118. Ribner, in contrast, notes the unorthodoxy of *Woodstock* (*English History Plays*, 2nd revised edition [London, 1965], p. 141). All citations from Ribner are to this edition. [*Thomas of Woodstock* is an anonymous history play probably written in the 1590s, and centred on the political career of Thomas Duke of Gloucester, uncle to Richard II. See George Parfitt and Simon Shepherd (eds), *Thomas of Woodstock* (Nottingham, 1977). Ed.]

3. See Tillyard, *History Plays*, pp. 261–2.

4. According to him (*History Plays*, p. 277), 'the subhuman element in the population must have been considerable in Shakespeare's day; that it should have been treated almost like beasts was taken for granted'. But apart from the fact that Francis generously gave Hal a pennyworth of sugar and wished that it had been two pennyworth, the only evidence of his character (and subhumanity) is the way he scurries about at Hal's behest.

5. 'What cunning match have you made with this jest of the drawer?' Poins asks when the game is done. 'Come, what's the issue?'

6. See Campbell, *Shakespeare's Histories*, pp. 211–12; Tillyard, *History Plays*, p. 261.

7. Complaining that the tragedy of *Richard II* 'was played 40 times in open streets and houses', Elizabeth is said to have remarked in 1601, 'I am Richard II, know ye not that?' (Campbell, *Shakespeare's Histories*, p. 191).

8. In his edition of *Woodstock* (London, 1946), A. P. Rossiter notes its quite unorthodox sympathy with armed rebellion against tyranny (p. 32).

9. *The Mirror for Magistrates*, ed. L. B. Campbell (Cambridge, 1938), p. 120.

10. There is no Tudor or Elizabethan chronicler who fails to document Richard's personal vices and political failings, his lawlessness and rapacity. The only completely sympathetic sixteenth-century view of Richard is, I think, the idealised portrait in *Jack Straw*, which is not a defence of the character of Richard II but rather an abstracted study in royal fortitude and clemency. The play focuses wholly on the uprising and makes no comment on other aspects of Richard's life or reign. [*The Life and Death of Iacke Straw, a Notable Rebell*, a dramatisation of the Peasants' Revolt of 1381, was published anonymously in 1593. Ed.]

11. See the discussion of the writings of the Jesuit Robert Parsons in Campbell, *Shakespeare's Histories*, pp. 173–81.

12. C. L. Kingsford, *English Historical Literature in the Fifteenth Century* (Oxford, 1913), p. 265.

13. Kingsford, p. 274.

14. See, for example, W. G. Zeefeld, 'The Influence of Hall on Shakespeare's English Historical Plays', *ELH*, 3 (1936), 317–53.

15. *Shakespeare's Histories*, p. 68.

16. *Shakespeare's Histories*, p. 125.

17. *History Plays*, p. 60.

18. That one or both of Shakespeare's tetralogies is founded on the Tudor myth of history has become practically a *donnée* of the scholarship on the History Plays. See for example, *Narrative and Dramatic Sources of Shakespeare*, ed. Geoffrey Bullough (New York, 1960), vol. 3, p. 355.

19. Although Hall returns again and again to the theme of faction and division, he does not speak of the deadly sin of rebellion. His plea for unity is quite different from the Homilies' execration of rebellion.

20. See the new Cambridge edition of *Richard II*, ed. John Dover Wilson (Cambridge, 1939, reprinted 1961), pp. lxiv–lxxvi.

21. See for example, Wilson's introduction to *Richard II*, pp. lxiv–lxv.

22. That the two great uprisings of the sixteenth century (The Pilgrimage of

Grace in 1536 and the Northern Rebellion of 1569) were essentially conservative protests against revolutionary political, social and religious changes is noted by Christopher Morris, *Political Thought in England: Tyndale to Hooker* (Oxford, 1953), pp. 58–9, and by J. B. Black, *Reign of Elizabeth* (Oxford, 1936), pp. 103–8.

23. Black, *Reign of Elizabeth*, pp. 107–8.

24. It was a time-honoured custom for usurpers to bastardise those they overthrew. Richard III, for example, spread rumours of the illegitimacy of Edward IV, his own brother.

25. See Act III, scene i, of *Henry VI, Part III*, where the gamekeepers explain their loyalty to Edward IV to their former king Henry VI.

26. See the discussion of the 'Puritan Protest' in Morris, *Political Thought*, chs 2, 6 and 8; see also Franklin Le van Baumer, *The Early Tudor Theory of Kingship* (New Haven, 1940), pp. 91, 112–13, for the reversals of Catholic and Protestant positions during the sixteenth century.

2

Rituals of State / Strategies of Power

LEONARD TENNENHOUSE

. . . My objective is to determine what figures allow the materials of chronicle history to authorise the state in characteristically Elizabethan ways. . . . I will not be concerned with the march of literature, on the one hand, nor with the history of institutions of state on the other. It is the representation of power that commands my interest, by which I mean specifically that cultural logic or general economy of meaning within which the monarch's body was inscribed and achieved value. I will show that the theatre which idealised state power did not observe either its own logic or that of any individual author's development. Quite the contrary, as the inherited prerogatives of the monarch were challenged, first by a contending faction within the aristocracy, and later by dissenting voices outside the oligarchy, literature had to employ radically discontinuous artistic strategies to remain politically consistent. Indeed, we find that a whole set of literary genres fell out of favour with the accession of James I, and new forms provided the appropriate means of situating oneself in proximity to political power. Along with romantic comedy, Petrarchan poetry, prose romance, and other genres as well, the chronicle history play enjoyed a period of unprecedented popularity during the 1590s. And just as clearly as it shared their popularity, the chronicle history play also participated in the demise of many of these Elizabethan genres; with few exceptions, such plays ceased to be produced after *Henry V* (1599), the most notable exception being *Henry VIII*.

To explain why history plays became virtually unwritable after 1600, I would like to consider what this dramatic form shared with romantic comedy and Petrarchan poetry that enabled these genres to address the interests of the same audience and then hasten into obsolescence together. For all their differences, chronicle history uses the same strategy to produce political order out of political conflict as romantic comedy uses to reinforce the dominant rules of kinship. Both represent patriarchal hierarchies in a state of disorder, in this way creating two bases for authority, and thus two competing hierarchies of power, which only the monarch can hold together in harmonious discord.

If we recall for the moment the example of *A Midsummer Night's Dream*, a play surely characteristic of Shakespeare's romantic comedies, we can see that the problem which authority has to master is a problem with authority itself. . . . Oberon represents the traditional alternative to patriarchal law, the elements of carnival. Thus we find his introduction into the play triggers a series of inversions.[1]. . . Such inversions – of gender, age, status, even of species – violate all the categories organising the Elizabethan social world. . . . But the romantic comedies demonstrate that festival breaks down the hierarchical distinctions organising Elizabethan society only – in the end – to be taken within the social order where it authorises a new form of political authority. . . .

If Theseus authorises certain inversions of power relations by permitting them to exist within the frameworks of festival and art, it is also true that the introduction of disorder into the play ultimately authorises political authority. . . . The equation of juridical power with patriarchal power gives way to a new set of political conditions where competing bases for authority are held in equipoise by the duke. This form of authority constitutes an improvement over the punitive power he threatened to exercise at the play's opening. The entire last act of the play consequently theorises the process of inversion whereby art and politics end up in this mutually authorising relationship. This process is reproduced on the stage in the form of an Elizabethan tragedy – *Pyramus and Thisbe* – which has been converted into a comedy as rude mechanicals play a range of parts from those of noble lovers to the creatures and objects of the natural world.

The popularity of inversions which bring the law into contradiction with patriarchal authority cannot be fully understood unless one sees how Elizabeth used these forms of authority against one another. It is not enough to say that the transfiguration of authority in romantic comedy resembles Elizabeth's actual style of exercising the power of the monarch. To be sure, she used her power as a patron to curb the power of the ruling families and set economically-based authority in opposition to that based on blood. But the facts would indicate this strategy was more than personal ingenuity on her part. They indicate her characteristic strategies for expressing power were no less dependent upon the political conditions of the time than the form of a comedy such as *A Midsummer Night's Dream*. The Acts of Parliament of 1536 and 1543 gave Henry VIII the power to determine succession. His will not only specified the crown would pass to Edward, Mary and Elizabeth in that order, it also determined that, if his children should die without issue, the crown would pass to his younger sister's children in the Suffolk line and not to her older sister's children in the superior hereditary Stuart line.[2] Henry thus treated the crown as property, governed by the same common-law rules against alien inheritance as any other piece of English property. By exploiting his legal prerogative to authorise this line of descent, Henry used the civil authority of a property owner to define the monarchy as such a juridical form. This tautology set the dominant principle of genealogy against the one which was invoked later by supporters of Mary Queen of Scots and her line. During Elizabeth's reign, both Catholic and Stuart spokesmen insisted on the traditional view of the monarch as two bodies, a body natural and a body mystical, in the same body.[3] Theirs was a monolithic view of power that saw the body politic as the corporate body of the crown in perpetuity. The mystical body purged the body natural of attainder; it joined the king with his royal predecessors to constitute them as one and the same corporate person; and the metaphysical body was joined to the natural body of the king, they argued, like an affair of the heart in a marital pre-contract of the blood royal.

A similar logic operates in *A Midsummer Night's Dream* as the law and the father temporarily come into contradiction in the last act of the play. In this instance, however, the splitting of one form of power into two competing voices is hardly the dramatic problem. It is rather the comedic resolution to a problem which develops when authority assumes an absolute and monolithic form. Since Elizabeth's ascendancy could be justified according to her father's will and primogeniture both, her very person temporarily reconciled the competing viewpoints formulated during the debates concerning her succession. Elizabeth was a paradox, in other words, by virtue of the contradictory definitions of monarchal authority her succession had occasioned. Much the same contradiction resolves the dramatic conflict of *A Midsummer Night's Dream* with the divergence of Theseus's authority from that of Egeus. Indeed, in turning back to courtly poetry, we find the same strategy for idealising power obtains as the patron is endowed with the attributes of the reluctant lover. The puns characterising the Petrarchan mode of poetry effectively create a gulf between the power of property (in the form of economic favours) and that of blood (through marriage into the aristocracy), even as the two modes for representing power are brought together in one figure of speech.

If the Petrarchan lyric or romantic comedy are shaped by the strategies for idealising the state, this rhetorical behaviour should be all the more evident in the chronicle history plays. The obstacle one encounters in identifying these strategies in the material of chronicle history is not quite the same as the obstacles that stand in the way of historicising romantic comedy. Shakespeare's use of political rather than sexual subject matter entices many to make the history plays allude to contemporary events. While such a procedure anchors 'the text' to events taking place in a 'context', such an allusory or allegorical construction prevents us from seeing the drama as a symbolic activity of a piece with and giving shape to the events we call history. It is fair to say that the form of the history play is so completely one with certain Elizabethan controversies, that the materials of chronicle history could no longer be so assembled once the official strategies for mastering those controversies changed.

Richard II exemplifies the strategies by which Shakespeare stages the struggle for legitimate authority. It is significant that few if any monarchs in the entire sequence of history plays are represented at the outset of their dramas with a more secure claim to the throne. Yet within the first two acts Shakespeare creates the impression that no monarch is more irresponsible and finally more threatening to the stability of the state. He makes Richard appear as a tragic version of the patriarch who exercises his authority for penurious and exclusionary ends. In contrast with the anointed king, then, Shakespeare makes the displaced and dispossessed Bullingbroke into the figure who rescues the principle of genealogy and links it to the law.

Shakespeare first has Richard act as if he had absolute authority over the law by virtue of his solid claim to the throne. At the same time, Richard disregards the other principle that secures his position. In the opening scenes, the king is unwilling – or, more likely, unable

– to entertain Bullingbroke's charge that Mowbray was responsible for Gloucester's murder. There is even the possibility Richard is complicit in that crime, which would implicate the king in a crime against the state. An impossible semiotic dilemma would arise in the event of such a conflict within the body politic between the monarch's two bodies. The notion that the bearer of blood could also betray the state requires one to imagine the state and the blood as separate entities. Although several of the sources for the play suggest the possibility of Richard's implication in his uncle's death, then, Shakespeare leaves the whole issue in a cloudy state. . . . In assuming the authority of blood is absolute, Richard neglects those displays of political authority which establish the absolute power of the monarch over the material body of the subject. To settle the charges about Mowbray's role in the murder of the Duke of Gloucester, Richard stages a trial by combat, only to cancel this ceremony before it gets underway. His subsequent banishment of Mowbray and Bullingbroke demonstrates the monarch's right to exercise royal power arbitrarily. But with a consistency that suggests he could not do otherwise, Richard avoids those occasions where scenes of violence ordinarily would be staged. Even late in the play, Shakespeare does not allow Richard to do battle where he would show an ability to exercise the force of state. Hearing of the uprising led by Bullingbroke, Richard instead invokes the metaphysics of kingship to protect his crown. It is from his position as the magical body of England that he urges the earth,

> Feed not thy sovereign's foe, my gentle earth,
> Nor with thy sweets comfort his ravenous sense,
> But let thy spiders, that suck up thy venom,
> And heavy-gaited toads lie in their way,
> Doing annoyance to the treacherous feet,
> Which with usurping steps do trample thee.
> (III.ii.12–17)

He believes angels will fight on his behalf, that stones will become soldiers for the anointed king, and that 'the king's name' is worth 'twenty thousand names' (III.ii.85). In contrast with Richard III, then, Richard II threatens to break the bond between the king's two bodies.

Although Shakespeare raises the matter of Gloucester's death, he stops short of making it the central issue. Instead, he uses Gaunt's deathbed speech to represent Richard as 'the careless patient' who fails to prevent the spilling of royal blood. Of equal importance is Richard's insensitivity to the dangers of leasing the royal lands, for both policies – or lack of policy – cause the body politic to fall dangerously ill. Giving up his control over royal land threatens the very basis of the monarch's authority ('This land . . . Is now leas'd out – I die pronouncing it – / Like to a tenement or pelting farm' [II.i.57–60]). The danger, of course, is one and the same as that troubling the participants in the succession debate. By so representing Richard, Shakespeare has the king undermine the bond among the claims to power which Elizabeth embodied. In Gaunt's opinion, Richard threatens to destroy the equipoise between the king's two bodies by making that body subject to contract. 'Landlord of England art thou now, not king.', the dying Gaunt charges, 'Thy state of law is bond-slave to the law' (II.i.113–14). Besides the spilling of aristocratic blood and the leasing of the aristocratic body, Shakespeare represents yet another assault by Richard on the institutions of power, his arrogant disregard for the principle of primogeniture. When the king seizes Bullingbroke's inheritance following the death of Gaunt, York rightly accuses him of challenging the principle on which his own power rests. '. . . How art thou a king', York asks, 'But by fair sequence and succession'(II.i.198–9). This act threatens the entire nobility and provides as great a threat to the body politic as the 'grievous taxes' that have stripped the common people bare and 'quite lost their hearts' (II.i.247).

In the comedies, as we have seen, such a split in the body politic is repaired as the state contains all the heterogeneous elements of carnival. This makes the hierarchy of state seem less at odds with nature, at once more inclusionary and less arbitrary in its laws. Although we do not usually think of Henry Bullingbroke in such terms, Shakespeare does give him the features of inversion which necessarily challenge the law. In preparing for battle against Mowbray, Bullingbroke is 'lusty, young, and cheerly drawing breath' (I.iii.66). As Henry leaves England, Richard accordingly describes his rival as one who enjoys the popular support of the 'craftsmen', 'an oyster-wench', and a 'brace of draymen'. These elements, Richard notes, regard Henry as if 'England [were] in reversion his, / And he our subjects' next degree of hope' (I.iv.35–6). Even the support enabling Henry to challenge the king – in its mixing of ages, sexes and social ranks – sounds more like a carnivalesque troop than a disciplined military force. And indeed, Scroop employs figures of inversion to describe the raggle-taggle supporters of Bullingbroke:

> White beards have arm'd their thin and hairless scalps
> Against thy majesty; boys, with women's voices,
> Strive to speak big, and clap their female joints
> In stiff unwieldy arms against thy crown;
> Thy very beadsmen learn to bend their bows
> Of double-fatal yew against thy state;
> Yea, distaff-women manage rusty bills
> Against thy seat: both young and old rebel.
>
> (III.ii.112–19)

This is not the figure of a revolutionary army assaulting the traditions of patriarchy. To the contrary, as E. P. Thompson has noted, such are the elements of an essentially conservative form of riot staged to demand better adherence to a patriarchal ideal.[4] . . .

I would like to suggest that the history plays all turn on this use of the materials of carnival. The popular energy embodied in carnival legitimises authority, provided that energy can be incorporated in the political body of the state. In effect, such energy lends the power of autochthony to a rigidly hierarchical form of patriarchy. In this respect, it is significant to find Richard describing Bullingbroke in language more appropriate for a Falstaff than an English king; Bullingbroke is 'a thief', as well as 'a traitor', one 'Who all this while hath revell'd in the night' (III.ii.47–8). It is especially significant that Bullingbroke embody these features as he rescues the principle of inheritance which underwrites Richard's right to wear the crown. Bullingbroke repeats his uncle's words as he lays claim to a title and, with it, to the authority of the blood, 'Wherefore was I born? / If that my cousin king be King in England, / It must be granted I am Duke of Lancaster' (II.iii.122–4). If Richard had dissociated the power of blood from the exercise of force, then Henry restores the body politic to wholeness. His England incorporates the robust features of festival, while Richard's is a state that lets the family blood and leases the royal land. Gaunt characterises Richard's body politic as a place where Edward III's 'son's sons . . . destroy his sons' (II.i.105), and it 'is now bound in with shame, / With inky blots and rotten parchment bonds . . .' (II.i.63–4). It is for this reason that the figure of carnival is associated with Henry, while the figure of a mutilated England characterises Richard's monarchy. The rhetorical contrast between them shifts legitimate authority from Richard to Henry.

The shift begins when Bullingbroke arrests Bushy and Green on charges of treason for assaulting the king's body. Not even the loyal York questions Henry's authority in this, for Bushy and Green have,

. . . misled a prince, a royal king,
A happy gentleman in blood and lineaments,
By you unhappied and disfigured clean.
                                    (III.i.8–10)

They 'disfigured' Richard we should note, by dividing the king from
the queen, thus breaking 'the possession of a royal bed', as well as by
dividing Bullingbroke from the king. As Henry says, 'you did make
him misinterpret me'. While critics have puzzled over the charge of
divorce, (there is no evidence in the play or in the chronicles of any
such divorce), the play simply suggests that anything dividing the
aristocratic body against itself disfigures the king. Assaults on
Bullingbroke's estate constitute the same treasonous act of disfigure-
ment, then, as Bullingbroke further details the crimes of Bushy and
Green:

. . . you have fed upon my signories,
Dispark'd my parks and fell'd my forest woods,
From my own windows torn my household coat,
Ras'd out my imprese, leaving me no sign,
Save men's opinions and my living blood,
To show the world I am a gentleman.
                                    (III.i.16–21)

This representation of aristocracy divested of its natural body indicts
not only Bushy and Green, we must note, but also Richard. In
allowing the body of England to be split apart and himself disfigured,
he has disfigured the official iconography of state. He has become the
'other' against whom popular support may be legitimately invoked.
    Richard has been called the poet king by critics who want to read
him in the nineteenth-century manner, as a poet king who was a
political failure, rather than as a sixteenth-century monarch who
destroyed the sign of his own legitimacy.[5] In actuality, it is Henry IV
rather than Richard in whom Shakespeare invests the power of the
artist, not a power detached from matters political, that is, but the
power to incorporate disruptive cultural elements within the official
rituals of state. Henry successfully stages Richard's resignation of the
crown and the procession and coronation that legitimate his own
claim to the throne.[6] York contrasts Richard's poor appearance to
Bullingbroke's triumphant processional; while Henry drew everyone's gaze, he says Richard appeared

> As in a theatre the eyes of men,
> After a well-graced actor leaves the stage,
> Are idly bent on him that enters next,
> Thinking his prattle to be tedious.
>   (V.ii.23–6)

Another occasion for Henry to display his authority occurs when Aumerle, his conspiracy discovered, begs forgiveness, and Henry grants it. With this, Shakespeare completes the contrast between Richard and Henry. Richard lacks the power of generosity as well as the capacity for ruthlessness. Henry possesses both and can manifest either power in extreme as he so chooses. No less important than granting his cousin Aumerle forgiveness is Henry's condemnation and pursuit of all those who plotted against him. He vows, 'Destruction straight shall dog them at their heels . . . / They shall not live within this world, I swear' (V.iii.139, 142). Thus in one scene he shows both sides of the coin of power: he vows to exercise unlimited force in the interest of the state, and he displays generosity in the interest of the blood. It is significant that by staging this scene of forgiveness for Aumerle's parents, the Duke and Duchess of York, Henry recasts his authority in a comedic form. 'Our scene is alt'red from a serious thing' (V.iii.79), he observes, when the Duchess begs an audience to plead for her son. . . . By this stroke, we might say, Shakespeare acknowledges the conceptual link between his two major Elizabethan genres.

In certain respects, *Henry V* can be called a piece of political hagiography.[7] As if omniscient, Henry discovers domestic conspirators and punishes them. He secures his borders against Scottish invaders, unifies the dispirited and heterogeneous body under his authority, and wins the battle of Agincourt, thus taking control of territory which had been claimed by French inheritance law and contested by English laws of succession. The stability of the state having been won, and the promise of its continuance having been established by the king's marriage with the French princess, the Epilogue to this tetralogy takes on the features of a comic resolution:

> Thus far, with rough and all-unable pen,
> Our bending author hath pursu'd the story,
> In little room confining mighty men,
> Mangling by starts the full course of their glory.
> Small time, but in that small most greatly lived
> This star of England. Fortune made his sword;

By which the world's best garden he achieved,
And of it left his son imperial lord.

(ll. 1–8)

The history play stabilises the conflict among contradictory origins of power, it appears, only to define that stasis as nothing else but a moment of equipoise within a competitive process. The hagiographical theme of this play understands power as the inevitable unfolding of order. But to idealise political authority, Shakespeare evidently found it necessary to counter this theme with a contrary one.

In this other logic of history, history is nothing else but the history of forms of disorder, over which Henry temporarily triumphs. He alone embodies the contradictions that bring disruption into the service of the state and allows a discontinuous political process to appear as a coherent moment. Thus the Epilogue continues on past a comedic resolution to remind the Elizabethan audience that the very marriage which secured the peace with France and established the line of succession eventually led to the Wars of the Roses:

Henry the Sixt, in infant bands crown'd King
Of France and England, did this king succeed;
Whose state so many had the managing,
That they lost France, and made his England bleed.

(ll. 9–12)

Providence temporarily comes under the control of the monarch. Working against political order, however, providence offers a tide that one can ride into power but against which he must struggle vainly in order to remain there.[8] This levelling force effectively unseats every hierarchy. This seems to be the point of Richard III's rise, of Henry Richmond's victory over Richard, of Bullingbroke's successful challenge to Richard II, but particularly of Hal's defeat of Hotspur and his subsequent victory over the French. In each case, state authority does not descend directly through blood. Rather, it pursues a disrupted and discontinuous course through history, arising out of conflicts within the reigning oligarchy as to which bloodline shall legitimately rule. Together these chronicle history plays demonstrate, then, that authority goes to the contender who can seize hold of the symbols and signs legitimising authority and wrest them from his rivals to make them serve his own interests. What else is accomplished, however perversely, by Richard III's incarceration of the young princes? Or Bullingbroke's public ceremony in which Richard is forced to hand over the crown? And surely Hal's self-coronation in *II Henry IV*, pre-emptive though it may be, dramatises the same principle, that power is an inversion of legitimate authority which gains possession, as such, of the means of self-authorisation.

Such a rhetorical strategy guarantees the figures of carnival will play a particularly instrumental role in the idealising process that proves so crucial in legitimising political power. It cannot be accidental that the *Henriad*, which produces Shakespeare's most accomplished Elizabethan monarch, should also produce his most memorable figure of misrule. The complete king was by birth entitled to the throne. A youth misspent in low-life activities at the same time lends him the demonic features of the contender, a potential regicide, whose legitimacy has yet to be recognised. The various conflicts comprising *I* and *II Henry IV*, in actuality cohere as a single strategy of idealisation. In opposition to legitimate authority, Hal takes on a populist energy. In contrast, the law of the father seems to have atrophied and grown rigid to the degree that it can be inverted by the likes of Falstaff, whose abuses of legitimate authority, like those of Oberon, take on a menacing quality when unconstrained by the forest glade or tavern. Falstaff frequently anticipates the lawlessness he will enjoy when Hal assumes authority and authority is therefore not 'as it is with the rusty curb of old father antic the law' (I.ii.61). Upon hearing of Henry IV's death, again (in *Part II*) he looks forward to the dissolution of the state: 'I know the young king is sick for me. Let us take any man's horses, the laws of England are at my commandment' (V.iii.135–7). Thus Shakespeare uses the figures of carnival to represent a source of power contrary to that power inhering in genealogy. However, the various confrontations between licit and illicit authority comprising the *Henriad* more firmly draw the distinction between aristocracy and populace even as they appear to overturn this primary categorical distinction.

The figures of carnival ultimately authorise the state as the state appears to take on the vigour of festival. We see this, for example, in Vernon's account of Hal and his men preparing to do battle with Hotspur:

> Glittering in golden coats like images,
> As full of spirit as the month of May,
> And gorgeous as the sun at midsummer;
> Wanton as youthful goats, wild as young bulls.[9]
>
> (IV.i.100–3)

The same process transfers what is weak and corrupt onto the tavern folk where it is contained and finally driven even from that debased world. Criminalising the popular figures of inversion is as necessary to the poetics of power as incorporating a certain popular vigour within the legitimate body of the state. This capability of making rebellion serve the interests of the state by including it within the state is the proof of noble blood and the principle toward which the tetralogy moves. Legitimate order can come into being only through disruption according to this principle, and it can maintain itself only through discontinuous and self-contradictory policies.

If Henry V appears to be Shakespeare's ultimate monarch, it is because historical sources provided the author with material that met the Elizabethan conditions for idealisation. Yet these semiotic conditions for producing the ideal political figure are precisely what make Henry V so resistant to modern criticism's attempts at appropriating him for a post-Enlightenment humanism.[10] The king's identity coalesces and his power intensifies as he unifies those territories that are his by hereditary law. But as this occurs, one finds that the figure of the monarch breaks apart and disappears into many different roles and dialects. He uses the strategies of disguise and inversion to occupy a range of positions from soldier to lover, as well as several roles in between. As a consequence, the king is virtually everywhere. He occupies the centre of every theatre of social action and in this way constitutes a state that to modern readers appears to have no centre at all, neither a continuous political policy nor an internally coherent self. To make sense to an Elizabethan audience, we must therefore assume the king's body did not have to behave as if it were that of a self-enclosed individual. Rather the histories suggest that body had to behave, semiotically speaking, as if blood had conspired with the disruptive operations of providence to produce it. In becoming so many functions and dialects of a single political body, he makes the various social groups he thus contains lose their autonomy. At the same time, the people acquire an ideal identity as they are embodied by the king.

The most successful monarch of the Elizabethan stage plays displayed his power by incorporating political elements – people, land, dialects – within the body politic. So, too, the power of the monarch achieved legitimacy as recalcitrant cultural materials were taken up and hierarchised within the official rituals of state. Figuratively speaking, this notion of power argued against the idea of patriarchy whose authority was based purely on primogeniture and the metaphysics of blood. But since no challenge to patriarchal authority was successful unless the claimant also happened to possess the blood, the exercise of force alone could hardly convert the energy of the populace into a display of legitimate power. Thus a monarch's ability to convert carnivalesque activity into banqueting and procession was the sign of his entitlement to political power.

From Leonard Tennenhouse, *Power on Display* (London, 1986) pp. 72–85.

NOTES

['Rituals of State/Strategies of Power' is extracted from a chapter entitled 'Rituals of State: History and the Elizabethan Strategies of Power', in Leonard Tennenhouse's book. An American New Historicist, Tennenhouse was introduced into British radical criticism by the inclusion in Dollimore and Sinfield's *Political Shakespeare* (Manchester, 1985), of an earlier version of this essay ('Strategies of State and Political Plays: A *Midsummer Night's Dream, Henry IV, Henry V, Henry VIII*'), pp. 109–29). Ed.]

1. As C. L. Barber notes, 'In making Oberon, prince of faeries, into the May King, Shakespeare . . . presents the common May game presided over by an aristocratic garden god'. *Shakespeare's Festive Comedy: A Study of Dramatic Form and its Relation to Social Custom* (Princeton, 1959), p. 159.

2. The problems with Henry VIII's will have been detailed by Mortimer Levine in *The Early Elizabethan Succession Question: 1558–1568* (Stanford, 1966), see especially pp. 99–162.

3. This summary draws upon Marie Axton's fine study, *The Queen's Two Bodies: Drama and the Elizabethan Succession* (London, 1977), and Ernst H. Kantorowicz, *The King's Two Bodies: A Study in Mediaeval Political Theology* (Princeton, 1957).

4. E. P. Thompson, 'The moral economy of the English crowd in the eighteenth century', in *Past and Present*, 50 (1971), 76–136.

5. While a number of critics have held to some version of the thesis that Richard was more a poet than a king, the most extreme is Mark van Doren, *Shakespeare* (New York, 1939), p. 89.

6. Joseph A. Porter, *The Drama of Speech Acts: Shakespeare's Lancastrian Tetralogy* (Berkeley, 1979), argues Bullingbroke is the figure for the

drama itself as opposed to Richard whose theatricality is always contained by Henry, pp. 175–7.

7. See, for example, Sherman H. Hawkins, 'Virtue and Kingship in Shakespeare's *Henry IV*', in *English Literary Renaissance*, 5 (1975), 313–43.

8. Henry Ansagar Kelly, *Divine Providence in the England of Shakespeare's Histories* (Cambridge, Mass., 1970). Kelly shows that the workings of providence in the two tetralogies is neither consistent nor continuous.

9. I am indebted to Peter Stallybrass for calling these lines to my attention.

10. Norman Rabkin summarises the critical discomforts many have with this play, in *Shakespeare and the Problem of Meaning* (Chicago, 1981), pp. 33–62.

3

History, Tragedy, Gender

LINDA BAMBER

In the two tetralogies of English history plays, the feminine Other seems to change as we go along. From the beginning of the first tetralogy to the first play of the second, the desires and activities of women are differentiated more and more from those of the men. My series begins with Joan of Arc in *I Henry VI* and ends with Isabel in *Richard II*; Joan is in many ways similar to the masculine Self, whereas Isabel is very different. The masculine Self in history is always defined in terms of his place in the world of men. His central activity is the struggle to procure, maintain, or wield power, and his experience of what lies beyond this struggle is limited. At the beginning of the history cycles the woman is also defined in terms of her success or failure in the masculine-historical struggle for power. Joan of Arc fights and kills like a man, desires only victory for her party and power for herself. Isabel, at the other end of my series, embodies an idea of the feminine that is fully differentiated from the masculine Self. She is queen of an alternative realm, the realm of the garden where her major scene takes place. The world of men offers political and military adventure and a headlong struggle for power; Isabel's garden world is private, slow, full of a sorrow that cannot be released in action. In the histories the feminine develops from an almost undifferentiated participant in the masculine adventure into an emblem of what is left out in the masculine-historical mode. Initially similar to the masculine Self, the feminine changes into something essentially different. . . .

The one female character in these plays who is defined by something beyond history is Queen Isabel in *Richard II*. Isabel's sense of loss is resonant with more than the fortunes of the political moment. Indeed, in Act II, scene ii, she grieves a loss that has not yet occurred:

> Some unborn sorrow ripe in Fortune's womb
> Is coming towards me; and my inward soul
> With nothing trembles – at something it grieves
> More than with parting from my lord the king.
>
> (II.ii.10–13)

The conversation in which this speech occurs is itself an anomaly in a history play – leisurely, philosophical, dealing with the nature of emotion. Furthermore, Isabel rejects Bushy's commonsense analysis and insists on the reality of her 'inward soul' and its feelings. It is not merely Richard's departure that she grieves, as Bushy supposes, but something hidden, mysterious, ineffable. Isabel alone of the history women connects us this intangible world.

With Isabel's crucial scenes we get a sense of stop-action, a quick descent into a different world. Time moves differently when we are with her; nothing happens. It is the garden scene that most strikingly illustrates the alternative Isabel represents. Here we are aware of natural time, not historical time; of the growth of plants rather than the movement of the wheel of Fortune. The Queen, of course, is not the one who talks of grafting, pruning and binding the flowers. But it is she who supplies the emotion in this scene, and her emotion at the news of Richard's demise is what forges the bond between man and the natural things in the garden. As she leaves she says, 'Gard'ner, for telling me these news of woe, / Pray God, the plants thou graft'st may never grow' (III.iv.100–1). He answers,

> Poor queen, so that thy state might be no worse,
> I would my skill were subject to thy curse.
> Here did she fall a tear; here in this place
> I'll set a bank of rue, sour herb of grace;
> Rue even for ruth here shortly shall be seen,
> In the remembrance of a weeping queen.
>
> (III.iv.102–7)

The symbolic connection between the woman and the flower, even though it is unhappy, creates a sense of a female principle apart from history. Like Ophelia and Perdita distributing flowers, Isabel in the garden reminds us of our place in nature, which, unlike our place in society, is not subject to the wheel of time. Isabel's grief interrupts the momentum of the action; it surrounds Richard's downfall like a nimbus of sorrowful love.

With Isabel we arrive at an idea of the feminine similar to the one that operates in the tragedies. For the feminine in the tragedies is associated with unhistorical experience. From one point of view, of course, this is a pity. At one level, the progression I have been describing is nothing but a progression toward the cultural stereotype. Isabel is passive whereas the typical history hero is active; while she grieves, he fights. A feminine defined in terms of gardens, the ineffable, and natural cycles of time is certainly nothing new. What we are missing are images of women who *do* participate in history, and the progression I have been describing may seem to be a movement away from the feminine as an element in history. But the women in the early history plays do not participate in history *as women*. Joan is a kind of second-class man . . . . Since such characters participate in history only as inferior versions of the masculine Self, or as failed versions of the feminine Other, they do not offer the kind of images we might profit from. The women characters in these plays who are involved in the events of history either betray their own femininity or simply mimic the men. Nothing is lost, then, in the progression from Joan to Isabel. And from the perspective of what is to follow the histories, something is gained. For in the tragedies, the woman as Other becomes a powerful dialectical force, and the progression toward Isabel is a progression toward feminine Otherness. The separation of Isabel from the world of men prefigures the dialectical opposition in the tragedies between the world of men and the woman as Other. Only as the Other are women in Shakespeare consistently the equals of men. Only in opposition to the hero and the world of men, only as representatives of alternative experience do the women characters matter to Shakespeare's drama as much as the men.

In the tragedies the women characters oppose the world of men in several ways. Sometimes they represent an anti-historical world; sometimes they directly threaten the hero's place in history; sometimes they simply elicit such powerful and chaotic emotions from the hero that he can no longer play his public role. . . . The feminine in the tragedies is always something that cannot be possessed, controlled, conquered; it resists the colonising impulse of the imperial male Self. . . .

But in *Richard II* the challenge of Isabel's Otherness is only latent. The feminine offers too powerful a challenge to the idea of history itself for Shakespeare to deal with it in the history plays. The Otherness of the feminine challenges the ethos of power and conquest through aggression; history as a genre must ultimately base itself on that ethos no matter how it also criticises it. If we lose interest in the military-political adventure we have lost interest in history itself as a genre. The feminine is not the only challenge to the history ethos; the struggle for power in Shakespearean history is always as tawdry as it is glamorous, challenged by common sense, common decency, and a sense of the common good. But apparently there is something uncommon in the challenge offered by the feminine. The feminine Other is too explosive a figure for history; having arrived, with Isabel, at a feminine that is truly Other, Shakespeare seems to put her away for safekeeping until he is ready to abandon history for tragedy. Not until he is ready to abandon history altogether does the feminine return in force.

After Isabel, the women characters neither participate in history nor challenge it. They merely create a kind of contrast or background from which the hero rides off to his adventure. Hotspur's parting from his wife is illustrative. In *I Henry IV* Lady Percy tries to get a declaration of love from Hotspur as he is leaving her for the wars; he replies,

> Come, wilt thou see me ride?
> And when I am a-horseback, I will swear
> I love thee infinitely.
> (II.iii.99–101)

Shakespeare seems to have understood the implications of history-as-a-genre for relations with women, and here presents them in their starkest form. If women neither seriously challenge the values of the history world nor participate as women in the crucial activities of this world, then they are supernumeraries in a world of men. Relations with the feminine take place but do not much matter: 'This is no world', as Hotspur puts it, 'To play with mammets and to tilt with lips' (II.iii.90–1). If the woman is not a version of the Other, she is powerless to counteract the lure of the masculine-historical adventure. Hotspur, the true believer in history-as-an-ethos, demonstrates the irrelevance of the feminine to those who live up to this creed. Kate's response to Hotspur's rejection is illuminating:

Do you not love me? Do you not indeed?
Well, do not then; for since you love me not,
I will not love myself. Do you not love me?
Nay, tell me if you speak in jest or no.
                                    (II.iii.95–8)

Where the woman does not represent the Other, she is and perceives herself to be merely the adjunct of the man. She has no kingdom of her own, and if he abandons her she loses everything.

Of course, Hotspur and Kate are only one version of relations between men and women in the last three plays of the second tetralogy. A more significant version, perhaps, is the one represented by Henry V and Katherine of France. For Hotspur only represents history at its most unselfconscious, and therefore he verges on self-parody. Henry V is the opposite of Hotspur; he is thoroughly conscious of his own role as a history hero, as detached as can be from his role. But even Henry V is not confronted by the feminine Other. Katherine is no challenge to Henry's public role.

As one critic has put it, 'Katherine is regarded by everybody (including herself), and by Henry in the first place, as part of the war spoils resulting from the Agincourt victory.'[1] Henry may love Katherine, as he says he does, but she is no more serious an issue for him than Kate is for Hotspur. The greatest challenge to the hero's historicity comes not from Katherine but from Falstaff; although I shall return to Henry V and Katherine, it is worth digressing to consider the differences between the challenge of the feminine and the challenge offered by such a character as Falstaff. In *Shakespeare and the Energies of Drama*, Michael Goldman tells us that Falstaff represents 'our sensuality and our impulse to anarchy';[2] as such he is a threat to political organisation per se, not just to the feudal monarchy Hal inherits. Falstaff suggests a world beyond the dialectic of politics, just as the women do in the tragedies. But finally Falstaff is rejected completely: 'I know thee not, old man' (V.v.47), says Hal on becoming king. Maturity in history implies the brutal rejection of whatever is incompatible with the hero's public role; Falstaff is a part of Hal that is removed with surgical precision.

When, by contrast, the masculine-historical adventure is challenged by the Other as woman, the surgical solution is never adopted. In the tragedies the opposing principle is a sexual one rather than a general, asexual principle of pleasure; here Shakespeare never imagines so successful a rejection as Henry's of Falstaff. The hero who comes closest to rejecting the feminine outright is Othello; but of course he cannot long survive his murder of Desdemona. Henry, by contrast, goes on to dominate another whole play. In the tragedies the feminine cannot be dealt with as Falstaff is dealt with in history, by excision. When it is Falstaff who represents 'the vulnerable body of our sensuality',[3] it is possible to put that body aside; but when sensuality is what connects us to the other sex, we must simply come to terms with the constant threat it offers to our public identity. Falstaff shows history up for what it is, an enterprise that denies much of our experience; the feminine in tragedy is analogous to whatever finally makes history impossible, as a genre for Shakespeare and as an enterprise for his heroes.

Katherine of France, however, is no representative of the feminine that ends history. When women represent a significant challenge to the masculine-historical mode, the heroes are never so good-humoured as Henry is in his relations with Katherine. The great final wooing scene in *Henry V* is the most sustained encounter between a man and a woman in the histories, and it is worth looking at in some detail.

The most notable feature of this scene is the complete absence of anxiety with which this great hero of history approaches the feminine. Henry is relaxed and self-confident, animated by an enjoyment of his own performance. He begins with a little easy hyperbole: 'An angel is like you Kate, and you are like an angel' (V.ii.110–11). But things aren't going to be *that* easy. Katherine protests against the obvious flattery by murmuring something about language and deception; so Henry immediately switches to the plain style:

> I know no ways to mince it in love, but directly to say, 'I love you'. Then, if you urge me farther than to say, 'Do you swear in faith?' I wear out my suit. Give me your answer, i' faith, do; and so clap hands, and a bargain. How say you, lady?
>
> (V.ii.128–33)

If Kate wants plainness, Henry seems to say, how is 'clap hands, and a bargain' for plainness? Obviously, a little too plain. Henry will not be trapped into sincerity, even though his love may be sincere. His bluffness is a role he plays to reveal and conceal himself simultaneously. He does want to win Katherine of France, but he also knows he has already won her – at Agincourt. The bluffness is a way of being true to both these facts:

> I speak to thee plain soldier: if thou canst love me for this, take me; if
> not, to say to thee that I shall die, is true – but for thy love, by the
> Lord, no; yet I love thee too.
>
> (V.ii.152–5)

Henry's feelings are clear enough – to himself, to Katherine, and to us. Michael Goldman emphasises the element of performance in this scene, and the effort it costs Henry to put on *all* his performances. The wooing scene, says Goldman, is 'the right note of mirth to cap the play' because it is 'as much a performance as his speech on Crispin's Day'. It is consistent because it continues to illustrate, says Goldman, 'the effort of greatness'.[4] But surely it illustrates just the opposite. The Crispin's Day speech *did* require a great deal of effort; it was produced for a demanding audience whose assent was not a foregone conclusion. Henry's troops might have refused to be stirred and therefore to fight. The wooing speeches, by contrast, have an audience with no desire but to be charmed. If the Crispin's Day speech is a full-dress performance in front of an important and demanding audience, the wooing of Katherine is a piece of good-natured guerrilla theatre before an audience of one. Henry teases this audience with her own desire to be told stories; flirts with the possibility of breaking through the fiction and telling the bald truth; and amuses himself at her expense with his own doubleness. Henry's effort to speak French, for instance, is self-forgiving, exasperated at the need to make an effort at all, self-entertaining. It is reminiscent of Viola and Rosalind pretending to be men – delighted that they can pull it off at all, and certainly without the ambition to do it very well. The speech is preceded, moreover, by a quick insult to the listener, who must identify with the hypothetical 'new-married wife' to which Henry compares his own French:

> I will tell thee in French, which I am sure will hang upon my tongue
> like a new-married wife about her husband's neck, hardly to be shook
> off. Je quand sur le possession de France, et quand vous avez le
> possession de moi (let me see, what then? Saint Denis be my speed!),
> donc votre est France, et vous êtes mienne. It is as easy for me, Kate,
> to conquer the kingdom as to speak so much more French; I shall
> never move thee in French, unless it be to laugh at me.
>
> (V.ii.180–9)

Henry's speeches go wittily on and on, turning corners, leaping fences, backing into antitheses – while Katherine confines herself to dimples and coyness. Of Henry's insolent French, for instance, she says primly and conventionally, 'Sauf votre honneur, le français que vous parlez, il est meilleur que l'anglais lequel je parle' (V.ii.190–1). A heroine with the substance to challenge male strengths – a Desdemona or a Cleopatra – would never meet Henry's provocation with so mild and straight a response.

'Strain' and 'effort' are precisely what this scene is free of. Henry's power and desire is wholly unopposed by Katherine, who is a negligible presence in the scene. Henry has all the good lines. If this scene is the right one to 'cap' the play, as Goldman says, it is because Henry at ease is as compelling as Henry at his real work, not because Henry works as hard to play the lover as he does to play the general. The opposition by the French troops was real and dangerous; Katherine's opposition is non-existent.

Neither Hotspur's Kate nor Henry's Katherine offers any resistance to the exercise of masculine power. The one woman after Isabel who does challenge the masculine mode is the Duchess of York in *Richard II*, and her challenge is a comic one. In Act V, scene ii, York discovers that his son Aumerle is part of the Oxford conspiracy against the new king, Henry IV. York rides off to denounce Aumerle for a traitor; the Duchess follows to beg for the life of her son. York, of course, is behaving prudentially; but at one level he also represents masculine honour, patriotism and fealty as opposed to pure mother-love on the Duchess's part. The Duchess asks her husband incredulously,

> Why, York, what wilt thou do?
> Wilt thou not hide the trespass of thine own?
> Have we more sons? Or are we like to have?
> Is not my teeming date drunk up with time?
> And wilt thou pluck my fair son from mine age?
> And rob me of a happy mother's name?
> Is he not like thee? Is he not thine own?
> (V.ii.88–94)

And York replies,

> Thou fond mad woman,
> Wilt thou conceal this dark conspiracy?
> A dozen of them here have ta'en the sacrament
> And interchangeably set down their hands
> To kill the king at Oxford.
> (V.ii.95–9)

To York the king must be treated as an absolute even when he is guilty, like Henry IV, of usurpation. To the Duchess the idea of the king is meaningless. She follows her husband to Windsor to plead her cause; but when she is heard at the door Bolingbroke says, 'Our scene is alt'red from a serious thing, / And now changed to "The Beggar and the King"' (V.iii.78–9). The arrival of the woman turns the tense political situation into a family comedy. In fact the seriousness of the conflict is undermined in the previous scene where Aumerle and the Oxford conspiracy are treated as the occasion for a domestic dustup. When York calls for his boots, for instance, the Duchess tries to prevent his departure by driving off the servant who brings them. She shouts to Aumerle to strike the servant, but Aumerle is dazed and does not obey. The Duchess then attacks the servant herself, 'Hence, villain, never more come in my sight'; but York bellows, 'Give me my boots, I say' (V.ii.86–7), and rides off, furious. There can be no real question of Bolingbroke's verdict on Aumerle when it has been preceded by such family antics. The conflict between the Duke and the Duchess is obviously comic and will not have serious consequences. Aumerle is forgiven and the Duchess tells Bolingbroke extravagantly, 'A god on earth thou art' (V.iii.135). The Duchess as Mother offers only a comic contrast to the seriousness of the world of men.

From Joan to Isabel, then, the feminine in history follows a progression away from second-class citizenship in the world of men and toward a separate identity; but as soon as Shakespeare establishes the separateness of the feminine, he shelves the feminine as an Other until he is ready to write tragedy. The challenge of the feminine would destroy the historical mode; or, to put it the other way around, when Shakespeare is finished with history and ready for tragedy, the challenge of the feminine, heretofore latent, suddenly becomes central to his drama.

From Linda Bamber, *Comic Women, Tragic Men: A study of gender and genre in Shakespeare* (Stanford, 1982), pp. 137–47.

NOTES

[Linda Bamber's essay is taken from her book *Comic Women, Tragic Men*, which argues that the drama of Shakespeare is gendered in terms of a binary opposition between the writer's maleness and various manifestations of female Otherness which challenge the masculine Self. The original chapter title of the essay is: '*1 Henry VI* to *Henry V*: Toward Tragedy'. Ed.]

1. Zdenek Stribrny, '*Henry V* and History', in Arnold Kettle (ed.), *Shakespeare in a Changing World* (New York, 1964), p. 96.

2. Michael Goldman, *Shakespeare and the Energies of Drama* (Princeton, 1972), p. 57.

3. Ibid., p. 57.

4. Ibid., p. 73.

4

The Shadow of the Male

COPPÉLIA KAHN

> Thy mother's son! Like enough, and thy
> father's shadow. So the son of the female is the
> shadow of the male; it is often so, indeed – but
> much of the father's substance!
> (*II Henry IV*, III.ii.128–30)

The patriarchal world of Shakespeare's history plays is emphatically masculine. Its few women are relatively insignificant, and a man's identity is determined by his relationship to his father, son, or brother. The two tetralogies are a continuous meditation on the role of the father in a man's self-definition. . . . In these plays, it is the father from whom men strive to separate themselves or with whom they merge.

The shift from mother to father can be explained both in psychoanalytic and in historical terms. In Freud's developmental scheme, the father looms mainly as the castrating forbidder of the oedipal phase. But Mahler and others posit an earlier, more supportive role for him. The child's awareness of the father, they hold, begins at about the same time (eighteen months of age) he becomes decisively conscious that he and his mother are distinct entities. Concurrently, the child learns to walk, and if he is a boy, discovers he has a penis.[1] These several discoveries – of his separateness from his mother, the existence of his father, his possession of a penis, and his ability to stand upright and move freely – coincide, with important ramifications. Associating phallic consciousness with upright mobility, the boy is strongly motivated to turn away from his mother and toward his father. Furthermore, he feels profoundly ambivalent toward his mother, because he wants both to regress into symbiotic union with her and to move away from her into realistic interaction with the world. His father, associated with this newly perceived world of objects to be manipulated, places to be explored, and people to know, can help the child resist re-engulfment with the mother.[2] In the history plays, the intensity of the son's identification with the father measures the strength of the pull toward such re-engulfment, and the son's difficulty in separating from the mother.

In historical terms, Shakespeare makes late medieval society a mirror of his own by stressing its obsession with paternal authority and power. . . . Shakespeare uses history to test the lineal principle of patriarchy – that the son inherits his identity (the name and role by which he is known in society, and his inner sense of self) from his father. What Roland Barthes says of the father in Racine is also true of the father in the history plays:

> . . . his being is his anteriority; what comes after him is descended from him, ineluctably committed to a problematics of loyalty. The Father is the past . . . he is a primordial, irreversible fact: what has been *is*, that is the code of Racinian time. . . . Thus Blood is literally a law, which means a bond and a legality. The only movement permitted to the son is to break, not to detach himself.[3]

As historical event and psychological experience, the history plays present the problematics of loyalty to the father.[4]

. . . *Richard II* can be seen as an *agon* between maternal and paternal images of the kingship, Richard identifying himself with England as an all-providing mother, Henry with the patriarchal principle of succession. Both heroes invoke the principle, both violate it, and both suffer for that violation, but Richard's tragedy is that he fails to comprehend its meaning for his kingship or his identity as a man.

Throughout the play England is imaged in the traditional *topos* as a maternal presence, nurturing its people as her babes. In the tournament scene (I.iii), Richard deplores the enmity threatening to 'wake our peace, which in our country's cradle / Draws the sweet infant breath of gentle sleep' (132–5), and Bolingbroke departs for exile saying,

> Then, England's ground, farewell: sweet soil, adieu,
> My mother and my nurse that bears me yet!
> (I.iii.306–7)

Gaunt's famous death speech (II.i) combines a fantasy of boundless maternal provision – England as 'Eden', 'nurse', and 'teeming womb of kings' – with the idea of England as fortress, 'built by Nature for herself', a walled and moated 'seat of Mars'. Mother and child, land and people, constitute a self-contained defensive alliance against external threat. Gaunt reproaches Richard for using this communal refuge as his own preserve, but Richard never fully understands the distinction between himself and the realm as belonging to all. He uses his country as the nurturant source of his own grandeur, literally, when he 'farms' the crown's revenues, and figuratively, when he lands at Barkloughy, kissing 'my earth'. Though he calls himself the 'long-parted mother' reunited with her child the earth, as his speech unfolds it is the earth who mothers. As the good mother, she comforts Richard with flowers and sweets, while as the bad mother, she repulses his enemies with spiders, toads, nettles and adders.

First Gaunt, then York, reminds Richard of his paternal heritage, with its strict responsibilities, its well-delineated hierarchy of fathers and sons:

> O, had thy grandsire with a prophet's eye
> Seen how his son's son should destroy his sons. . . .
> (II.i.104–5)

> Take Herford's rights away, and take from time
> His charters, and his customary rights;
> Let not tomorrow then ensue today:
> Be not thyself. For how art thou a king
> But by fair sequence and succession?
> (II.i.195–9)

But Richard seems not to hear them; he even makes York his deputy after York's stinging reproof of his conduct. Bolingbroke, on the other hand, identifies with his father from the first moments of the play; when Richard bids him throw back Mowbray's gage, he replies, 'Shall I seem crest-fall'n in my father's sight?' (I.i.188), and in the tournament scene he addresses John of Gaunt, the noble embodiment of 'the fathers' in every sense.

> O thou, the earthly author of my blood
> Whose youthful spirit in me regenerate
> Doth with a two-fold vigour lift me up. . . .
> (I.iii.69–71)

When he returns from exile, Bolingbroke . . . claims only his paternal rights. But he stresses to York, as York stressed to Richard, the analogy between them and Richard's right to rule, implying that denial of the first endangers the second:

> You are my father, for methinks in you
> I see old Gaunt alive. O then my father,
> Will you permit that I shall stand condemned
> A wandering vagabond, my rights and royalties
> Pluck'd from my arms perforce, and given away
> To upstart unthrifts? Wherefore was I born?
> If that my cousin be King in England,
> It must be granted I am Duke of Lancaster.
>   (II.iii.116–23)

. . . When he cannot call upon his identification with mother England, Richard becomes a hollow king. . . . For him there is no mean between fullness and emptiness, omnipotence or total dejection, because he is emotionally dependent on a boundless supply of reassurance, maternal in origin and quality, which the real world cannot supply.

Richard II portrays a loss of identity through a loss of kingship; the *Henry IV* plays, an identity won through kingship. The story of how Henry and his son reciprocally validate each other as father and son, king and prince, begins in the last act of *Richard II*, when Henry cries, 'Can no man tell me of my unthrifty son?' (V.iii.1). Henry's anxiety about Hal is complexly related to his two last actions in the play: pardoning Aumerle's treason and arranging for the murder of Richard. The two actions are depicted so as to present a spectrum of attitudes toward the father-son bond. Though York at first defends Richard as the divinely appointed king who rules by successive right, he finally opts for loyalty to Henry as de facto king, but not without misgivings. In accusing his own son of treason, he acts on this new loyalty but violates the blood tie between himself and his son – the tie that, the Duchess argues, far outweighs any other. Surprisingly, Henry pardons Aumerle and goes against his own characteristic allegiance to patriarchal order by failing to punish a man who would betray both father and king. Henry gives no explanation for his action except to say, 'I pardon him as God shall pardon me' (V.iii.129). Since this scene is followed by the scene in which Exton pins the responsibility for Richard's murder on Henry, we may infer that Henry pardons Aumerle's treason because he already feels guilty for his own. In order to be king, he kills the king, his brother-cousin, and must suffer Cain's guilt. Henry regards Hal as his punishment long before he explicitly admits (in *II Henry IV*) having committed any crime. He who righteously invoked the principle of succession even as his troops massed before Richard at Flint Castle, and claimed to seek only his 'lineal royalties', is appropriately punished by his own son's seeming unfitness to inherit the crown.

In the course of the two *Henry IV* plays, Shakespeare presents a conception of the father-son bond and its part in the formation of a masculine identity . . . with some give to it, literally some free play, some space for departure from paternal priority and for experiences fundamentally opposed to it. . . . He tries to portray a successful passage negotiated, paradoxically, as lawful rebellion and responsible play. He makes Hal the stage manager of his own growing up, the embodiment of a wish to let go – but to let go only so far, without real risks. In the end, Falstaff's regressive appeal is so dangerously strong for Shakespeare that he cannot afford to integrate it into Hal's character, and must, to Hal's loss, exclude it totally. . . . He begins to see how the father's identity is shaped by his son, as well as the son's by his father. In Henry and Hal he uses the renewal of the principle of succession as a way to validate Henry's kingship as much as Hal's; identity becomes a reciprocal process between father and son.

The relationship between the two men has three focal points of overdetermined needs and signals at which crises are defined or resolved. The first is the Boar's Head and Hal's reign there as madcap prince under the tutelage of Falstaff, who is usually seen as anti-king and anti-father, standing for misrule as opposed to rule.[5] But he is also the opposite of the king in the sense of being his predecessor psychologically, the king of childhood and omnipotent wishes, as Henry is king in the adult world of rivalry and care. Franz Alexander describes Falstaff as the personification of 'the primary self-centred narcissistic libido of the child', commenting that

> the child in us applauds, the child who knows only one principle and that is to live. . . . Since the child cannot actually overcome any external interferences, it takes refuge in fantastic, megalomaniac self deception.[6]

'Banish plump Jack, and banish all the world!' Falstaff cries. Because of his sophisticated adult wit, however, he makes social capital out of his megalomania; men love his gloriously ingenious lies better than their own truth. Falstaff is a world unto himself, shaped like the globe and containing multitudes of contradictions as the world itself does; fat and ageing in body, but ever young in spirit and nimble in wit; a shape-shifter in poses and roles, yet always inimitably himself; a man with a curiously feminine sensual abundance.

A fat man can look like a pregnant woman, and Falstaff's fatness is fecund; it spawns symbols. In the context of Hal's growing up, its feminine meaning has particular importance.[7] As W. H. Auden says, it is 'the expression of a psychological wish to withdraw from sexual competition and by combining mother and child in his own person, to become emotionally self-sufficient'.[8] Falstaff is said to be fond of hot wenches and leaping-houses, but he is no Don Juan even in *Part II* when his sexual relations with Doll Tearsheet and Mistress Quickly are made more explicit. They are fond of him rather than erotically drawn to him. It is not only tactful regard for Hal's legendary dignity as the perfect king that keeps Shakespeare from compromising him by making Falstaff a lecher. Rather, Falstaff represents the wish to bypass women; he has grown old, but remains young, and yet in terms of women has 'detoured manhood', as Harold Goddard says.[9] . . . The fat knight desires food and drink more than he desires women. And though women are devoted to him, he cheats and deceives them, giving his own deepest affections to a boy. No wonder that, for Hal, Falstaff incarnates his own rebellion against growing up into a problematic adult identity.

Hal himself is unaware that his affinity for the fat knight constitutes rebellion; he conceives it, rather, as part of his long-term strategy for assuming a proper identity as king. That strategy reveals his likeness to his father, his ability to think and act in the same terms of political image-building as his father, his fitness for the very role he seems to be rejecting. . . .

Neither man can freely express his true self, whatever that is, because each has something to hide. Hal hides his sympathy with his father, while Henry hides his guilt over the deposition and murder of Richard. Nonetheless, that guilt is revealed in the way he splits his son into two contending images: the bad son, Hal the wastrel; and the good son, Hotspur the king of honour. For Hal to become his father's son personally (to be loved) and politically (to be trusted as fit to succeed his father), he must restore his reputation as heir apparent, triumph over Hotspur, and assume Hotspur's identity as

French campaign – a strategem suggested by his father's dying advice to 'busy giddy minds with foreign quarrels . . . to waste the memory of former days' (*II Henry IV*, IV.v.213–15). In the scene that takes place on the eve of Agincourt, Shakespeare is at pains to compare Henry and Hal as kings, showing how Hal has infused his new role with qualities he could only have gained through his regression and rebellion in Eastcheap, while at the same time revealing what of the father lives on in the son.

Henry V mingling unrecognised with his common soldiers just before a crucial battle is a far cry from Henry IV hiding behind the many 'counterfeit kings' marching in his coats at Shrewsbury. The common humanity from which Hal seemed to exclude himself by rejecting Falstaff with neither love nor regret now inspires him to share both his fear and his courage with his men. He does it by acting – not the image-building his father used to get the crown, but the self-expressive role playing that he and Falstaff indulged in when they pretended to be king and each other (*I Henry IV*, II.iv). Speaking as Harry le Roy, Hal really speaks from his own heart as king:

> For, though I speak it to you, I think the king is but a man, as I am: the violet smells to him as it doth to me; the element shows to him as it doth to me; all his senses have but human conditions: his ceremonies laid by, in his nakedness he appears but a man; and though his affections are higher mounted than ours, yet when they stoop, they stoop with the like wing.
>
> (IV.i.100–8)

Intending to practise what he preaches, Hal declares he will refuse ransom and face death like any common soldier – then picks a quarrel with the soldier who doubts him. He perpetrates the same kind of creative, illuminating trickery as he did in the Gadshill robbery. Williams, maintaining his honour honestly as Henry knows he will, is not afraid to protest his own innocence before the king, saying, 'I beseech you, take it for your own fault and not mine' (IV.viii.54–6). Hal contrives the whole incident with a combination of insight, humour, and sympathy he could only have gained in Eastcheap, pursuing his own eccentric course of growth.

The topic of Henry's conversation with the soldiers is the question of whether the king is morally responsible for the deaths of those who fight in his wars. Hal's argument is earnest and his logic convincing when he says, 'Every subject's duty is the king's; but every subject's soul is his own' (IV.i.182–4). However, he might well add,

'and every king's soul is not just his own but his father's as well'.
When the soldiers leave, Hal delivers a long soliloquy that recapitulates and combines the major motifs from two great speeches in *II Henry IV*: his father's meditation on sleep (III.i) and his own on the crown (IV.v). The theme of all three speeches can be stated as the ironic disparity between the tangible majesties of kingship and its emotional burdens. Hal's soliloquy might be uttered by any of Shakespeare's kings: its truths are universal. But its context makes it a telling comment on Hal's particular identity as king. Not only does it refer backward to the troubled circumstances of Hal's succession to the throne, it leads into the prayer in which he confesses his fear that God will punish him for his father's crime by giving the victory to the French:

> Not today, O Lord!
> O not today, think not upon the fault
> My father made in compassing the crown!
>   (IV.i.298–300)

Despite his ability to succeed where his father failed, unifying his kingdom and winning the love of all his people; despite the originality of his kingship, his playfulness and *joie de vivre* in such marked contrast to his father's careworn formality, he has inherited his father's sense of guilt along with his father's crown.[11]

Plus ça change, plus c'est la même chose, it might be said. The same mixture of originality and repetition characterises attitudes toward women, and relationships between men, in this final play of the two tetralogies. Henry bases his claim to the French crown on the Salic Law, which forbids inheritance through the female and thus expresses the principle underlying masculine identity in the two tetralogies: men are defined by other men, not by women. Yet while the play contains an episode of masculine friendship that strongly recalls the idyllic warrior bonding of the Talbots, and while it evokes powerfully the brotherhood of warriors under a strong father-king, it concludes with a marriage that blesses rather than subverts that brotherhood. Though Katherine is actually part of Henry's French spoils, the first article in a treaty her father can hardly refuse to sign, like the Kate of an earlier comedy she is a woman willing to submit, and *Henry V* is a comedy, resolving discord in a symbolic marriage. Thus Shakespeare attempts to round off happily the story of Prince Hal's troubled progress to manhood: he is a successful father-king and a lusty bridegroom. Shakespeare leaves it to us to decide whether the terms in which his kingship and manhood are won – the French campaign with its doubtful rationale, its cruelty and destruction, as well as its effective political unification of England – can win our full approval. Before he sets off for France, Henry must contend with treachery at home: Scroop's betrayal. . . . Love and trust have no place at court; it is only in battle that friendships between men can flourish even unto death, as does that between York and Suffolk. Their dual death scene (IV.vi) is a sharply etched cameo of homoerotic martial pathos: York kissing Suffolk's wounds and lips, and envisioning their souls flying into heaven together – a complete merging of one man with another, . . . evoking a desire for the peaceful dual unity of mother and child, a unity based on sameness, before self is differentiated from other or male from female, it stands in high contrast to the infrequent, dangerous, and unbalanced liaisons with women in the history plays.

These loving pairs of warriors invite comparison with the common band of warriors. Henry's first speech before Harfleur (III.i) employs heavily sexual imagery to exhort his men to courage and strength. The analogies between besieging a walled city and rape are brought to the surface when Henry urges each man to make himself, in effect, a battering ram or erect phallus: stiffening his sinews, making his eye a cannon and his brow a rock, setting his teeth and holding his breath. In the second half of the speech, he makes this martial virility a test of legitimacy (they must emulate their fathers in this collective erection, or dishonour their mothers by seeming bastards) as well as of nationality (the virile English as opposed to the effete French). Several other speeches by Henry and Exeter threaten the French with sexual violence against their mothers, wives and sweethearts. Thus until Henry's wooing of Katherine, love is felt only between men as a form of complete pregenital merger, and sexuality takes the form of men's collective violence against women.

. . . After exploring the richly shaded, complex relationship between father and son in the *Henry IV* plays, after showing how problematic, psychologically as well as politically, the principle of succession is, Shakespeare returns to the simple, idealised male comradeships he began with. Henry woos Kate as a soldier – that is at once the charm and the necessary condition of his courtship; it sets the distance between them on which his manhood depends.

From Coppélia Kahn, *Man's Estate: Masculine Identity in Shakespeare* (Berkeley, 1981), pp. 47–9, 66–81.

NOTES

['The Shadow of the Male' forms a chapter of Coppélia Kahn's book *Man's Estate* which is concerned with the question of masculine identity in the whole of Shakespeare's plays. Kahn's work represents a pioneering synthesis of psychoanalysis and feminism. All quotations in the essay are from the Arden editions of Shakespeare. Ed.]

1. See Margaret S. Mahler, Fred Pine and Anni Bergman, *The Psychological Birth of the Human Infant: Symbiosis and Individuation* (New York, 1975), on the third subphase of separation individuation, especially pp. 91, 102–6.

2. See Ernest L. Abelin, 'The Role of the Father in the Separation-Individuation Process', in *Separation-Individuation: Essays in Honor of Margaret S. Mahler*, ed. J. B. McDevitt and C. F. Settlage (New York, 1971), pp. 229–52.

3. Roland Barthes, *On Racine*, tr. Richard Howard (New York, 1964), pp. 37–8. Sir Robert Filmer's *Patriarcha, and Other Political Works*, ed. Peter Laslett (Oxford, 1949) in effect translates Barthes' Racinian paradigm into a comprehensive justification of the father's absolute and eternal supremacy as the source of all social order. He holds that all men are subjected to their fathers because they were created after them in time, and that their subjection even as adults ends only when they themselves become fathers and, at the will of the king their supreme father, transfer their allegiance to him.

4. The only critics who have specifically addressed father-son relationships in the history plays are Ronald S. Berman, 'Fathers and Sons in the *Henry VI* plays', *Shakespeare Quarterly*, 13 (1962), 487–97; Robert B. Pierce, *Shakespeare's History Plays: the Family and the State* (Columbus, Ohio, 1971); and Edward I. Berry, *Patterns of Decay: Shakespeare's Early Histories* (Charlottsville, Va., 1975), ch. 3, '*3 Henry VI*: Kinship'.

5. Notably, by Ernst Kris, 'Prince Hal's Conflict', in *The Design Within: Psychoanalytic Approaches to Shakespeare*, pp. 389–407, who takes Hal's friendship with Falstaff as an outlet for and defence against his hostility towards his father. Kris's case depends too heavily on the hypothesis that Hal had a previous friendship with Richard II, and on reading a parricidal urge into Hal's taking of the crown, however evident it is that Falstaff is a father-figure.

6. Franz Alexander, 'A Note on Falstaff', *Psychoanalytic Quarterly*, 2 (1933), 392–406.

7. Suggested subtly and convincingly by Sherman Hawkins in 'Falstaff as Mom', a talk given at the Special Session on Marriage and the Family in Shakespeare, at a meeting of the Modern Language Association, Chicago, 30 December 1977.

8. W. H. Auden, 'The Prince's Dog', in his *The Dyer's Hand* (New York, 1963), p. 196.

9. Harold C. Goddard, '*Henry IV*', in his *The Meaning of Shakespeare*, 2 vols (Chicago, 1951), vol. 1, p. 184.

10. See discussions of the Wild Prince legend and *The Famous Victories of Henry V* (which has a similar structure) by A. R. Humphreys in his introduction to *I Henry IV*, Arden edition (London, 1960), pp. xxix–xxxi, xxii–xxiv, and Geoffrey Bullough, *Narrative and Dramatic Sources of Shakespeare*, 7 vols (New York, 1966), vol. 4, pp. 155–80, especially pp. 159–60.

11. In a paper forthcoming in *Modern Language Studies*, ' "The fault/My father made": The Anxious Pursuit of Heroic Fame in Shakespeare's *Henry V*', Peter B. Erickson offers a searching interpretation of Henry as a son still burdened by his father's guilt, and hears in Henry's soliloquy on the eve of Agincourt, describing the penance he has performed for the murder of Richard, 'a clear note of futility about the absolution which Henry V seeks for himself'. He finds tension and ambivalence between a desire for epic fame and a fear of oblivion, and between anger and pity, in Henry's character throughout the play, because 'Henry must surpass his father . . . that is the prearranged means of atoning for and with him'.

5

Shakespearean Authority

ROBERT S. KNAPP

A crucial part of the creation of literary drama in England involved
the differentiation of mongrel tragicomedy into a system of struc-
tured and more or less determinate generic shapes. Without such a
sorting into coded emphases upon the individual image and its sexual
or textual deflection, English drama could not have set its own
frame, could not have transcended the determinants of civic ritual
and ideological occasion. Yet part of the peculiarity of Elizabethan
theatre also has to do with its reaching beyond the classically certi-
fied set of dramatic genres, thereby complicating the opposition
between tragedy and comedy with mutants – history and romance –
that neither the playwrights nor we moderns know for sure how to
name.[1]. . .

Shakespeare's insistence on impurity exemplifies his own unusual
authority: in their intricate blending of presence and absence, his
plays recapitulate the defining essence of drama itself, its uncertain
intersection of word and deed, text and other, literature and excessive act. Yet his apparent awareness of this mirroring interplay, while
it prevents him from letting drama succumb to conscious or unconscious code, never leads him to pretend that suspension can persist
forever. For another mark of Shakespeare's peculiarly dramatic authority is his insistence on judgement, his forcing events to a crisis
which issues in a defining shape, a shape which seems to depend not
upon the author's will, but upon a reality whose demands could be
refused only by an ideologue or a sentimentalist. It is as if the
Shakespearean genres each responded to the claims of finitude, as if
each were a way of giving the formula for a particular interaction

between anaclitic pairs. . . . The claims of finitude, the claims of presence and position; which also rest upon the absent, not quite contrary other, the might-have-been. . . .

. . . I want to claim that Shakespeare's management of the three (or four) Elizabethan and Jacobean genres displays the logically different possibilities of preserving a real – and therefore wounding – indecidability within these variously named but similar antinomies that have governed my discussion: theatre and book, symbol and function, cognitive and performative, non-natural and natural, metaphor and metonym, word and deed.[2] . . .

. . . Since more than any other of the histories, *Richard II* has come to stand for Shakespeare's meditation on the loss of medieval certainties about the order of things and the nature of representation, this initial play of the *Henriad* best introduces the basic problematic.

The first and certainly most influential critic to identify medievalism in the play seems to have been Tillyard, who described Richard's characteristic actions as 'symbolic rather than real', and who saw in the contrasting Bullingbrook one whose world 'displays a greater sincerity of personal emotion.[2] . . .

It testifies to the power of allegory, and to the persistence of modern anxieties about the loss of tradition, that this interpretation of *Richard II* has won such general assent.[3] For we know, of course, that Shakespeare cannot have had in mind what modern authorities would consider real medieval kingship. Even though the historical Richard II somewhat anticipated Tudor monarchs in contemplating a claim to divinely granted absolute authority, standard late medieval doctrines of kingship fell short of the needs of a monarchy intent on demonstrating the virtues of effective and thoroughgoing governance.[4] We know that the state apparatus therefore promulgated the doctrine of divine right through midcentury Tudor homilies, and that the contrary Anglo-Norman theory of the monarch's two bodies – which Kantorowicz proved central to this play – was revived only during the early years of Elizabeth's reign as a lawyerly device to define the 'relationship between sovereign and perpetual state', usually in ways that frustrated the queen's efforts to exercise the sort of imperium that her father had hoped to secure.[5]

The issues at stake in *Richard II*, then, were 'modern', alive throughout Elizabeth's reign and thereafter. The struggle between Richard's will to be the single, unassailable representative of God and his unruly subjects' desire to split the king's being into one natural body capable of death and another immortal body capable of succeeding to a different person, reflects a familiar and immediate controversy as to the powers and identity of the monarch. No doubt the lawyers' theory of two bodies and the Tudor theory of divine right both have medieval and indeed sacramental origins. But the tension displayed by means of such historically rooted theories shaped Shakespeare's own era and took a more extreme form in the century thereafter, partly because of new demands upon and resistance to sovereign authority, and partly because of the increasingly sharp ideological contention over these competing claims and theories.[6] As for the obtrusive ceremony and symbolism of the play, that too has medieval origins, but it was Tudor and Stuart monarchs – like their continental brethren – who made spectacles of state into major (and in that way very modern) vehicles of ideological control.[7]

Yet apart from questions of medievalism and modernity, *Richard II* plainly enacts a conflict between two interdependent yet partly incompatible sorts of authority, and it is this conflict which engages me here. . . . One can say that Richard has the name of kingship, whereas Bullingbrook is the man who can gather and wield its power.[8] . . . On the one side, an authority signified in names, forms and ceremony; on the other, an authority enacted, empowered and embodied. Whatever the precise terms of contrast . . . , *Richard II* obviously explores antinomies of language and action, symbol and function, public duty and private alliance, cognitive structure and performative force.

But personification, especially that which would set verbal Richard against active Henry, can make us miss the greater difficulty of the play, which is that neither Richard at the beginning nor Henry at the end can bring the words and deeds of monarchy together. Neither can successfully personate an undivided, fully legitimate crown, or make power conform to its ideal image. Richard, of course, is as profligate in expenditures and conduct as he is in speech. Far from maintaining any sort of divinely authenticated match between either the name of kingship and his political practice or between the image of God and his deputised likeness, Richard is altogether too much the 'figure of God's majesty', too given to an erotic troping and turning in both language and behaviour. His apparent complicity in the murder of Gloucester, his leasing of tax revenues, his perverting the ceremonies of chivalry, like his delight in 'lascivious metres' and the 'fashions in proud Italy', testify to 'unkindness' in the richest meta-

physical sense.[9] Though possessed both of the blood and name of proper kingship, he warps that legacy to deviant and improper ends.
. . .

But Bullingbrook, as critics regularly point out, and as Richard insists all through the play, equally fails to maintain propriety, either as a subject whose deeds match his obedient speech and symbolic gestures or as a sovereign with secure and lawful title to the crown that Richard 'wills' him. The riddle in his reiterated insistence that he has 'come but for mine own' will not come clear, since the scope of that property depends not solely on his name but on the power that informs it. Which is likewise a power to transform names and alter forms, changing first his 'own' name from Hereford to Lancaster, then crowning that alteration with another, the improper name that Richard scornfully gives him, 'King Bullingbrook', and finally assuming the image that makes 'high majesty look like itself' (II.i.295). Yet no more for Bullingbrook than for Richard does the power to change names and forms confer the power to create a stable reality. The crown, like any other property or sign, can move from one head and person to another, but that very capacity for motion and re-assignment prevents possession from being single: the kingdom still has rebels, the succession is still insecure, Henry still has an 'unthrifty son' whose adolescence promises to be still more riotous than Richard's.

For both the last of Edward's elder line and the first Lancastrian king, then, a problem exists with respect to identity. Both have trouble keeping the king's two bodies in harmony, but from different causes and in different ways. The one, though possessed of the proper name of kingship, cannot keep it free of figures, cannot subdue conceits of language and of youth so as to inspire continued belief that the 'king is himself', that his body private exhibits the undisfigured image of high majesty. The other, though his performance at least temporarily inspires confidence in such a public image, has come to his name only through the 'indirect crook'd ways' to which Shakespeare makes him allude when old and dying.[10]

Such indirection and deviation as afflicts King Bullingbrook, however, has curiously little to do with his apparent will – except the will to possess his own. For Bulingbrook's entrance to the throne seems oddly without intention, almost passive. We never see him plan the deposition, except after Richard has seemed to volunteer it. Scene by scene, events move inexorably through Henry's ascent and Richard's decline, but we never hear Bullingbrook express a treasonous or ambitious sentiment. At most, he agrees to Richard's prophecies and York's stage-management of a political theatre meant to baffle complaints of illegitimacy, a theatre that also baffles us in probing for the right or wrong intentions of the new king. All the turns of fortune, changes of name, and swervings of alliance and affection which lead Bullingbrook to assume the crown are but roads which he traverses, patterns which he follows, conceits in the unravelling of time to which he conforms himself.[11]

Richard's conceits, on the other hand, seem both wilful and deliberate. His alertness to the figurative possibilities latent in the grimmest situation – like his penchant for rhyme – dominates the play from beginning to end. . . . This difference between kings – that Bullingbrook follows out tropes within history whereas Richard gives conceit a voice – generates a dilemma that neither characters nor interpreters can resolve. The breath of kings, as Gaunt remarks at the moment of Richard's reduction of his son's years of banishment, can shorten days and 'pluck nights from me, but not lend a morrow' (I.iii.227–8); Richard's eloquent conceits can wrong plain language and plain dealing, can trick prophecies of woe and doom out of occasions that might otherwise seem innocent, but cannot charm the world into obedience. Though he can as aptly deck out figures for the defence of sacred kingship as for the Christological implications of its betrayal, he cannot call forth revenging plagues – except after it is too late to do him any good, after he has suffered the crucifixion also invoked in his despairing figures. Conceits that spring from grief – even the as yet nameless grief which his queen shrinkingly possesses 'in reversion' (II.ii.33–40) – come true for Richard; the rest do not. Yet history, though it has this tragic dimension, being full of the falls of princes and the defeat of plans, has its successful – or at least surviving – actors too, whose deeds work out designs that go beyond any individual's positive conception, depending on interactive patterns that no single wit can articulate, except, perhaps, by indirection.

The problem for both readers and enactors of history, then, is that the figures of thought and language – those conceits which always outrun and undo pure structure and idea – give only negative knowledge, after the fact. Even the gardener's 'model' can show only how infirm England's estate really is; 'old Adam's likeness' can divine Richard's downfall, but neither his pruning nor the queen's cursing of the gardener's grafts can improve the state (II.iv). The self, too – that putative origin of all such figures – is equally a vain conceit, as

Richard implies in the first despair of his acknowledgment that 'nothing can we call our own but death' (III.ii.152). Not the manifestation of an essence, this kingly self is but a name-shrouded nothing which must submit, must be deposed, and can never – so long as the king remains a man – be 'pleas'd, till he be eas'd / With being nothing' (III.iii.143–4; V.v.39–41). Or if not that – if Bullingbrook rather than Richard – then an impenetrable actor, an image of authority that outweighs empty names with theatrical power and with 'all the English peers' and commons who have preferred Lancastrian performance over Ricardian conceit (III.iv.85–9). For becoming Richard's heir does not solve the riddle of Bullingbrook's identity, does not reveal the essence that Mowbray accuses him of having: 'But what thou art, God, thou, and I do know, / And all too soon, I fear, the King shall rue' (I.iii.204–5). Yet the curse of being a successful image, ironically, is that one's words have a performative power that exceeds an ownable origin or intention. 'A god on earth thou art', says the Duchess of York upon Henry's pardon of her old, errant son. Already risking parody in the comic context of that scene, this bald affirmation of an ideology for Renaissance princes turns bitter in the very next episode when Sir Pierce of Exton convinces himself to act on Henry's words and rid him of the 'living fear' of Richard. And even this one undoubted coincidence of word and deed gives no clue to Henry's meaning, either to his real will or to the sense his actions ought to have in the book of life or in the hell where Exton's deed 'is chronicled' (V.v.116).

One could say with some justice that such a balance of imperfections – of hollow or at best negative conceits against successful but impenetrable performances – seems like a suspension of judgement between tragedy and comedy. Certainly the juxtaposition of Aumerle's pardon and Richard's murder, which encapsulates the larger juxtaposition of the rise of one prince and the fall of another, suggests as much. So, too, does the still larger suspension within the *Henriad* as a whole between the tragedy with which the quarto titles *Richard II* and the recurrent comedy of the two parts of *Henry IV*, a suspension resolved only by a further impenetrable, theatrical image, *Henry V*, flanked by two textual disclaimers of the power of the image: the prologue, which unfavourably compares the resources of the stage to the lost reality of history, and the epilogue, which takes note of the fleeting and unstable character of the momentary model, the 'brief garden' that Henry made of England.[12] . . .

But this formulation, though it names one way in which these plays depend upon implicit generic alternatives, does not obviously pick out any special logic that the histories exemplify. To begin to get at that, I want to work out more of an issue that troubles *Richard II* from the start. I have argued that the play engages the difficulty of legitimate personation, a difficulty which arises from the impossibility of keeping present words and deeds in harmony with the absent symbolic order that should confer identity and meaning. At the root of this difficulty lies a now familiar paradox of repetition. For there to be any person positioned within and measurable against symbolic order, repetition – as of shifter pronouns, proper names, qualities and attributes – must seem to return the same, fixed meaning and being. Yet in any return is an alteration, a displacement, that belies the sought-for sameness: from the tidy couplets of Richard's speech to the structural parallels which invest Henry with the terms that failed Richard or which seem to make him as culpable of murder as the king that he deposed, repetition differentiates and exceeds even while enabling position and comparison. On the one hand there is what we might – with Owen Barfield – call legal fiction, the repeated terms of which constitute the persons and entities of any governable order.[13] On the other hand, there is an uncanny and illicit doubling that divides both royal and ordinary persons from origins, intentions and authority. And each of these effects of repetition seems as necessary, and as irreducible, as the other. The structural doubling that prevents our establishing a stable moral opposition between Richard and Henry serves at the same time to construct positions that each actor fills in turn, despite intentions, even while simultaneously preventing anyone from being more than an impersonator, one who lacks authority of his own.

York's impassioned question – addressed to Richard in hopes of dissuading him from seizing Gaunt's estates – thus cuts deeper than he understands: 'how art thou a king / But by fair sequence and succession?' (II.i.198–9). For nowhere in the background or the action of this play does *fair* sequence and succession occur; no repetition, no doubling from father to son, king to governor, God to king, or one king to another, takes place in a way that preserves justice.[14] Richard does not adequately embody 'Edward's sacred blood'; York – though 'he is just and always loved us well' – cannot effectively serve as deputy of the anointed king; however much 'God's substitute', Richard has only an uncreating word; and Henry, despite his party's fictions, succeeds in name only but not in blood (except the blood of violence) to his cousin's crown.

Henry's unthrifty son, of course, fails also – until the miraculous fulfilment of his most self-interested and self-fulfilling prophecy – to successfully repeat his father's politic ascent to the throne. Only by repeating, but in a fictive and self-knowing way, that father's excess – that part of his inheritance which is illegitimate, transgressive, and 'merely' mimetic – can Hal truly, but still only in an *image*, become a perfect repetition, the mirror of all Christian kings. And in that very perfection, Henry V seems excessive in another way: too good to be true, too calculating to be good, too fully merged with the demands of office to show a self, too much the successful mime to be quite trusted or believed. He becomes so perfect a repetition, in fact, that actors and stage cannot but parody him in their gross attempt at homage.

This 'perfect' repetition – this mirror of perfection, of a perfect and paradoxical unity of spirit and flesh, God and man, sovereignty and humility – achieves his stature by means of a double gesture of negation, in effect cancelling both of the possible ways to mistake the nature of repetition in so far as the self participates in its perpetual activity of alienation and reconstitution. It is easy to specify these ways of misapprehension: one can take oneself as primary rather than secondary – as Lacanian signifier rather than as effect of signification; or, one can suppose oneself a free, perpetually ironic *dédoublement*, a repetition pure and simple and therefore unconditioned, unmixed with effects of significance. These are not just theoretical errors. The *Henriad* embodies them in its characters, arranging these in a dialectical progression which prepares Hal's succession to seeming legitimacy. Richard wilfully errs in both ways, taking himself as primary, as the source of meaning, yet denying connection, consequence and significance in his own 'giddy' play at being king. Bullingbrook – compelled by necessities of state and driven by the will to possess his own – commits both errors despite himself: improper and illegitimate from the start of his rise to power, he never becomes for his kingdom more than a 'counterfeit' king, fixed forever in the role of usurper, of the one (like Lucifer, but without an obviously Luciferian will) who mistook himself for primary and can therefore never be more than a temporarily ascendant lie.

But it is Hotspur and Falstaff, of course, who exemplify these errors in their most striking and opposed forms. And as everyone knows, Hal's successive overcoming these two threats to his future enables his impossibly fair succession.[15] Here the *Henriad* becomes as overtly dialectical as a play can be. On one side, the sincere egoist of honour, who hates the vile politician's hypocrisy, who scoffs at Glendower's fantasies, who yet behaves like an automaton of chivalry, so spirited, so filled with 'great imagination, / Proper to madmen' (*II Henry IV*, I.iii.31–2), that he lives an allegory of his own devising, in which he only 'apprehends a world of figures here, / But not the form of what he should attend' (*I Henry IV*, I.iii.209–10). On the other side, that reverend vice, the perfect nominalist for whom honour is air and life a continuous improvisation and jest, the actor who ironises everything but his own flesh, that perfectly insignificant literality which only death can counterfeit: 'Counterfeit? I lie, for I am no counterfeit. To die is to be a counterfeit, for he is but the counterfeit of a man who hath not the life of a man; but to counterfeit dying, when a man thereby liveth, is to be no counterfeit, but the true and perfect image of life indeed' (V.iv.114–19).

Between these, as double negation, is Hal, who only imitates the simulacrum of his father's thievery, who lets Percy serve as factor and simulacrum of the honour he will attain (and of the purified father he would succeed), who allows the credit for slaying that representative to go to the one for whom all (or nothing) is counterfeit, who in the process imitates an archetypal incarnation and ascension into and out of this world, and then, like 'Alexander the Pig', does away with his (counterfeiting, fleshly) friend: 'I speak but in the figures and comparisons of it: as Alexander kill'd his friend Clytus, being in his ales and his cups; so also Harry Monmouth, being in his right wits and his good judgments, turn'd away the fat knight with the great belly doublet. He was full of jests, and gipes, and knaveries, and mocks – I have forgot his name' (*Henry V*, IV.vii.43–50). On the one side, position that mistakes itself; on the other, displacement that fails to avoid significance: between them, shuttling back and forth between the spirit of a failed representative and the flesh of an impure mimic, is the soon-to-be king who knows and mocks and negates both, who can himself be known only through impossible comparisons, lame figures and bad actors: 'Yet sit and see, / Minding true things by what their mock'ries be' (IV. Pro. 52–3).

Still the necessity of a negative gesture: we must cancel out mockery to get at truth; we must see through theatrical counterfeits to an inexpressible logos. And what is the true thing that Harry has become? Having negated both Hotspur's unactable allegories and Falstaff's unmeaning ironies does not make Hal the ideal synthesis of word and deed, however much his success at seeming to recuperate and preserve what he cancels out. Not the ideal king (whether Shakespeare's or his audience's) nor even the kingly idealist (living his own allegory); not the perfect Machiavell (enacting a politic lie) nor yet the agent of others' interests and fancies (whether conniving churchmen or desiring audience): Henry V is neither architectonic idea nor mere actor. To be one or the other of these would simply repeat – on a grander scale – what he has already known, mocked, and negated in Hotspur and Falstaff. But to be *neither* of these – or to thereby conjoin such contraries – is to be a charismatic something that cannot be known as such, to be the political equivalent of repetition 'itself', a surface that seems to hide and reveal at the same time, a surface whose specular interior is always just another such surface, just another public meaning.

It is also – like it or not – to be the embodiment of power, the King of all, given in a theatrical image. Which is to be something that *we* can experience only as allegory – with its necessary distance from functional circumstance – or as a lie; in either case, as *mere* image. If we read that image as ideal, it must provoke a certain mourning, for as mere image (which even the best of kings can only be, on or off the stage), it reminds us of the unavailability, the loss, even the failure and decay, of the paradoxical union that it figures. If on the other hand, we take that image as a knowing construct (which even the best of kings must knowingly construct), it becomes something that we can view only with apprehension, something that through self-interested artifice separates us from the desired union of spirit and flesh. Either an irrecoverable Eden or an alienating, modern imitation: in either case, this image forces us to feel the power behind and within repetition, the power of that nameless authority which repetition cannot control, which we experience in and as history, and which keeps us from finding in history anything more than an unrent veil or a succession of unacknowledgeable masks.[16]

For that power to work upon us, it must both promise to reveal itself and resist our efforts to know and name it. . . . How to present power in its 'proper' embodiment and on the open stage, without its going flat; how to show power in its public form while holding something back, something which can elicit and yet frustrate all our desires to know and thus usurp that power – this is the task that Shakespeare and his mirror of all Christian kings confront in *Henry V.*

Creature and creator employ many devices toward accomplishing this end, most of which serve to position Henry as one not yet come into his 'own'. For instance, having surprised the clergy not only with his reformation but with at least indifference toward a bill that would strip the church of temporal holdings, Henry submits to their interested interpretation of his right to the French crown. Putting on 'my gracious Lord of Canterbury' all the burden for establishing the justice of his cause, while more than hinting (I.ii.13–32) what we already know, that the Archbishop has reason to 'fashion, wrest, or bow' his reading of the law, Henry thus keeps his motives and ultimate identity secret. His cause is God's – as God's interpreters read it and as God will grant him victory. With another legacy and crown in view, Henry can then once again become the heir apparent, can put off having a history or even a name until he has broken through another set of clouds:

> Or there we'll sit,
> Ruling in large and ample empery
> O'er France and all her almost kingly dukedoms,
> Or lay these bones in an unworthy urn,
> Tombless, with no remembrance over them.
> Either our history shall with full mouth
> Speak freely of our acts, or else our grave,
> Like Turkish mute, shall have a tongueless mouth,
> Not worshipp'd with a waxen epitaph.
>   (I.ii.225–33)

Then threatening to defy the Dauphin's expectations and successfully cutting off the hopes of the treasonous Cambridge, Scroop and Grey, Henry further establishes himself as one more knowing than known. Whereupon Shakespeare places these several moments into a complex figural relationship: God's discovery of the conspirators' purposes becomes an omen of his as yet unacknowledged vicar's success abroad, and the now legitimated heir can exit with the cry, 'No king of England, if not king of France' (I.ii.193).

Such figurative patterns pervade the histories. It is essential to their logic and to their characteristic temporal suspension, their open-endedness and sense of futurity, that Henry V receive definition from those sacred and profane figures in all things which neither Fluellen's theology nor Shakespeare's stagecraft nor the constant reminders of the transience in glory quite let us triumph in this royal actor's fulfilling.[17] Henry's refusal to give ransom to the representative of the effete French recapitulates Hotspur's rebuff to the perfumed milliner who brought the elder Henry's request to him at

Holmedom, just as his speech before the battle at Agincourt fulfils what in Percy at Shrewsbury was mere bravado. Harry's wooing of his Kate displays far more wit and erotic vitality than Hotspur's his, yet equally subsumes the personal in the public; and he copes with his bride's foreign tongue far better than Mortimer can, just as he also far more securely wins the affection of the unfashionable Welch.

But the power evoked within these patterns still keeps its seductive secrets, largely by keeping the Henry we see from perfecting any such figures. In part, this erotic frustration occurs through Shakespeare's stringing us along with hopes that Harry can break free of the very meanings that such patterns create and sustain. In another part (perhaps simply the converse of the first), it develops from Shakespeare's insisting on the suspect theatricality which is Harry's only being – on the stage and in his kingship. Whatever the origin, this frustration of fulfilment reminds us that Henry is not the idea of kingship, but a trope of that idea, a veiled or veiling excess. . . .

Yet it is just this theatricality that gives Henry power, that keeps his power imperfectly revealed, that thus empowers this history. For by continually reminding us how poor the stage is by comparison with its great exemplar while at the same time presuming upon that greatness with the antics of harlotry players. Shakespeare gives Henry the private reserve he might otherwise lack. There are, I think, three effects to be noticed here. First, Shakespeare's references to his 'unworthy scaffold' keep us imagining that the original of this history has a being that exceeds what the stage can hold: 'may we cram / Within this wooden O the very casques / That did affright the air at Agincourt?' (Pro. 12–14). Second, the constant references to theatricality both lead us to attribute to the actor's 'crooked figure' rather than to Henry himself any actual incapacity to reveal the person behind the office, and cause us to see that problem as an effect of theatricality in history itself. And third, by reminding us that we watch theatre rather than these events themselves, Shakespeare forces an indecorous and therefore also excessive fleshly body upon the warlike Harry, who would otherwise, 'like himself, / Assume the port of Mars' (Pro. 5–6). Insisting on the materiality of his medium, Shakespeare thus reasserts the metonymic contrary to the equally theatrical metaphors of kingship.

This last effect seems most important, both for defining the generic logic of Shakespearean history and for situating that history within some story about representational space in England. Throughout this account of the *Henriad*, I have suggested that Shakespeare's kings live in the dangerous middle ground between mimesis and figuration, between being the player king and being the specular consequence of some figural pressure or procedure. The danger here is not keeping to the middle, losing power and place by slipping toward one pole or the other: so Henry IV (were it not for his son) would finally be exposed for one poor counterfeit player among the many who wear the king's armour; so Richard, led by his own disfiguring conceits, finally becomes a fallen allegory of that betrayal and death which waited on the only God who ever came to earth. Henry V keeps his balance – or Shakespeare keeps it for him – not just by never allowing us to know him, but by constantly reminding us that this king is both a theatrical body and a figure in a play of signs. Because he has a body, because his is the sort of kingship that can be played, he remains one of us – and the history he enacts thus remains 'ours', believably associated with our motives, our mortality and our Falstaffian awareness that some part of life escapes the play of signs. Yet because this Henry also participates in several partly overlapping figurative patterns, he is more than a 'mere' player: not just a 'self' like us, he is also a significance, an effect of signifying processes. Since we cannot know and master that significance, however, it retains its own kind of hold upon us. . . .

In a later era – not much later – the English political nation would consolidate its power in the person of a monarch much more the representative of a system than a power in his own right. But at this Shakespearean moment, the idea of kingship has become an idea that theatre can encompass. For it is still conceivable that a person like us can wield and be accountable for such power, accountable in the same ways that we are held accountable. The monarch still goes on progresses, still washes paupers' feet on Maundy Thursday, still sponsors the same plays that anyone else can see, and is still threatenable by a clever usurper. And yet that same person has acquired a mythic and ideological structure – and source of potency – unprecedented in English history. Much of this new source of potency consists in the audience's – and commonwealth's – will to have itself personated by such an actor, and in this way . . . desire has become central to the structure of monarchical authority. Monarchy – and governance – has thus become conceivable as an art that seems impossibly to join body private and body politic in one royal person. The construction of such a person is the subject and structure of Shakespearean history, as it was the (failed) project of Tudor 'absolutism'. Part of the power – and most of the nostalgia – of

Shakespeare's histories consists in their acknowledging what the
state could not: that such erotic unions are always just out of reach.

From Robert S. Knapp, *Shakespeare: The Theatre and the Book*
(Princeton, NJ, 1989), pp. 183–201.

NOTES

['Shakespearean Authority' is extracted from Robert Knapp's study of the
relationship between authority and dramatic genre, especially history and
tragedy. While the essay draws on a number of modern critical approaches
– psychoanalysis, poststructuralism – it still locates the source of meaning,
like most traditional criticism, in Shakespeare as author. All quotations are
from the *Riverside Shakespeare*, ed. G. Blakemore Evans *et al.* (Boston,
1974). Ed.]

1. David Scott Kastan, *Shakespeare and the Shapes of Time* (Hanover,
   New Hampshire, 1982), pp. 37–41, notes that until the Folio, no settled
   nomenclature distinguishes histories from tragedies (or comedies). The
   Folio itself distributes what we call 'romance' between comedy and
   tragedy.

2. Stephen Melville, *Philosophy beside Itself: On Deconstruction and
   Modernism* (Minneapolis, 1986), p. 148: 'For criticism, "indecidability"
   is not a thesis but a fact – the fact that is no longer acknowledged, no
   longer even recognised, by "richness"'. As Melville argues, what matters for criticism is reading, with an almost Arnoldian emphasis on the
   purchase of criticism on life, and on 'responsibility to and contestation
   of a canon, of literature, of criticism'. As Graham Holderness rightly
   insists, though with a Marxist disavowal of the aesthetic which finally
   seems undialectical, Shakespeare's authority – and his apparent freedom
   from orthodoxy's authoritarianism – has historical determinants and
   limitations: some issues of our lives bear on the plays (even if indecidable
   in their imagined worlds); others do not. See Graham Holderness,
   Shakespeare's History (Dublin and New York, 1985), esp. pp. 1–13.

3. E. M. W. Tillyard, *Shakespeare's History Plays* (London, 1944), pp.
   280, 295. See also Alvin B. Kernan, 'The *Henriad*: Shakespeare's Major
   History Plays', in *Modern Shakespeare Criticism*, ed. Alvin B. Kernan
   (New York, 1970), pp. 245–75. For the governing formula of this
   argument, Kernan relies on C. L. Barber, *Shakespeare's Festive Com-
   edy: A Study of Dramatic Form and its Relation to Social Custom*
   (Princeton, 1959), p. 193. See also J. L. Calderwood, *Metadrama in
   Shakespeare's Henriad* (Berkeley, 1979), pp. 22, 169, 219–20; Murray

M. Schwarz, 'Anger, Wounds and the Forms of Theatre in *King Richard II:* Notes for a Psychoanalytic Interpretation', in *Assays: Critical Approaches to Medieval and Renaissance Texts*, ed. Peggy Knapp (Pittsburgh, 1983), 2, p. 128. One major, early exception is A. P. Rossiter, *Angel with Horns and Other Shakespeare Lectures*, ed. Graham Storey (London, 1961).

4. Richard H. Jones, *The Royal Policy of Richard II: Absolutism in the Later Middle Ages* (Oxford, 1968), and Gianfranco Poggi, *The Development of the Modern State: A Sociological Introduction* (Stanford, 1978), pp. 16–85. Cf. Peter Saccio, *Shakespeare's English Kings: History, Chronicle and Drama* (New York, 1977), p. 23: 'Richard certainly held a theory of the kingly dignity and power more exalted than that of his predecessors. Shakespeare picks this up from Holinshed and has his Richard express a grandiose notion of monarchy, though it is couched of course in language and concepts developed by Elizabethan political theorists rather than in medieval terms.' Holderness, *Shakespeare's History*, esp. pp. 42–79, plausibly argues that Shakespeare was well aware of the real character of medieval kingship.

5. E. H. Kantorowicz, *The King's Two Bodies* (Princeton, 1957), esp. pp. 24–41, and Marie Axton, *The Queen's Two Bodies* (London, 1977), esp. pp., 17–18, 11–37.

6. For an account of the medieval origins of both the theory of absolute rule and the theory of limited monarchy, in the context of an argument that the monarchy's seventeenth-century apologists gave a new, unbalancing emphasis to the sacramental grounds of absolutism, see Robert Eccleshall, *Order and Reason in Politics* (Oxford, 1978). Cf. J. P. Sommerville, *Politics and Ideology in England, 1603–1640* (London, 1986).

7. Sydney Anglo, *Spectacle, Pageantry, and Early Tudor Policy* (Oxford, 1969); Stephen Orgel, *The Illusion of Power: Political Theatre in the English Renaissance* (Berkeley, 1975).

8. Kernan, for instance, calls Bullingbrook, a 'practical, efficient man', in contrast to Richard, who 'mistakes metaphor for science': 'The *Henriad*', pp. 248, 260.

9. Quoting II.i.19, 21, 133.

10. *II Henry IV*, IV.v.184.

11. James Winny, *The Player King: A Theme of Shakespeare's Histories* (London, 1968), pp. 94–100, discusses Bullingbrook's passivity.

12. For an especially useful account of the interplay between comedy and other generic implications in the histories, see Moody Prior, 'Comic Theory and the Rejection of Falstaff', *Shakespeare Studies*, 9 (1976), 159–71.

13. Owen Barfield 'Legal Fiction and Poetic Diction', in *The Importance of Language*, ed. Max Black (Englewood Cliffs, NJ, 1962), pp. 51–71.

14. For an extended account of the problem of succession in the second tetralogy, see Sigurd Burckhardt, *Shakespearean Meanings* (Princeton, 1968), pp. 144–205.

15. Arthur Quiller-Couch, for instance, found in the plays 'a Contention for the Soul of a Prince', *Notes on Shakespeare's Workmanship* (New York, 1917), pp. 125–7.

16. Cf. Jonathan Goldberg, *James I and the Politics of Literature: Jonson, Shakespeare, Donne and their Contemporaries* (Baltimore, 1983): 'it is precisely in ambiguity that power resides, making it as capable of direct as of indirect action. . . . A kind of infinite regress is established in which the affirmation of power is cloaked in denials, and the assumption of power is effected by erecting one's truth as absolution and submitting to the invention' (p. 12). Cf. Norman Rabkin, *Shakespeare and the Problem of Meaning* (Chicago, 1981), p. 62: 'the inscrutability of Henry V is the inscrutability of history'.

17. Cf. Kastan, *Shakespeare and the Shapes of Time*, on the open-endedness of the histories, esp. pp. 37–55.

6

Making Histories

CATHERINE BELSEY

I

Shakespeare's history plays are not commonly taken seriously as history.[1] Everyone knows that they are not accurate. Much of the material is pure invention, so the argument goes, and even when it is not, both story and characterisation are significantly modified in the interests of vital and enduring drama on the one hand and the glorification of the Tudor dynasty on the other. Brilliant fictions, and perhaps equally brilliant propaganda, the history plays are understood to be precisely art, not life, imagination and not truth.

Is it possible that this account reveals as much about the literary institution and the distinctions it takes for granted as it does about Shakespeare's texts? History, it is assumed, enables us to measure the accuracy of the plays and find them wanting – as truth. At the same time, and paradoxically, imagination throws into relief the dullness of mere empirical fact: art is dazzling where history is drab. In either case the term 'history play' is something of an oxymoron. History, *real* history, stands outside literature as its binary antithesis, fact as opposed to fiction.

Or it did. Our postmodern condition has called into question that antithesis, and perhaps in the process identified 'history plays' as a more sympathetic category for us now. I want, not purely perversely, to read Shakespeare's second tetralogy as history.

II

This project necessitates a preliminary examination of the relationship between history and the literary institution. A generation ago, because it was understood to be outside literature, history constituted the final court of appeal for readers of Renaissance texts. The truth – which is to say, the authority – of an interpretation could be guaranteed by its historical accuracy in the light of our linguistic, cultural, social and political understanding of the period. . . .

When it came to cultural history, political predisposition became more evidently part of the hermeneutic circle. E. M. W. Tillyard read a number of Renaissance plays to find a commitment to order, and found in consequence that most of the other plays of the period were also committed to order. . . . This investment in the past was symptomatic of an anxiety about the present, the crisis of the postmodern, precipitated by the Second World War. In the world of the Holocaust and Hiroshima, what price the optimism of the Enlightenment? What purchase now had the conviction that reason and truth must finally inevitably prevail? Nostalgia was the quest for an authentic reference point in the past, a moment of plenitude from which to fend off an uncertain modernity,[2] and history guaranteed the truth of that moment, its reality and its certainty. History, in each of its manifestations, was the single, unified, unproblematic, extra-textual, extra-discursive real that guaranteed our readings of the texts which constituted its cultural *expression*. If it was never fully mastered, never absolutely known, if the matter of history was never settled, that meant only that there was more work to be done.

But meanwhile, the same postmodern anxiety also produced a contrary symptom, a counter-current in the literary institution, which called into theoretical question all realities, all certainties, and with them the certainty of history. The work of Saussure, suddenly given a new prominence in the post-war period, put in doubt the possibility of mapping in language the extra-linguistic real. There was, Saussure's work implied, no sure place beyond language to draw from. History was consequently dethroned: it too was linguistic, precisely a story, a narrative, a reading of the documents, and thus no longer able to constitute a guarantee of our readings of other documents. What, after all, could be invoked to guarantee the truth of history itself?

It was Jean-François Lyotard who finally brought it out, who made explicit in *The Postmodern Condition* exactly what had changed. History itself, the grand narrative, the one story of the single extra-discursive truth, was no longer authoritative. Lyotard defined the postmodern condition as 'incredulity toward metanarratives',[3] and incredulity in consequence towards the knowledges and the competences the grand narratives had traditionally legitimated. The authority of the single historical story, with its heroes and voyages and goals, is, Lyotard argues, deeply political. The knowledge it transmits 'determines in a single stroke what one must say in order to be heard, what one must listen to in order to speak, and what role one must play (on the scene of diegetic reality) to be the object of a narrative' (p. 21). (Feminism and the Civil Rights Movement could, of course, have told him as much. The history of man, they were well aware, was the history of white men, and licensed their continued dominance.) History as progress, as the grand narrative of emancipation, legitimates the bourgeois state, in which the people have finally won the right to decide, to prescribe norms. History as the story of freedom represses the role of the economy; it suppresses difference. In the liberal narrative 'the name of the [single] hero is the people, the sign of legitimacy is the people's consensus, and their mode of creating norms is deliberation' (p. 30). . . .

Is there no alternative to the master-narrative of inexorable and teleological development, but only a (dis)continuous and fragmentary present, a world of infinite differences which are ultimately undifferentiated because they are all confined to the signifying surface of things, Lyotard's notorious degree zero of the postmodern: 'one listens to reggae, watches a western, eats McDonald's food for lunch and local cuisine for dinner, wears Paris perfume in Tokyo and retro clothes in Hong Kong' (p. 76)?[4] Is there in practice only a leap of faith, a willed commitment to an increasingly implausible narrative on the one hand, or on the other contemporaneity endlessly deferred, the repeated encounter with absence which must ensue if the fullness of presence is recognised as a chimera? . . .

Lyotard is not opposed to narrative: his own book tells the story of the emergence of the postmodern within modernism. Narration, after all, constructs objects of discourse, 'objects to be known, decided on, evaluated, transformed . . .' (p. 18). How else but by telling new stories are we to challenge the limits of what one must say in order to be heard? But the *petits récits* lay no claim to extra-discursive authority, to mastery or to the absolutism of truth. They acknowledge the process that Derrida calls differance, by which signifying practice itself necessarily differentiates and distances all that is extra-linguistic.[5] They explicitly make meanings, make histories.

From the perspective of the literary institution it might be argued that the New Historicism has replaced the old historicism of Tillyard and C. S. Lewis in something like the way Lyotard's short stories supplant the grand narrative. Offering a generalisation which necessarily suppresses important differences, I want to suggest that at its most brilliant, its most elegant, New Historicism is characteristically postmodern. It records no heroic quests, no voyages of discovery, no dangers triumphantly overcome. On the contrary, its expeditions are more commonly voyages of colonisation and ruthless conquest. It is anything but nostalgic in its account of a world dominated by power, which produces resistance only to justify its own extension. Sophisticated to the point of scepticism, the work of Stephen Greenblatt, Jonathan Goldberg, Steven Mullaney and others is self-consciously fragmentary, arbitrary. But its degree zero is the eclecticism of the anecdote, the single esoteric text, the improbable reading. Its theme is not change, since the history it recounts is rarely diachronic. The sleek surfaces of New Historicist writing propose no programme; they offer the minimum of evaluations and transformations, except in so far as they transform into its opposite the grand narrative itself; and in consequence they legitimate no political intervention.

In the analysis of Jameson and Eagleton the postmodern is a single, unitary, undifferentiated, non-contradictory phenomenon, the deadly cultural manifestation of late capitalism.[6] (Marx would perhaps have been surprised by this unwillingness to acknowledge contradictions.) But in Lyotard's account the postmodern is itself divided. If functionalism produces an analysis of society as a single whole, in which culture is non-contradictory, or power always succeeds in pre-empting challenges to its own increased mastery (produces them, indeed, for that purpose), there is another sociology, derived this time from the Marxist account of society as a site of struggle. It follows that there is also another postmodernism, this time of the left, which emphasises dissension,[7] difference as opposition, and a possible consequent historicity which tells of the *resistance* that continues to challenge power from the position of its inevitable, differentiating other.

Is it not this emphasis on struggle which is above all important for us in Marxism now? What distinguishes Marxism is not, in other words, its grand narrative, the inexorable succession of the modes of production, but its analysis of contest, the classes confronting each other locked in contradiction and conflict. Marx's grand *history* is intelligible now as breathtakingly inventive, ingenious myth, the story of a struggle for power which repeats itself and differs from one historical moment to the next.[8] Though it offers a brilliant framework, the attempt to work in detail with the Renaissance as the encounter between feudalism and capitalism runs, it seems to me, into endless problems of historical specificity. Marx's account of *the relations of production*, however, so daring in the nineteenth century, and still politically indispensable now, has not been superseded by postmodernism or poststructuralism. Marx saw labour as the other of capital: not its binary opposite, but the condition, at once necessary and menacing, of its existence.[9] And his dangerously radical gesture was to analyse capital from the position of the other. . . .

To attempt to speak on behalf of subversion, to write a history of the working class, or to give women a voice, is in the end to reaffirm the oppositions which currently exist. Our more radical and more modest narratives set out to undo those oppositions themselves, to throw into relief the precariousness of power, of capital, of patriarchy and racism, showing them as beleaguered to the degree that the resistances they produce return to endanger their seamless mastery.[10] This too is a postmodern project, but it is not satisfied with an elegant pessimism. Its mode is to activate the differences and promote political intervention. It tells short stories which are nevertheless stories of change. There are many histories to be made, meanings to be differentiated, dissensions to be emphasised. And if the practice does not promise utopia, it has at least the advantage that it offers the possibility of making a difference. . . .

III

. . . It is possible to read Shakespeare's history plays otherwise, in ways which have explicit resonances for us now. The second tetralogy tells a story of change which begins in nostalgia for a lost golden world and ends in indeterminancy. Early in *Richard II* John of Gaunt speaks wistfully of a time when kings were kings and went on crusades (II.i.51–6), but by the end of *Henry V* the legitimacy of kingship itself is in question. The issue is power. Similarly, the beginning of *Richard II* seems rooted in the simple unity of names and things, but the plays chart a fall into differance which generates a world of uncertainties. The issue is meaning. And the texts themselves bear witness to the difference within textuality. Read from a postmodern perspective, they reveal marks of the struggle to fix meaning, and simultaneously of the excess which necessarily renders meaning unstable.

IV

The vanishing world to which the opening of *Richard II* alludes is an imaginary realm of transparency, plenitude and truth, where the essential link between signifier and referent has not yet been broken. Names, their meanings and the condition they name are apparently one:

> K. Richard   What comfort, man? How is't with aged Gaunt?
> Gaunt   O, how that name befits my composition!
>   Old Gaunt, indeed; and gaunt in being old.
>   Within me grief hath kept a tedious fast;
>   And who abstains from meat that is not gaunt?
>   For sleeping England long time have I watch'd;
>   Watching breeds leanness, leanness is all gaunt.
>   The pleasure that some fathers feed upon
>   Is my strict fast – I mean my children's looks;
>   And therein fasting, hast thou made me gaunt.
>   Gaunt am I for the grave, gaunt as a grave,
>   Whose hollow womb inherits nought but bones.
>   (*Richard II*, II.i.72–83)

For Richard this reiteration of Gaunt's name, specifying in a series of figures its meaning and its cause, is no more than an instance of the play of the signifier: 'Can sick men play so nicely with their names?' (II.i.84). But from the point of view of the audience, the sequence has the effect of producing a convergence on a single truth, identifying a unified state of being, gaunt by name and gaunt by nature.

Ironically, this affirmation of plenitude, of the fullness of truth in the signifier, is also an assertion of absence, of leanness, fasting, the hollow womb of the grave. Its occasion is the absence Richard has made in the political and the symbolic order. John of Gaunt is dying of grief for a land which has no heirs, a realm whose lineage is coming to an end as Richard fails to *live* the true and single meaning of sovereignty: 'Landlord of England art thou now, not King' (II.i.113). Richard divorces the name of king from the condition, leasing out the realm and banishing Bolingbroke.

Gaunt's grief is also for his own heir. The name of Duke of Lancaster has a material existence: it is a title, an entitlement, meaning land, a position, an army, power. By sending his son into exile, Gaunt protests, 'thou dost seek to kill my name in me' (II.i.86), to end the dynasty and expropriate the land.[11] Thus Richard, already identified as the murderer of Gloucester, is now represented as causing the death of Lancaster.

It is not, of course, to be done by fiat. Lancaster is not merely a name but a material presence. Since the title is precisely an entitlement – to property and to power in the realm – the inscription of power in the symbolic order cannot be created or destroyed by an act of individual will, not even the sovereign's. In the opening scene of the play Bolingbroke, Duke of Hereford, nephew of the dead Gloucester, challenges the king in Mowbray. In Act II Bolingbroke, his identity transformed by his father's death, returns to challenge the king again by reclaiming his title, in all its materiality: 'As I was banish'd, I was banished Hereford; / But as I come, I come for Lancaster' (II.iii.113–14); 'I am come to seek that *name* in England' (II.iii.71, my emphasis).

But as in Gaunt's sequence of figures, here too the names of England and Lancaster are linked as elements in a system of differences where meanings are interdependent. All names are authorised by inheritance, as fathers are authors of their children. The inscription of authority in a name is reciprocal and differential, not individual, and it is specified by blood. In consequence Bolingbroke is entitled to argue, 'If that my cousin king be King in England, / It must be granted I am Duke of Lancaster' (II.iii.123–4). It is not granted, of course. In the event, the king's repudiation of the symbolic order, which also guarantees his own succession, impels civil war to manure the ground with English blood – in another but, of course, related sense of the word 'blood'.

There is thus only a brief moment in Act I when the truth of things is perceived to reside in names, when the grand simplicities appear to be in place, or when the (royal) sentence seems absolute. By naming the banishment of Mowbray and Bolingbroke the king is able to bring it about – or to repeal it. Richard sees Gaunt's grief signified in his tears and reduces the term of Bolingbroke's exile. Bolingbroke draws attention to the inscription of power in the signifier:

> How long a time lies in one little word!
> Four lagging winters and four wanton springs
> End in a word: such is the breath of Kings.
>   (I.iii.213–15)

But within the system of differences which gives meaning to kingship, inscribes the power in royal utterances, kings are only the location of authority, not its origin. In practice Richard cannot give meaning to his sentences or deny meaning to the names of his subjects. His words are absolute only on condition that they remain within the existing system of differences. He, like his subjects, is subject to the symbolic order, which allots meaning to the orders he gives.

Richard transgresses this system of differences when he tries to remake the meaning of kingship in the image of his own desires. His predecessors lived the regality of their name, Gaunt complains. Their sovereignty was thus synonymous with England's, and the realm was a '*sceptr'd* isle', an 'earth of *majesty*' (II.i.40–1, my emphasis). But this world of unity and plenitude is already lost. Richard-as-England has consumed England's material wealth in riot, misusing his sovereignty to mortgage the land, devouring in the name of his title his own entitlement. He has thus turned the sceptre against the isle, majesty against the earth itself, and in consequence fragmented the singleness of the realm.[12] The 'teeming womb of royal kings' (II.i.51) is now, according to the logic of Gaunt's rhetoric, empty, and it is this absence of heirs which propels one of its few remaining denizens towards the grave, 'Whose hollow womb inherits nought but bones' (II.i.83). Richard violates the symbolic order, and in consequence his words lose their sovereignty. Bolingbroke returns, repudiating the royal sentence of banishment.

Richard makes a gap between names and things, between kingship and its referent, majesty, and Gaunt cannot live in the new world he makes. But Bolingbroke belongs there already, and thus proleptically identifies himself as Richard's heir even more surely than he is his father's. Gaunt offers consolation for exile in the supremacy of the signifier:

> Go, say I sent thee forth to purchase honour,
> And not the King exil'd thee; or suppose
> Devouring pestilence hangs in our air
> And thou art flying to a fresher clime.

Look what thy soul holds dear, imagine it
To lie that way thou goest.
                                    (I.iii.282–7)

But his son recognises the power to remake the referent in accordance with the signifier as precisely imaginary:

O, who can hold a fire in his hand
By thinking on the frosty Caucasus?
Or cloy the hungry edge of appetite
By bare imagination of a feast?
Or wallow naked in December snow
By thinking on fantastic summer's heat?
                                    (I.iii.294–9)

But if Bolingbroke recognises the differance that Richard has made, or has made evident, the difference and the distance between the signifier and what it re-presents, Richard himself is tragically unable to do so. This is the dramatic irony of what follows, as Richard, deserted by 12,000 Welshmen, clings to the imaginary sovereignty of the signifier:

Is not the King's name twenty thousand names?
Arm, arm, my name! a puny subject strikes
At thy great glory.
                                    (III.ii.85–7)

In practice, we are to understand, the unity of the king's name and kingship itself have fallen apart. The realm has deserted him for Bolingbroke, and Richard is king precisely in name only.

Meanwhile, the new and silent sovereign says nothing, uses few words, or none (IV.i.289). It is Richard himself who employs the breath of kings to strip away the signifier of his own monarchy: 'What must the King do now? . . . Must he lose / The name of king? A God's name, let it go' (III.iii.143–6). But like Gaunt, he cannot survive in the world of differance, where if he is not king he has no identity at all: 'I must nothing be' (IV.i.201). 'What says King Bolingbroke? Will his Majesty / Give Richard leave to live till Richard die?' (III.iii.173–4). As Marjorie Garber points out, the King performs an act of erasure, as differance thus invades his identity, enters into the selfhood of Richard:

> I have no name, no title –
> No, not that name was given me at the font –
> But 'tis usurp'd. Alack the heavy day,
> That I have worn so many winters out,
> And know not now what name to call myself!
> O that I were a mockery king of snow,
> Standing before the sun of Bolingbroke
> To melt myself away in water drops.
>   (IV.i.255–62)

He is already a mockery king, other than himself, figured here as insubstantial, a snowman visibly melting away, though it is worth remembering, of course, that his name, his entitlement, will return to haunt the remainder of the second tetralogy.[13]

V

Richard fails to find a means of holding the signified in place, guaranteeing his title. The Bishop of Carlisle proffers the grandest of all grand narratives:

> Fear not, my lord; that Power that made you king
> Hath power to keep you king in spite of all.
>   (III.ii.27–8)

And Richard reiterates it (III.ii.54–62). But the play at once subjects the master-narrative of divine protection for divine right to ironic scrutiny, as first Salisbury and then Scroop deliver their *petits récits* of desertions and defeats. If God has the power, he signally fails in a fallen world to exercise it on behalf of his anointed deputy. The only power on earth that supports the materiality of titles is the law of succession, and Richard breaks it by seizing Bolingbroke's title (II.i.195–208).

Bolingbroke's regime becomes in consequence one of bitter uncertainties, of conflicts for meaning which are simultaneously conflicts for power. These constitute the story of the reign of Henry IV, but the uncertainty begins in the deposition scene in *Richard II*, when it becomes apparent that the world is no longer anchored in the referent, no longer names a single, consensual object. The Bishop of Carlisle defends Richard's sovereignty in the name of the transcendental signified: the king is 'the figure of God's majesty' (IV.i.125). In consequence, he argues, 'My Lord of Hereford here, whom you call king, / Is a foul traitor to proud Hereford's king' (IV.i.134–5). As he concludes his argument, Northumberland steps forward on behalf of Hereford (now Lancaster; now England?) and turns the verbal and political tables on Carlisle: 'Well have you argued, sir; and for your pains, / Of capital treason we arrest you here' (IV.i.150–1).

In a world of difference who is the traitor? Who is the king? When in Act I Mowbray and Bolingbroke accuse each other of treason, the truth is available: in the following scene the exchanges between Gaunt and the Duchess of Gloucester make clear to the audience that Richard is responsible for Gloucester's murder. But in the new world of differance, who can be sure? If Richard is king, Bolingbroke is a traitor. But is he? If Bolingbroke is king, Carlisle is a traitor. But is he? Richard's breach of the symbolic order has divorced the name of king from the power, laying bare a world of political struggle for possession of meaning, property and sovereignty. In this new world it is not a name but the allegiance of the Duke of York and of 12,000 Welshmen which proves decisive. The orders of the mockery King are now subject to confirmation by Bolingbroke:

> For do we must what force will have us do.
> Set on towards London. Cousin, is it so?
> **Bol.**   Yea, my good Lord.
> **K. Richard**   Then I must not say no.
> (III.iii.207–9)

Bolingbroke comes back to claim his title in the name of law, but his victory, the play makes clear, is an effect of force, not legality. Nevertheless, the repressed law of succession returns to disrupt the reign of Henry IV. It is Mortimer's legal title as Richard's heir which cements the quarrel between Hotspur and the King (*I King Henry IV*, I.iii.77 ff., 145–59), and if Mortimer is not the motive, he is none the less the legitimating occasion of the rebellion which constitutes the main plot of the *Henry IV* plays.[14]

Henry V is legally and unequivocally king, and he manages to bring the law of succession into line with political strategy when his Archbishop of Canterbury adduces legal authority for the war with France. Part of Henry V's claim to reunite the name of king and the power that belongs to it depends on his identity as a man of the people. He himself declares his ordinariness as he wanders in disguise among the common soldiers on the eve of Agincourt: 'Though I speak it to you, I think the King is but a man as I am'. And if the utterance is an equivocation, exploiting the plurality of the signifier, the speech goes on to specify more clearly the unexceptional nature of the king: 'all his senses have but human conditions; his ceremonies laid by, in his nakedness he appears but a man' (*King Henry V*, IV.i.100,103). The scene presents the king as a popular hero and thus helps to legitimate his sovereignty.

In Williams, therefore, who is also a man of the people, Henry encounters a figure who represents both his similitude and his differentiating other. At the moment of victory Williams, a man as he is, will apparently give back to Henry in his own person the king's desired self-image, while still preserving his independence, his defining alterity (IV.vii.45–55). But on the eve of Agincourt, the climactic battle of the play, Williams challenges on behalf of the people the justice of the king's war. The issue is ostensibly what it means to die well. The official position is apparently that if the king's cause is good, and the soldiers' consciences clear, death is no real threat to them. Williams sees it differently. From the point of view of the ordinary soldier, death is not simply a question of conscience, an affair of the soul, but a matter of 'legs and arms and heads, chopp'd off in a battle', of mutilated bodies on the battlefield, 'some swearing, some crying for a surgeon, some upon their wives left poor behind them, some upon the debts they owe, some upon their children rawly left. I am afeared', Williams continues thoughtfully, 'there are few that die well that die in battle; for how can they charitably dispose of anything when blood is their argument?' (IV.i.133–43).

If Williams's role in the play identifies his as the voice of the people, his final sentence specifies the nature of the challenge he delivers: 'Now, if these men do not die well, it will be a black matter for the king that led them to it; *who to disobey were against all proportion of subjection*' (IV.i.143–5, my emphasis). Williams does not propose disobedience to the king: he accepts his subjection. But what he says locates the initiative for the war and the consequent responsibility for the legs and arms and heads, the widows and orphans, solely with the monarch. . . .

Williams speaks, fluently and persuasively, on behalf of the people. And the people put a strong case that the king has no moral entitlement to risk *their* bodies, *their* lives and the security of *their* families in *his* war. Henry's answer evades the issue, although he has the last word and to this extent Williams seems to concede his case.

The whole question is apparently dissipated in the victory celebrations, as the king fills Williams's glove with (ironically?) crowns (IV.vii.56). But it is not necessarily forgotten, and the audience is left to ponder the problem implicitly raised in the debate. Has the sovereign the right to demand obedience to the point of death? What are the rights of the people? What are the limits of sovereignty? Who is entitled to define them, to impose them? *What is the meaning of the king's title?* The encounter with Williams prompts Henry himself to ponder the last of these questions. What differentiates the king who is a man of the people from the people themselves? The answer he gives is no more than idle/idol signifying 'ceremony', but this only prompts further questions. Is ceremony material, substantial: 'What are thy rents? What are thy comings-in?' (IV.i.239). Does ceremony entail power, or is it no more than an empty signifier, a form, an illusion:

> O, be sick, great greatness,
> And bid thy ceremony give thee cure!
> Thinks thou the fiery fever will go out
> With titles blown from adulation?
> Will it give place to flexure and low bending?
> Canst thou, when thou command'st the beggar's knee,
> Command the health of it? No, thou proud dream.
>   (IV.i.247–53)

What, then, does it mean to say, as Henry does, 'I am a king . . .' (IV.i.255)? . . .

Since the play cannot settle on an answer to the problem of what it means to be a king, it throws into question the nature of both sovereignty and meaning. In a world of differance presence is necessarily an illusion, to the extent that absolute meaning, whether as material substance or pure intelligibility, is always deferred, relegated, supplanted by the signifier itself. But if meaning is not fully present, it is not an absence either, not a space to be vacated at will. Henry V's 'ceremony' is not in that sense illusory: it is precisely an instance of the materiality of the signifier, 'place, degree, and form/ Creating awe and fear in other men' (IV.i.242–3). It elicits obedience, though it cannot ensure it, and in that sense it represents power, but a power which, without metaphysical guarantees, is always unstable.

Ultimately, outside the fictional world of the history plays, the people were to repudiate, in the name of law, the law of succession, the power of ceremony, and the monarchy with them. In the 1590s the revolutionary struggle was half a century away. Are the questions posed by Shakespeare's history plays among the conditions, nevertheless, of the possibility of that struggle? If so, we are entitled to read the plays not only as interrogating the absolutist claims of the Tudor present, but as raising a broader issue for the immediate future. This is the question that Brecht was to reformulate in another political crisis: 'who does the world belong to?' Who is *entitled* to property and power?

Williams demonstrates that the royal meanings do not go uncontested. In the *Henry IV* plays it is Falstaff who consistently represents the refusal of monarchic order. His emblematic significance reaches its climax when he performs in play the role of king to Hal's prince – and recommends the company of Falstaff (*I King Henry IV*, II.iv.408–16). But resistance is evident throughout in Falstaff's repudiation of all orthodox values: heroism, military discipline, law, truth, honour and, inevitably, authorised meaning. . . .

Henry IV, we are invited to understand, deserves Falstaff. Eastcheap represents the inevitable return within his regime of the lawlessness by which he became king. Henry cannot exercise control – over the rebels or over Eastcheap – because he is not morally or legally entitled to the throne he holds. But Henry V changes all that. He does penance for his father's crime, rejects Falstaff, brings treason remorselessly to justice, and displays at Agincourt that he has secured the popular obedience that he thus so richly deserves. Act V of *Henry V* duly celebrates the victory of the ideal Christian king.

But at the end of the play, in a speech possibly written for Falstaff to perform, though attributed to Pistol in a version of the text from which Falstaff has been excised, it appears that resistance to the monarchic and symbolic order is about to begin all over again, and in exactly the same punning terms as before:

> Old do I wax; and from my weary limbs
> Honour is cudgell'd. Well, bawd I'll turn,
> And something lean to cutpurse of quick hand.
> To England will I steal, and there I'll steal.
> (*King Henry V*, V.i.78–81)

VI

It is worth remembering, whatever Tillyard may have argued about the unthinkable nature of rebellion in the sixteenth century, that it was the anarchic Falstaff whose reappearance Elizabethan audiences clamoured for. And for this reason too, when Stephen Greenblatt assures us that the audience of *II Henry IV* does not leave the theatre in a rebellious mood, or that the doubts raised about Henry V merely serve to heighten his charisma, I am compelled to wonder what can be the *grounds* of Greenblatt's certainty.[15] Not, I suspect, the text.[16] And not what we know of Elizabethan history. What then? A politics which faces the present in the conviction that domination, however regrettable, is inevitable, a fact of life? I hope not.

Shakespeare's own practice of history-making is more complex and, ironically, more contemporary. When Greenblatt urges in the same essay that we need 'a poetics of Elizabethan power', and goes on to argue that this 'will prove inseparable, in crucial respects, from a poetics of the theatre', I find myself in wholehearted agreement with him.[17] But a poetics of power would take account of the possibility of resistance, not simply as power's legitimation, its justification or glorification, as the New Historicists seem so often to argue, but as its defining, differentiating other, the condition of its existence precisely as power. And it would recognise the corresponding possibility that resistance is not tamed in the end. Meanwhile, a poetics of the theatre would take account of the ubiquity of resistance to power as a requirement of plot, and of the corresponding possibility that resistance is not always 'contained' by the reaffirmation of power. And finally, to do justice to the complexity both of power and of Shakespeare's theatre, we need in addition a theory of textuality which understands meaning as differed and deferred, differentiated by and distanced from the signifier, so that it cannot be fixed by any reading, however supple, which treats texts as ultimately undifferentiated, homogeneous and univocal.

Nostalgia for lost plenitude, for the unity of words and things, is a longing for the imaginary, a desire for the simplicity and certainty of a world which precedes the symbolic difference. This is a world without visible power, since power is a relation of difference. But because certainty implies metaphysical guarantees of the singularity of meaning and the truth of things, it is also a world which is in practice deeply authoritarian. The condition of differance, meanwhile, ensures only that nothing is certain. Presence is deferred, meanings no more than differential. Differance precipitates doubt. The questions about power that differance prompts are not answered by reference to metaphysics. On the contrary, they concern a political relation, and one which, since it is an effect of difference, always inclines towards struggle.

Shakespeare's history plays know this. The world of plenitude was always already lost. It has no place outside the memory of an old man whose name is his condition and signifies an absence. Differance invades the opening scene of *Richard II*, and the plays go on to depict a succession of struggles which pose questions concerning the proper location of power in the present and in the future. The second tetralogy charts a descent from absolutism to the moment when the people confront the King, who cannot give them an adequate answer. It ends at this point. Unable to foresee the Revolution of the 1640s, the history plays leave kingship in question. But do they not also indicate in the process that the world belongs to those who are prepared to take it?

Shakespeare's histories refuse to constitute a grand narrative. They do not recount Tillyard's story of legitimate monarchy betrayed by monstrous rebellion, of hierarchy divinely endorsed. (But then in practice Tillyard was never sure they did.) Instead, these pre-Enlightenment texts propel their audience towards the as-yet unpresentable, the possibility of histories made by the people. Rejecting the transparency of names, they tell of political struggle and of the difference within the signifier. Of course, Shakespeare made free with his sources in a way that no serious member of the literary institution could now countenance. But ironically, does he not in other ways, in spite of the historical difference, display some of the concerns which impel our own postmodern and radical *petits récits*?

Extraordinarily enough, the second tetralogy, read from the present, might perfectly well adopt as an epigraph Lyotard's call to arms at the end of his essay, 'What is Postmodernism?':

> Let us wage a war on totality; let us be witnesses to the unpresentable; let us activate the differences and save the honor of the name. (p. 82)

The difference between our histories and Shakespeare's is decisive, an effect in part of the intervening Enlightenment. At the same time, however, the Enlightenment is no longer the condition that our postmodern culture aspires to. And to that extent it constitutes a space across which we are able to perceive Shakespeare's questing, questioning stories otherwise, and perhaps also to accord them a new kind of recognition.

From Francis Barker, Peter Hulme and Margaret Iverson (eds), *Uses of History: Marxism, Postmodernism and the Renaissance* (Manchester, 1991).

NOTES

[Catherine Belsey's 'Making Histories' is a shortened version of her essay 'Making Histories Then and Now: Shakespeare from *Richard II* to *Henry V*', taken from *Uses of History*. This is a collection of papers presented to a conference on this theme at the University of Essex in 1989. Quotations are from Shakespeare's *Collected Works*, ed. Peter Alexander (London, 1951). Ed.]

1. One possible exception is Tillyard's glowing account of the depiction of the middle ages in *Richard II*; see Tillyard, *Shakespeare's History Plays* (London, 1944, reprinted 1969), pp. 258–65.

2. See Janice Doane and Devon Hodges, *Nostalgia and Sexual Difference: The Resistance to Contemporary Feminism* (New York, 1987).

3. Jean-François Lyotard, *The Postmodern Condition: A Report on Knowledge*, trans. Geoff Bennington and Brian Massumi (Manchester, 1984). Subsequent references to Lyotard are included in the text.

4. Eagleton, who seems to miss the venom in this French irony at the expense of American culture, solemnly reminds us that there are millions of people who never jet-set at all, but go to work every day and educate their children; see Terry Eagleton, 'Capitalism, modernism and postmodernism', *New Left Review*, 152 (1985), 60–73.

5. For an account of differance see Jacques Derrida, *Positions*, trans. Alan Bass (London, 1987), pp. 8–9, and 'Difference' in *Margins of Philosophy*, trans. Alan Bass (Brighton, 1982), pp. 1–27.

6. See Fredric Jameson, 'Postmodernism, or the cultural logic of late capitalism', *New Left Review*, 146 (1984) 53–92, and Terry Eagleton, 'Capitalism, modernism and postmodernism', *New Left Review*, 152, (1985) 60–73.

7. See Lyotard, *The Postmodern Condition*, p. 61, and Jacques Derrida, 'Cogito and the history of madness', in *Writing and Difference*, trans. Alan Bass (London, 1978), pp. 31–63.

8. I refer here to the story of successive modes of production. Specific analyses, like the *Eighteenth Brumaire*, for example, are in quite a different category, and in many ways a model for us now. [Karl Marx's *The Eighteenth Brumaire of Louis Bonaparte* (New York 1852) is an

analysis of the revolutionary struggles in France between 1848 and 1851. Ed.]

9. Ironically it is the non-Marxist Lyotard who draws attention to Marx's insistence on the spuriousness of the unity of capital. Writing of the postmodern fission of the pretension to a single purpose, he adds, 'since Marx, we have learned that what presents itself as unity . . . is the imposter-subject and blindly calculating rationality called Capital' (Lyotard, *Positions*, p. 180). Compare the Marxist Jameson: 'anyone who believes that the profit motive and the logic of capital accumulation are not the fundamental laws of this world . . . is living in an alternative universe' (Fredric Jameson, 'Cognitive Mapping', in Cary Nelson and Lawrence Grossberg (eds), *Marxism and the Interpretation of Culture* [Basingstoke, 1988], pp. 347–60).

10. For a feminist instance see Alice Jardine, *Gynesis: Configurations of Woman and Modernity* (Ithaca, New York, 1985).

11. Cf. Mowbray who, because he is accused of treason, stands to lose his name to Richard (I.i.167–9), and is therefore defending the rights of his 'succeeding issue' (I.iii.20). The titles and thus the estates of traitors were forfeit to the Crown.

12. This was pointed out to me by Gareth Edwards.

13. See Marjorie Garber, *Shakespeare's Ghost Writers: Literature as Uncanny Casuality* (New York, 1987), pp. 20–1.

14. And, of course, of the Wars of the Roses in *Henry VI*.

15. Stephen Greenblatt, 'Inyisible bullets: Renaissance authority and its subversion, *Henry IV* and *Henry V*', in Jonathan Dollimore and Alan Sinfield (eds), *Political Shakespeare: New Essays in Cultural Materialism* (Manchester, 1985), pp. 41, 43.

16. For a discussion of the ambiguity of the play see Norman Rabkin, *Shakespeare and the Problem of Meaning* (Chicago, 1981), pp. 33–62.

17. Greenblatt, 'Invisible bullets . . .', p. 44.

7

'Richard II': Metadrama and the Fall of Speech

JAMES L. CALDERWOOD

It is hardly surprising that a playwright like Shakespeare would project his concerns about drama not only into life but even into the fictional life of his plays, where the world may become a stage, history a plot, kings dramatists, courtiers actors, commoners audiences, and speech itself the dialogue or script that gives breath to all the rest.

In the *Henriad* the main metadramatic plot centres in the 'fall of speech'. To the Divine Rightness of Richard's kingship corresponds a kind of language in which words have an inalienable right to their meanings, even a divine right in so far as God is the ultimate guarantor of verbal truth. In this sacramental language of Richard's imagination God is an invisible third partner to every dialogue, the final verbal authority, even as He is the invisible third partner in every trial by combat, the final judgemental authority. Richard's sentimental, magical investment in royal semantics metaphorically reflects Shakespeare's own artistic investment in the poetic mode and in a language of ontological rightness, a language of 'names'. Not that Richard in any blunt sense 'is' Shakespeare – though he is surely his imaginative possession – for it is Shakespeare, after all, who supplies us with a critique of Richard's position. Metaphors are metaphors, in short, not allegorical equations.

For God as the third partner in dialogue Bolingbroke substitutes material force, human need, 'votes'. The determinant of meaning is now, like the occupant of a throne, whoever gets there first with the most. When Richard and Bolingbroke meet at Flint Castle, the royal name so tenuously held by Richard is without meaning, and the forceful meaning of Bolingbroke is without the royal name. Words and meanings generally are now disjunct. In the 'base court' (appropriately) the third partner to Richard's and Bolingbroke's dialogue, the verbal authority, is not God but Bolingbroke's twenty thousand silent soldiers, who help seize the word 'king' and give it the new meaning of 'Henry IV'. This 'debasement' of kingship involves the secularising of language as well, the surrender of a sacramental language to a utilitarian one in which the relation between words and things is arbitrary, unsure, and ephemeral.

Bolingbroke's usurpation of the name 'king' brings into dramatic being both the lie and metaphor. Falstaff, the corporealised lie, is also a low-life metaphor for kingship, as at a higher level is Hotspur, 'king of honour'. Prince Hal begins his ascent toward the throne as an apparent lie, the wastrel truant. And in the person of Henry IV the lie is on the throne of England. Even the dramatist Shakespeare must seem a liar, now that truth, meaning, and value are no longer naturally resident in words. Thus he and Hal, the interior dramatist, begin their plays as seeming liars and seek to transcend the fallen, lie-fraught world of Henry IV by restoring value and meaning both to kingship and to the King's English.

In the *Henry IV* plays the redemption of the word is commercially figured as the paying of verbal debts, by Hal, 'who never promiseth but he means to pay' (V.iv.43), and by Shakespeare, whose successful dramatic form depends on his fulfilment of structural promises. A lie is the price of bribing the temporarily rebellious Falstaff to re-enter the illusion of history in *I Henry IV*: 'For my part, if a lie may do thee grace, / I'll gild it with the happiest terms I have' (V.iv.161–2). And a more heinous lie is the price of subduing the rebel forces at the 'battle' of Gaultree Forest in *II Henry IV*. In this break-faith world one word is made good – Hal's promise to redeem time when men think least he will, particularly the implicit promise of his quiet reply to Falstaff's 'Banish plump Jack, and banish all the world' – 'I do, I will' (II.iv.526–8). A fuller redemption of speech is accomplished in *Henry V*. There the divinely guaranteed truths of Richard's reign and the ubiquitous lies of Henry's are succeeded by rhetoric, the language of conquest. The rhetorical word is no longer instinct with value, as in Richard's time, nor divorced from it, as in Henry's, but triumphant over it. In rhetoric, words take on an achieved, pragmatic value as instruments of persuasive action, even as English kingship takes on an earned, human value by virtue of Harry's victory at Agincourt. But Shakespeare's verbal achievement is no more enduring than Harry's brief reign; it is a fugitive solution to linguistic and dramatic enigmas that will vex the playwright to the end of his career. . . .

*

As the deposed Richard II sits alone at Pomfret Castle musing on his losses, his only apparent consolation is an abundance of metaphors bestowed upon him by a generous playwright. The most extravagant of these is his sustained conceit identifying himself as Time's 'numbering clock':

> I wasted time, and now doth Time waste me,
> For now hath Time made me his numbering clock.
> My thoughts are minutes, and with sighs they jar
> Their watches on unto mine eyes, the outward watch,
> Whereto my finger, like a dial's point,
> Is pointing still, in cleansing them from tears.
> Now sir, the sound that tells what hour it is
> Are clamorous groans, which strike upon my heart,
> Which is the bell. So sighs and tears and groans
> Show minutes, times, and hours. But my time
> Runs posting on in Bolingbroke's proud joy
> While I stand fooling here, his Jack o' the clock.
> (V.v.49–60)

The ironies of the time-waster now wasted by time, though they eloquently express the pathos of Richard's plight, seem a small semantic return on a poetic investment of twelve lines. However, if the plight of the unemployed sovereign in prison figures that of *his* sovereign, the poet-playwright Shakespeare, then at that level of interpretation this clock may tell us more than timely truths.

In the first place, as 'teller' (l. 55), that is, as true reflector or measuring device, the clock as such is notoriously prone to error, especially in an England that had yet to establish Greenwich as a final temporal authority (even though another great temporal authority, Elizabeth, was born there). In the second place, though Shakespeare probably considered time as part of the natural cosmic order, he could hardly help knowing that of all temporal units the

'minutes, times and hours' he emphasises here are the most arbitrary
– since days, months, seasons and years are at least based on period-
icity in nature. This stress upon the arbitrary and distorting features
of temporal representation is reinforced by the fact that Richard's
bodily clock reflects his internal state, so that the external representation of time (the 'outward watch' of eyes, finger, heart) is governed
by the subjective experience of time. The overall effect of the conceit
is to bring home to us the extent to which time is humanly created
rather than mimetically measured, and hence how fundamentally cut
off from time man is. The temporal *Ding an sich* is presumably out
there somewhere, but it is available to man only through the deflect-
ing prism of his symbolic representations. The clock thus asserts the
disjunction of man and nature (time) at the very moment that it
serves imperfectly to unite the two.

The wayward artificiality of the clock as a teller of nature's truths
is mirrored verbally by the strained, rhetorical self-consciousness (for
example, 'Now sir') of Richard's conceit telling of the clock. All of
Richard's metaphors during the latter part of the play and especially
at Pomfret Castle exhibit this air of uneasy contrivance. As metaphors they appear to assert an equation of tenor and vehicle – usually
of Richard and the world outside his prison – much as the clock
presents itself as a true teller of time. But they are metaphors in
which Richard no longer believes, and which therefore imply a
chasm between him and the world in the very attempt to bridge it:

> I have been studying how I may compare
> This prison where I live unto the world.
> And for because the world is populous
> And here is not a creature but myself,
> I cannot do it. Yet *I'll hammer it out.*
> My brain I'll prove the female to my soul,
> My soul the father, and these two beget
> A generation of *still-breeding thoughts,*
> And these same thoughts people this little world
> In humours *like* the people of this world.
> (V.v.1–10; my italics)

What Richard hammers out as a labour of will rather than of belief
is a series of metaphoric likenesses whose ambiguous success in
connecting him to the world outside is indicated by the fact that they
will prove 'still-breeding' – ever-and-never-breeding at once, always-
bearing and yet stillborn.[1] Ultimately, however, Richard's thoughts

can populate only 'this little world', the nursery of his own mind, unable to pass beyond likeness and become authentic citizens in the larger world outside. Metaphors, after all, are not the thing itself.

Symbols had not always seemed so isolated from reality. Indeed, on Richard's unexamined assumptions, language had been bonded to nature and the world order by virtue of God's certification of him as a Divine Right king. The original power of the divine Word remained actively at work in the King's English, just as divine authority descending by way of primogeniture was immanent in Richard himself. But it is the purpose of the play to divest Richard of these views – to drive a wedge between words and their meanings, between the world order and the word order, between the king and the man who is king, and between names and metaphors. Thus we find in *Richard II* not merely the fall of a king but also the fall of kingly speech – of a speech conceived of as sacramental and ontological, in which words are not proxies for things but part of the things themselves. With the fall of this King's English there falls also a view of reality contained within it, a view so similar to the 'world picture' attributed to Elizabeth's reign that the parallels might well seem vexing to anyone who worked in words. 'I am Richard II', Elizabeth told William Lombarde, 'Know ye not that?' In 1595 Elizabeth had not yet played Richard II to Essex's Bolingbroke, but her language – the English on which playwrights like Shakespeare drew – was already beginning to play Richard II to Sir Francis Bacon's Bolingbroke. I have outlined this general shift from verbal fideism to scepticism during the sixteenth and seventeenth centuries [elsewhere]. Shakespeare comes at these matters dramatically. Like Richard in Pomfret Castle, he addresses himself not to linguistic theory, but to homelier things like names and metaphors.

Losing his name, Richard loses everything. Cast out of his medieval world of pre-established order and significance, he is isolated in Pomfret Castle where he attempts, with stiff rhetorical flourishes, to hammer out meanings that had once simply been there for his taking. His resort to metaphor is inevitable once the old names are gone, for metaphor is the language of the unnamed. The process is familiar. Lacking a vocabulary for the unnamed, we steal from the already named. Each successful new metaphor is a creative insight and for a time gives off a spark of aesthetic pleasure. So long as tension exists between tenor and vehicle – so long as there is an element of the negative in our awareness that it is not what it literally claims to be – the metaphor remains metaphoric. With wear, however, this tension slackens, and the metaphor collapses into an inert name – or more familiarly 'dies'. Thus few people today hear the 'call' of the word *vocation* or feel the 'fusion of self and god' in *enthusiasm*. The fact that *baron* once meant roughly 'blockhead' had been forgotten even by Shakespeare's time, when noble reminders still abounded. Language, in short, is a cemetery of dead metaphors, as linguists are fond of saying; or as poets like Emerson prefer, it is fossil poetry.

In a sense metaphor is an improper use of words, a violation of the linguistic system. Its depth structure is that of the proposition 'A is B' – 'Honey is sweet' – whether the tenor is present or only implied in the surface structure. But whereas none of the properties of sweetness is incompatible with honey, a metaphor cannot be a metaphor unless some, perhaps most, of its properties are incompatible with its subject. 'For what else is your Metaphor', Puttenham asks, 'but an inversion of sense by transport.'[2] For this reason a metaphor may initially look like a terminological error, a misnaming. When Mistress Quickly cries out to the street-fighting Falstaff 'Ah thou honeysuckle villain!' and again 'Thou art a honey-seed', we may spend some long moments puzzling over the honeylike properties of plump Jack before realising that Mistress Quickly is playing hostess not to metaphor but to malapropism. She means, not 'honey-suckle' and 'honey-seed', but 'homicidal' and 'homicide' (*II Hen. IV*, II.i.55, 59).

In Mistress Quickly's usage, error must be distinguished from apparent metaphor. Normally, it is the other way round: metaphor must earn its title to truth in a contest against error. Any new metaphor must be tested, must win its way to acceptance, its truth competing for favour against the odds of its own more obvious falseness. When in *I Henry IV* Falstaff calls Mistress Quickly an otter, Hal challenges the term – 'An otter, Sir John! Why an otter?' – thus forcing Falstaff to defend the truth of his metaphor: 'Why, she's neither fish nor flesh; a man knows not where to have her' (III.iii.142–5). Mistress Quickly bustles forth a convincing denial – 'Thou or any man knows where to have me, thou knave, thou!' (III.iii.147) – but the point is that the question of truth has arisen.

The question of truth is precisely what does not arise in the case of dead metaphors. Here, the vehicle is no longer an illuminating similitude but literally the name of the tenor. No one questions whether 'far-seeing' is an appropriate term for the broadcasting of images by radiowaves to receivers that project them onto a picture tube. When the semantic batteries in a metaphor have gone entirely dead, as those of 'television' have for most people and certainly for those to whom it is merely 'TV', the metaphor ceases to be a metaphor and becomes a name. As such, it passes securely beyond challenges as to its truth, rightness and acceptability. Had Falstaff said 'Francis Bacon is a baron', Hal would no more have thought to challenge the dead metaphor – 'A baron, Sir John! Why a baron? – than he would to challenge the proper name, 'Why "Francis Bacon"?' To either question the only possible answer, even for a master of improvisation like Falstaff, would be a shrugging 'That's simply the name'. There is no relevance to search out, no insightful comparison or 'before unapprehended relation of things'. A name is a name is a name.

Now for Richard II kingship, *his* kingship, is as much beyond question as a proper name. It has the automatic warrant of Divine Right, which means not that Richard conceives of himself as the right king but that he conceives of himself simply as *the* king. For him 'King' and 'Richard' are not two words but one indissoluble name. The old metaphors linking kingly office and divine office are not analogical truths in Richard's imagination but anagogic ones, not metaphors but identities. The king is not *like*, he *is* the 'deputy elected by the Lord', 'God's substitute', 'the Lord's lieutenant', and so on. And because 'King' and 'Richard' are one entity, Richard is all of these things – and so he must carry his title with him to the grave, all successors disallowed.

This seems to be why Shakespeare, despite having established (in Act I, scene ii especially) Richard's criminal failures, even his murderousness, as king, then dramatises his deposition not so much as a trial of Richard's conduct as a trial of his concept of the royal office. At issue is whether King and Richard are in fact one word and whether the metaphors so royally taken for granted are literally true. Thus Shakespeare charts Richard's dramatic experience by the coordinates of name and person, thrusting him from a belief in the monistic divinity of name –

> Arm, arm, my name! A puny subject strikes
> At thy great glory
>
> (III.ii.86–7)

– to a recognition of dualistic separability –

> What must the King do now? Must he submit?
> The king shall do it. Must he be deposed?
> The King shall be contented. Must he lose
> The name of king? O' God's name, let it go!
> (III.iii.143–6)

– to an ultimate loss of name and a consequent dissolution of personal identity and meaning –

> I have no name, no title;
> No, not that name was given me at the font,
> But 'tis usurped. Alack the heavy day,
> That I have worn so many winters out
> And know not what name to call myself!
> (IV.i.255–9)

Ernst Cassirer remarks that, among primitives, 'the being and life of a person are so intimately connected with his name that, as long as the name is preserved and spoken, its bearer is still felt to be present and directly active'.[3] In Richard's case the ambiguity of the life-giving powers of the name is given full expression. Richard 'lives' only so long as his name is honoured; once that is gone, he becomes in his own word 'nothing', even before his death at the hands of Exton. In Pomfret Castle he realises that the name of king is merely arbitrary, that he has an identity apart from the name. Yet this knowledge, instead of sustaining him, instead of making him feel that he has lost 'merely' a name and not life itself, destroys him. There are no 'mere' words, it seems, only meaningful ones. Exton kills a man who is, in his namelessness, already dead.

*

Richard's world is dead too. It is a world conceived of in metaphors that had died into names, as Richard discovered too late. The metaphors he has taken literally were also taken literally in the sixteenth century, and implicit in them was a world view. Pattrick Cruttwell remarks:

> Shakespeare is not really a philosopher; he had no philosophy of his own. He didn't need to have one; it was given him. He had simply to describe human life as honestly, vividly, and completely as he knew,

and then, through the very terms of reference by which alone he *could* describe it, a philosophy emerges.[4]

The philosophy that emerges, Cruttwell says, is the 'integrated medieval view' that E. M. W. Tillyard has more famously, if somewhat metachronically, called the Elizabethan world picture. This world view, inherited from medieval culture, was intimately bound up with Elizabethan language, also inherited from medieval culture. The conception of a world essentially animistic, full of anthropomorphic life, dancing, ceremony, order, harmony – a hierarchical world of Platonic dualities and microspheres fashioned on the principles of analogy and parallelism – this world was not merely a set of theories in which men believed; it was what most of their key words implicitly *meant*. The world picture was a word picture. It was not for nothing that reality was thought to be composed of 'elements' and nature conceived of as a 'book'.

But in Richard's dramatic experience – as in England's historical experience during the sixteenth and seventeenth centuries – the Book of Nature becomes incomprehensible. Things no longer answer to their assigned names. Once upon a time, in a fairytale world, 'four lagging winters and four wanton springs [could be made to] end in a word, such [was] the breath of kings' (I.iii.214–15). Once upon a time the king's name was twenty thousand names, and the king and God were consubstantial. That fairytale time had its historical counterpart in Shakespeare's England, as the fictive Richard had his real-life spokesman in, among others, William Tyndale, who said that

> he that judgeth the King judgeth God, and he that layeth hands on the King layeth hands on God, and he that resisteth the King resisteth God. . . . The King is in this world without law, and he may at his lust do right or wrong and shall give accounts but to God only.[5]

These claims echo again and again through the Tudor homilies, especially in that 'Concernyng Good Ordre and Obedience to Rulers and Magistrates' (1547) and that 'Against Disobedience and Wilful Rebellion' (1574).[6] That kingship confers quasi-divine status and inviolability upon its holder is owing in part to God's direct appointment of kings, an appointment renewed through primogeniture, and in part to God's establishment of hierarchical order throughout the universe. As the visible symbol of human order, the king mediates between 'earthly men' and both God and God's grand design. If he falls, all else falls with him, as Ulysses, the domino theorist of *Troilus and Cressida*, so eloquently details it.

Bishop Carlisle, the Ulysses of *Richard II*, sounds a similar theme. Just before the deposition of Richard, when Bolingbroke says 'In God's name, I'll ascend the regal throne', Carlisle cries 'Marry, God forbid!' and in effect reads the Tudor homilies to him:

> . . . shall the figure of God's majesty,
> His captain, steward, deputy elect,
> Anointed, crowned, planted many years,
> Be judged by subject and inferior breath,
> And he himself not present?
> (IV.i.125–9)

The Earl of Northumberland applauds Carlisle's performance – 'Well have you argued, sir' – but adds, 'and for your pains / Of capital treason we arrest you here' (IV.i.150–1). So much, it would seem, for Divine Right!

And so much, also, for a sacramental language in which words have a kind of divine, inalienable right to their referents. Unlike Richard, Bolingbroke has never subscribed to such a language. From the opening scene of the play he has regarded words as mere vocal conveniences whose substance lies not in themselves but in what they designate. Thus he employs words as promissory notes in gathering followers in his venture for kingship, and reinforces what few words he does utter with material force. At Flint Castle, where Richard descends to the base court with many words and few soldiers, Bolingbroke listens politely and says little: his twenty thousand soldiers are all the eloquence he requires. If Richard is a regal name that is gradually divested of its meaning, Bolingbroke is a kind of material force or meaning in search of the name that will give him public expression.

The name Bolingbroke seeks is, of course, 'king', and the bond between word and meaning is analogous to that between kingship and the holder of that office. If the king's name or title normally goes unquestioned, it is not, Richard discovers, because it is divinely guaranteed but because it is humanly conferred and assumed. Names fit their referents not because of an underlying correspondence or substantive unity but by virtue of informal covenants among speakers. Kings and meanings rule by custom. It follows, as Bolingbroke well knows, that the name of 'king' will as readily answer to the meaning of 'Henry IV' as to that of 'Richard II'. The next step in this reduction of language from the sacrosanct to the purely arbitrary is registered by Falstaff's remark to Prince Hal at the opening of *I Henry IV*: 'I would to God thou and I knew where a commodity of good names were to be bought' (I.ii.92–4). Like money, language is now reckoned a merely useful social instrument. Its meaning and value are no longer intrinsic but manufactured in response to the vicissitudes of the marketplace. In the inflationary times of *II Henry IV* the value of the word will fall still further. But that is to get ahead of the story.

When words are divorced from things, when names are seen to have neither a magical nor an inherently natural connection to their referents, then meaning comes into question, both in language and in kingship. What, during the reign of Bolingbroke, does the name of 'king' mean? *Richard II* has presented us with the gradual estrangement of the name 'king' from the meaning which, in the person of Richard himself, it has expressed, a meaning underwritten by God. If the royal name still presumes to mean 'the Lord's lieutenant' or 'God's substitute', then the proposition 'The King is Henry IV' can only be a lie, as Hotspur and the other conspirators feel. If, on the other hand, the proposition is true, if Bolingbroke *is* 'King Henry IV', then the old meanings are, and must always have been, not literal but only metaphorical. If so, the king is not a participant in divinity but an actor in a secular role, as Richard appears to realise in his tiring-room at Pomfret Castle:

> Thus play I in one person many people,
> And none contented. Sometimes am I king,
> Then treasons make me wish myself a beggar,
> And so I am. Then crushing penury
> Persuades me I was better when a king;
> Then am I kinged again – and by and by
> Think that I am unkinged by Bolingbroke,
> And straight am nothing.
> (V.v.31–8)

Richard's world of names has cracked apart to reveal the metaphor that was inert but not entirely dead within. Between 'king' and such meanings as 'God's substitute' stands, not an equals sign, but an 'as-if'. If what is true of the king's name is also true of the King's English – or, in Shakespeare's time, of the Queen's English – then the implications for the poet-playwright are inauspicious indeed.

*

Why, we may wonder, should Shakespeare fashion in *Richard II* not merely the fall of a king but also the fall of kingly speech? Kings have died from time to time and worms have eaten them, but not for words. Henry VI, Richard III and John, all fall without our feeling that a world of words topples with them. Yet there is clearly a sense in which Richard's verbal experience can be seen to reflect issues of paramount interest to the poet-playwright. Indeed, Richard has often been called a poet-king, not because he speaks excellent verse – as the 'unpoetic' Bolingbroke does also – but because his attitude toward language is poetic. After his return from Ireland, he ignores his captains' calls to action, preferring instead to 'sit upon the ground / And tell sad stories of the deaths of kings' (III.iii.155–6). That is, rather than enter on actions that would assert his authority in England, Richard lapses into forms of lyric narcissism. These sentimental verbal kingdoms are gratifying to him because within their imagined borders he holds uncontested sway; no Bolingbroke may enter there.

It is not quite accurate, however, to say that the poetic Richard whiles away his time with symbols and ceremonies at the expense of reality and action, which fall under the aegis of Bolingbroke, because in Richard's view language participates in reality, and words constitute actions. Yet Richard's journey through the play from Windsor Castle to Pomfret Castle, from Highness to nothingness, dramatises the breakdown of this conception of symbolism and language. He experiences in miniature the whole cultural metamorphosis of language, the long historical process in which the marriage of word and thing, signifier and signified, was put asunder and man's thought divorced from his world. For Bacon, Hobbes, the Royal Society and modern linguists, this process is a melioristic one – not a breakdown of the union between word and thing but a liberation of the word from the thing.[7] For the poet, however, such a process is analogous to the Fall – or, in *Richard II*, to the deposition of a Divine Right king. For if language even in its post-Edenic, fallen form were sacramental – if its words either contained divinity, as in the figure of Christ the Logos, or even represented divinity, as in the figure of the Divine Right monarch – then the man who held dominion over language – whether king, priest, magician, or poet – would in some degree hold dominion over things and men's minds as well. Merely by practising his craft the poet would participate in the divine order, bringing the Book of Art into direct alignment with the Book of Nature, and acquiring by virtue of his mastery of words something of the creative authority deeply embedded in them from the beginning. He would then rebut the philistine claim that poetry is a pleasant lie, not by saying with Sidney that the poet nothing affirmeth and hence cannot lie, but by saying that his loving attendance upon language affirms a divine order and truth already implicit in words.

But for poet as well as king, it is not so. In *Richard II* Shakespeare dramatises his awareness that his verbal medium is founded not on names but on metaphor. More precisely, within a language of names, seemingly bonded to Elizabethan reality and warranted by God, lies the altogether human presence of metaphor, its once creative energy long since hardened into conventional definition.[8] This descent from names to metaphors implies a fall from truth also. For it is the nature of metaphor to assume the appearance of the lie, since both, as the Houyhnhnms put it, 'say the thing that is not'.

The linguistic issue is dramatised in terms of the royal 'name'. In Richard's Divine Right view, 'king' is part of his own proper name – inherently legitimate, inviolable, even unquestionable. Usurped by Bolingbroke and applied to himself as 'Henry IV', the name of 'king' becomes ambiguous – at best, a term abruptly redefined in meaning, at worst, a lie that invades all of the King's English and breaks the bonds of meaning. What, then, of the young Prince Hal, the future king? Applied to the wastrel prince, the title of king must appear a lie too. Or, from the perspective of the tavern world, it must seem a delicious joke whose punch line will burst riotously on England shortly after Hal's coronation.

Hal is himself willing to exploit the appearance of a lie, as his first soliloquy informs us, but in the long run his view of his relation to kingship is metaphoric, and in this regard he distinguishes himself from both Richard and Bolingbroke. For him, the title will no longer possess the Divine Right status of a personal name, as it did for Richard, because he maintains a metaphoric doubleness of focus between vehicle and tenor, name and person, never forgetting that there are ironic distinctions between His Highness Henry the Fifth and the man whom the drawers called 'a Corinthian, a lad of mettle, a good boy (by the Lord, so they call me)' (*I Hen. IV*, II.iv.11–13). If the royal title is not part of his personal name, neither is it merely a piece of stolen property, like 'King Henry the Fourth'. As with all metaphors, Hal must somehow demonstrate the truth of his kingship in the teeth of his apparent – in fact, his heir apparent – falseness. For a Divine Right he must substitute an earned human right to the crown. Only then can kingship be invested with meaning.

And Shakespeare? He, no less than Prince Hal, is called in doubt by Bolingbroke's usurpation and the fall of speech. If the king is a lie in the political realm, the lie is now king in the verbal world – and he who practises in that world must needs seem a liar. So the would-be king Hal and the would-be playwright Shakespeare must acknowledge themselves apparent liars to begin with, and somehow wrest truth from that false appearance. Both must transcend Bolingbroke and achieve authentic sovereignty in their separate realms of politics and art.

From James L. Calderwood, *Metadrama in Shakespeare's 'Henriad'* (Berkeley, 1979), pp. 5–29.

NOTES

[James Calderwood's essay is excerpted from his book on 'Metadrama' in Shakespeare's history plays, which focuses on the self-reflexive aspects of Shakespeare's second historical tetralogy, exemplifying a concern with language analogous to much poststructuralist criticism. Ed.]

1.   Eric La Guardia, 'Ceremony and History: the Problem of Symbol from *Richard II* to *Henry V*', in *Pacific Coast Studies in Shakespeare*, ed. Waldo F. McNeir and Thelma N. Greenfield (Eugene, Oregon, 1966), p. 74.

2.   George Puttenham in *Elizabethan Critical Essays*, ed. G. Gregory Smith (London, 1904), 2:160. Puttenham's view that figures are trespasses of speech, and my own emphasis in this chapter on metaphor as a violation of the linguistic system, should be qualified to take account of the fact that language so abounds with figurative speech that we can hardly call it a deviation from the norm. Metaphor is a trespass in so far as it is non-logical; it says what literally is not. But a very great deal of language is non-logical in this sense. Moreover, some metaphors, truly creative, name the previously unnamed – get a line on aspects of experience and reality that lie quite outside the received vocabulary of a culture. Others, however, simply rename the already named; they are not exploratory but inventive, products of Coleridge's fancy rather than Imagination.

3.   Ernst Cassirer, *Language and Myth* (New York, 1946), p. 52.

4. Pattrick Crutwell, 'Physiology and Psychology in Shakespeare's Age', *Journal of the History of Ideas*, 12 (1951), 75–89.

5. Quoted by Philip Wheelwright in *The Burning Fountain* (Bloomington, Indiana, 1954), p. 215.

6. To be sure, the increased stress in the sixteenth century on the divinity of kingship need not entail an increased belief in the concept, much less an exceptionally godlike crop of kings. The homily 'Against Disobedience and Wilful Rebellion' (1574) was issued not as a spontaneous expression of belief in the divinity of Elizabeth but as a propagandistic response to the Northern uprising of 1569. With the horrors of the civil wars still alive in public memory, both commoner and king wanted sacred as well as secular support for the established order. Even so, need is the fuel of belief, none more powerful, and it is quite impossible to dismiss the enormous prestige that monarchy had for men like Ascham, Spenser, Hooker and Bacon, or to ignore the ubiquitous metaphors linking order in the state with divine orderings of the universe and the laws of nature.

7. Ernst Cassirer regards this linguistic development as a three-phase movement from a 'mimetic' through an 'analogical' to a 'symbolic' relationship between signs and meanings. He sees this process as a teleogical maturing of language, an achievement of 'inner freedom'. See his *The Philosophy of Symbolic Forms* (New Haven, Conn., 1953), vol. 1, *Language*, pp. 186–98.

8. In discovering the metaphor within the name, Shakespeare could be said to have recognised something like the Sapir–Whorf hypothesis, according to which each distinct language encapsulates a world view that is untranslatable. (See Benjamin Whorf, *Four Articles on Metalinguistics* [Washington, DC, 1949] and also *Language, Thought and Reality: Selected Writings of Benjamin Lee Whorf*, ed. John B. Carroll [Cambridge, Mass., 1956]).

8

'Henry IV Part I': Rituals of Violence

DEREK COHEN

Hotspur is a character whose career runs the gamut of dramatic expression. Commencing on a note of furious, even farcical, comedy, his life concludes on a note of tragic grief so poignantly realised as to have inspired Northrop Frye's perception that his dying remark, 'thoughts, the slaves of life', comes out of the heart of the tragic vision.[1] Hotspur's brave death is placed squarely and deliberately before the audience and provides the final means by which they can comprehend the nature and meaning of his life. Gradually the character has been moulded and determined by forces and events that culminate in the great encounter between himself and Prince Hal. The forces, both those seen by and those hidden from Hotspur, are the means by which the audience and reader are able to apprehend and absorb the development of a character whose existence has been bent into the shape of tragic suffering shown by that last speech:

> O Harry, thou hast robb'd me of my youth!
> I better brook the loss of brittle life
> Than those proud titles thou hast won of me;
> They wound my thoughts worse than thy sword my flesh:
> But thoughts, the slaves of life, and life, time's fool,
> And time, that takes survey of all the world,
> Must have a stop. O, I could prophesy,
> But that the earthy and cold hand of death
> Lies on my tongue: no, Percy, thou art dust,
> And food for –
>
> (V.iv.76–85)

This speech, to which I shall return, is the apotheosis of Hotspur. By virtue of the transmogrifications wrought in drama through deliberately vivid depictions of dying moments, Hotspur becomes, during this quiet, nearly still, moment in the play, hero, god, and sacrificial creature of society.[2] The fallen hero speaking and looking upwards at his conqueror commands the world he has lost just as he leaves it; and he does so in a manner and with a completeness that have been denied him up to now. It is the concentration of the audience's, the reader's, the prince's passive energy upon the spectacle of the dying soldier that emphasises his role as the sacrificial victim of his and our world – a transcendence which involves us with his conqueror and his society in a silent collusion in the sacrifice. The production and reproduction of this play over the centuries testifies to a persisting pleasure (aesthetic and moral) in what is arguably the central emotional event of the drama.

Hotspur's death, a palpable and carefully prepared ritual, is directly referable to Prince Hal's vow of fealty to the king, his father.

> Do not think so; you shall not find it so:
> And God forgive them, that so much have sway'd
> Your Majesty's good thoughts away from me!
> I will redeem all this on Percy's head,
> And in the closing of some glorious day
> Be bold to tell you that I am your son;
> When I will wear a garment all of blood,
> And stain my favours in a bloody mask,
> Which, wash'd away, shall scour my shame with it:
> And that shall be the day, whene'er it lights,
> That this same child of honour and renown,
> The gallant Hotspur, this all-praised knight,
> And your unthought-of Harry chance to meet.
> For every honour sitting on his helm,
> Would they were multitudes, and on my head
> My shames redoubled! For the time will come
> That I shall make this Northern youth exchange
> His glorious deeds for my indignities.
> Percy is but my factor, good my lord,
> To engross up glorious deeds on my behalf;
> And I will call him to so strict account
> That he shall render every glory up,
> Yea, even the slightest worship of his time,
> Or I will tear the reckoning from his heart.
> This, in the name of God, I promise here:
> The which, if he be pleas'd I shall perform,

> I do beseech your Majesty may salve
> The long-grown wounds of my intemperance:
> If not, the end of life cancels all bands,
> And I will die a hundred thousand deaths
> Ere break the smallest parcel of this vow.
>   (III.ii.124–59)

The power of the speech derives not only from the solemnity of the vow and its invocation of the imagery of blood sacrifice, but also from the variegation of mood within it. The telling first line contains a note of beseeching which hovers on the verge of the imperative. It takes strength from its repeated negatives and urgent exhortation: 'Do not think so; you shall not find it so': – the first 'so' neatly dividing the line and balancing with the second in a parison of rhythm and harmony of logic. The monosyllables of the line, coming as they do immediately after King Henry's latinate, almost otiose, 'degenerate', emphasise the contrast between the speakers.

Hal's speech is the climax of the play in the sense that here the death of Hotspur is given substance and form as an inevitable consequence of what is occurring between the king and the prince.[3] Thus is the destruction of Hotspur by Hal transformed from a shadowy probability into a central fact of the play. It is the fact by which Hotspur becomes the ritual object of a revenger's quest. Resolution through death, as Lawrence Danson argues, 'is necessary to assure the sort of enduring memorial [the hero] and his creator seek, and is an integral part of the play's expressive form'.[4] This shift in emphasis from the probable to the actual takes force less from the known historical details on which the play is based than from the nature of the sacred vow, taken in private and hedged with such images of bloodshed as are traditionally identified with ancient, pre-Christian rites of purification.

As the willing captive of drama's most private moments and thus the willing possessor of the secret thoughts and desires of characters in a play, the audience becomes, perforce, a collaborator in the action. That is, the mere fact of silent observation of a ceremony (social, religious, theatrical) compels one into a posture of collusion. That the audience is forced to collude in Hal's oathtaking is a consequence of the natural, but nonetheless dramatically contrived, fact of Hotspur's absence which further separates the warrior from the ethical circle of 'right' action to which the audience is willy-nilly a party. The confrontation of father and son, with its ramifying features of paternal accusation leading directly to the solemn blood oath, is a re-enactment of a mythical encounter, a direct step towards purification in a blood ritual through which society itself will be saved. The blood images of this speech are unlike almost all of the other blood images in the play. Where those elsewhere are emotionally and morally neutral, in Hal's vow the images of the bloody mask and the garment all of blood harness the full force of traditional, even archetypal, mythic sanctity. Hal's promise to redeem himself by shedding Percy's blood is the moment to which the play has logically tended from his first soliloquy – 'I know you all . . .' (I.ii.190) – where he promised to reveal his hidden and greater self to the world. In this later private scene, the playwright significantly extends the circle of confidence by one; to the theatre audience is added King Henry himself.[5] In staking his life upon his honour, Hal adds potency to his promises by reference to a set of quasi-magical acts and symbols which help to conjure up dire images of fulfilment through the enactment in blood of timeless rites. Such primitive ceremonies inform the conventional concepts of honour and loyalty with new depth and so diverge from the mainstream of acts and images of the drama as to reinforce the idea of Hal's separateness and superiority. Virginia Carr has noted the violations of the ceremonies of kingship in the Henriad, commencing with Richard II's part in the murder of Thomas Duke of Gloucester and reaching their extreme form with the murder of Richard himself in which 'we see the ultimate violation of the sanctity of kingship'.[6] If we accept this view of the causes and manifestations of the destruction of ceremony, we might recognise in Hal's highly ritualised oath and performance of his vow a gradual, but concrete, reintroduction of the substances and linked ceremonies of kingship into the state.[7]

It is in distinguishing between beneficial and harmful violence that this drama advances through mime and illusion an age-old practice of blood ritual. Ritual, René Girard reminds us, 'is nothing more than the regular exercise of "good" violence'.[8] He adds: 'If sacrificial violence is to be effective it must resemble the nonsacrificial as closely as possible.' Hal's is a promise to commit a deed of 'good' violence, and the elements of ceremony with which he intends to inform the deed only add to its ritualised nature. To Hal, his blood-covered features and the garment of blood are the necessary stage of pollution precedent to the promised regeneration. In these images, Hal imagines himself stained with Hotspur's blood and presenting himself to his father as the conqueror of his father's – and of 'right' society's – enemy, and thus the saviour of the nation. The bloody mask is a token or a symbol of his effort on behalf of established order and will publicly proclaim him as hero.

And yet it is a mask. As such, it can possess the power to disguise the wearer. Hal imagines himself not precisely bloody or blood-smeared, but as wearing bloody robes. To *wear* a garment of blood is different from bloodying one's own garments: it can mean to wear outward dress or covering which is stained with blood or to be so covered in blood as to seem to be wearing such a robe. It is likely that both meanings are intended. The latter is used as an assurance of heroic behaviour, as a part of the ritual of purification being described and, furthermore, the latter use accords more literally and immediately with the notion, two lines later, of washing away the accumulated gore on garment and face. The idea of the garment, however, as a separate robe and of the mask as an adopted guise enforces an impression of Hal as separate from the bloody object. In part, the self-imagined picture of the prince clad in his garment and mask has the effect of portraying Hal as priest or ritual slaughterer. As such, the image helps make concrete the early notion, gleaned from Hal's first soliloquy, that Prince Hal is in control of the events of this drama. Seeing himself in this functionary role, Hal is enforcing upon our attention his confident knowledge of himself as director of events. The idea of the garment is more usually associated with the softness of the priest's robes than with steely armour. The mask, too, is a part of the garb of the priest of the common imagination and known tradition who participates in the ritual.

If this is convincing – if Hal's perception of his killing of Hotspur can be accepted as an act of cleansing ('Which washed away shall scour my shame with it') – then we might also accept that Shakespeare has identified yet another crucial, if not *the* crucial difference between the hero and his heroic antagonist. The image of their encounter is variously imagined by Hal and Hotspur, and in this very variety of imagination lies the key to their essential characters. Hal shows his own control of his emotions and of his imagination. As Hotspur can be driven beyond the bounds of patience by imagination of huge exploits, so Hal remains firmly anchored within his own sensible sphere. He is the most entirely self-controlled character in the play, perhaps in the canon. In identifying the difference between Hal and Hotspur, James Calderwood notes that, 'as a future king Hal knows very well that his business is to shape history, not to be shaped by it. To Hotspur history is a fixed and final reality to which he is irrevocably committed. He has given his word, as it were; he cannot alter his role. To Hal on the other hand history is a series of roles and staged events'.[9] Hal decidedly lacks what Maynard Mack once characterised as the first quality of the tragic hero – the driving impulse to overstatement,[10] which is possessed in such impressive abundance by Hotspur. For many, Hal seems to have an over-developed sense of right and wrong. Equally, and equally unlike Hotspur, part of Hal's amazing political success in the play has to do with his ability to move familiarly through a variety of speech styles, each apparently selected with a view to the occasion. We have noted in the speech quoted above the impressive opening line – its straight-forwardness, its rhythm, its explicit contrast with the words to which it is a response. Immediately thereafter follow seventeen lines in which Hal commits himself to fulfilment of a mission. These seven-teen lines form a unit which is separate from that dramatic, assertive first line whose loneliness in the speech lends it an air of authenticity of emotion separable from the carefully contrived rhetoric of all that follows it. Within the following lines lies deep the notion of ven-geance sanitised by reference to the cleansing ritual described. The idea of revenge is concentrated in the imagined destruction of an even greater Hotspur than exists – 'For every honour sitting on his helm, / Would they were multitudes, and on my head / My shames redoubled!' – and give an even sensual texture by the use and placing of the two key latinate words in the sentence, 'multitudes' and 'redoubled'. The contrast of these words and this entire section of the speech with the blunt monosyllables of line one, of the large and conventionally noble concepts of this part of the speech with the sound of outrage and grief conveyed by that first line, lends the speech the tinge of self-consciousness. What follows these seventeen lines seems to me, even more obviously, to point to a kind of cleverness in Hal that diminishes the felt rage he is trying to express: for he overlays it with metaphors too mundane to be able to carry with them the burden of moral distress by which he is ostensibly moved. I refer to the mercantile terminology by which Hal concludes his plea: 'factor', 'engross up', 'strict account', 'render every glory up', 'tear the reckoning from his heart', 'cancels all bands', 'smallest parcel', establish in this oath-taking a tone of marketplace transac-tion which tends to dull the burnishing imagery of ritual and heroism with which he begins. He introduces here a new mode of speech that contrasts with the heroically extravagant promise of the culminating lines of the preceding part – 'For the time will come / That I shall make this Northern youth exchange / His glorious deeds for my indignities.' Norman Council observes that the speech demonstrates the pragmatic side of the prince who determines here 'to use Hotspur's reputation for his own gain . . . . Hotspur's honourable reputation is useful to Hal and he means to acquire it'.[11] The speech as a whole speaks of the sheer, even miraculous, *competence* of the speaker. The manipulation of styles and the variegation of tones and metaphors all denote a virtuosity which, while commendable in itself, is somewhat vitiated when compared to the different kind of virtuosity of Hotspur's speeches. Finally we must note that the rhetoric of Hal's speech, in all its variety, accomplishes its end of gaining the king's good opinion. In this sense, of course, the speech is bound to be suspect, since the whole is motivated by a desire or need of the prince to persuade the king, his powerful father, of his loyalty. And there must be satisfaction for Hal and his partisans in Henry's clear change of heart, conveyed by his confident assertion, 'A hundred thousand rebels die in this' (II.ii.160).

All theatre audiences are accustomed to seeing people temporarily transformed into other people for the duration of the play. Audiences of and participants in rituals, however, see the process and function of ritual as a means to permanent transformation of a person into, essentially, another person – a boy becomes a man, a girl a woman, a man a priest. Shakespeare critics have been reasonably united in recognising the transformation of Hal from wayward boyhood to manhood after this speech; Harold Jenkins, for example, sees this exchange between father and son as the 'nodal point' of the play.[12] One may go further, I believe, in recognising the transformation of Hal as being the transformation of the protagonist of the play into a hero – and one may identify the moment of transformation as the first line of this speech. To recognise the transformation as made permanent by virtue of a ritualised oathtaking has the effect of strengthening and universalising the nature and extent of the change and, hence, of anticipating with certainty, the triumph of this hero in a drama which seems to depend frequently upon the formal modes of myth.

I say 'this hero' because the uniqueness of *I Henry IV* resides very largely in the fact that this is a play with two heroes, each of whom stands at the centre of a world which has been conceived in opposition to that of the other. Those worlds are separately defined units of place and ideology which cannot coexist; for their separate existences are partially defined by the pledge of each to destroy the other.

The ideologies for which the two heroes stand are at bottom the same – those of power and control. The encounter between them is the occasion of the play's greatest emotional intensity. The moment has been predicted, vaunted, hoped for by participants and heroes alike. The privacy of the confrontation – interrupted briefly by Douglas and Falstaff – does not in any sense diminish the timeless ritual with which it is informed. We note the common expressions of recognition and identification, whose tone of defiance maintains the note of hostility necessary to such life-and-death meetings as these. And we note the nearly compulsive need of each hero to articulate to the other his sense of the meaning of the moment. The form of the expression of each is remarkable: Hal's chivalry and Hotspur's haste are appropriate symbolic denotations of each as he is given the opportunity to express his sense of the significance of the moment, demonstrating that he knows, as his opposite knows, that for one of them it is a last encounter. It is this awareness of finality that endues the moment with solemnity and the ritual with its form – that of a last accounting in the dazzling light of a certain death to follow.

The encounter, when it finally comes, is preceded by a provocative ritual of boasting in which each of the combatants – almost as if to rediscover the basis of his hatred of the other – recalls the very spirit of his own animosity. In Hal's recollection of the Ptolemaic principle that 'Two stars keep not their motion in one sphere' (V.iv.64) he falls back upon the natural law, resistance to whose principles he has begun to abandon since his vow to the king. And indeed it is in obedience to the laws of nature that Hal has ritually dedicated himself. Hotspur's over-weening vanity makes him hark back, compulsively almost, to the lust for greatness that dooms him. But it is when Hal, oddly and mockingly, borrows Hotspur's own demotic language and metaphors of violent action, that the Northern youth is finally left without images and must act:

> Prince I'll make it greater ere I part from thee,
> And all the budding honours on thy crest
> I'll crop to make a garland for my head.
> Hotspur I can no longer brook thy vanities.
> (V.iv.79–4)

Hal's words, his image of Hotspur's 'budding' honours, suggest to his adversary that those honours are not yet full-grown, not really the honours of an adult hero. His threat to 'crop' them from his crest contains an insulting contempt: to crop, according to the *OED*, is 'to poll or to lop off'. The term, in other words, carries all the easy arrogance of a simple, almost casual, single deadly blow. In Hal's brilliantly infuriating image we and, more important, Hotspur are presented with the image of Hotspur as an unresisting plant and the prince as a carefree courtier in search of 'a garland for [his] head'. Hotspur's single line of reply is, thus, reasonably one of powerful anger: his only possible reply to Hal's vanities is the testing action of combat.

Of the dying Hotspur, George Hibbard has written that he 'eventually becomes capable of seeing all human endeavour, including his own, in relation to the great abstract ideas of time and eternity, and voices this vision of things in the moving lines he utters at his end'.[13] This observation in part explains the tragic element of this character in the coalescence of his comic and tragic selves into mutually supporting images of comedy and tragedy whose very extremism lends intensity to the character. There is tragedy, too, in the dying man's sheer magnificent truth to himself, to what he is and has ever been; 'I better brook the loss of brittle life / Than those proud titles thou hast won of me', comes not from the large heart of the tragic vision but from the authentic, single, separate self of Harry Hotspur, uniquely and eternally apart. That difference from his fellows, from all other heroes, is gloriously captured in the penultimate realisation that the instrument by which he has lived, by which his life and character have been defined, has been stilled – 'the cold hand of death / Lies on my tongue'. Hotspur, whose eloquence has elevated him, is unimaginable in a silent state, and Shakespeare, knowing the absolute truth of this for the character and the audience, rivets all attention upon the death of his hero's speech. Thus does silence become synonymous with tragedy.

The prolonged antagonism of Hal and Hotspur has no obviously alternative outcome to this final violent conflict. And in the conflict itself we can discern the fact that the physical closeness of the antagonists is a metaphor for a larger issue evident in the spectacle. That, as the two have been driven gradually closer through the play, so have they become with the subtle aid of ritual, more and more alike until, in the moments of and those immediately after, the fatal fight, they are almost images of each other. So utterly does violence dominate mimetic and dramatic action that it can result in the obliteration of individuality. During the violent encounter differences between combatants tend to evanesce: the violence itself is the correlative by which individuals are connected as their whole selves are absorbed by physical contention. Hal and Hotspur do not speak during their fight and thus are transformed by their attempts to kill each other into a single unit of dramatic action – the differences between them disappear; their personalities meld. And, indeed, it would seem that in killing Hotspur, and through the combat itself, Hal has absorbed something of his opponent's vital essence. There is an indication, in his tribute to the fallen hero, of love and something, too, of the generosity of soul which is Hotspur's hallmark.

> **Prince** For worms, brave Percy. Fare thee well, great heart!
> Ill-weav'd ambition, how much art thou shrunk!
> When that this body did contain a spirit,
> A kingdom for it was too small a bound;
> But now two paces of the vilest earth
> Is room enough: this earth that bears thee dead
> Bears not alive so stout a gentleman.
> If thou wert sensible of courtesy,
> I should not make so dear a show of zeal;
> But let my favours hide thy mangled face,
> And, even in thy behalf, I'll thank myself
> For doing these rites of tenderness.
> Adieu, and take thy praise with thee to heaven!
> Thy ignominy sleep with thee in the grave,
> But not remember'd in thy epitaph!
>
> (V.iv.86–100)

The ritualistic element of the speech takes the form of a loving tribute to the fallen hero and an action of passing symbolic import. Hal, Herbert Hartman has convincingly argued, disengages his own royal plumes from his helmet to shroud the face of his dead rival.[14] These plumes are equivalent to Hotspur's 'budding honours' so contemptuously referred to by the prince at the commencement of the encounter. If we can suppose Hal actually to have fulfilled his threat and, as the text allows, to have cropped Hotspur's plumes, then surely the removal of his own plumes and the act of placing them upon the face of the beloved enemy is a gesture of weight. In the purest sense of the phrase, Hal *identifies with* Hotspur, and that identification is given a poignant depth by the ritualistic means through which it is achieved.

In other ways the speech contains evidence of this identification which seems so much stronger than sympathy. By concluding Hotspur's dying speech Hal has appropriated to himself something of the power of his rival's speech; he has almost literally absorbed his last breath. Despite the obviousness of the tendency of Hotspur's last words, Hal's mere capacity to utter them cements the identification. Ten lines later, concomitantly with his 'rites of tenderness', Prince Hal bends over the body of Hotspur to lay his favours on the soldier's face. In so doing he closes once again – and for only the second time in the drama – the physical space between them as he touches his erstwhile adversary. Hal thus bathes his own favours which clearly have immensely strong symbolic, even religious, meaning for him – in the blood of Harry Hotspur. And thus, ironically, does Hotspur acquire a mask soaked in his own blood *and* the blood of the prince. For, as Hal performs his act of homage, we are powerfully reminded of his solemn oath to the king to 'stain my favours in a bloody mask'. In the mingling of the blood of Prince Hal and Harry Hotspur is the fusion of their two souls symbolically extended. The words by which Hal accompanies his gesture complete the connection: 'And even in thy behalf I'll thank myself . . .' The pronouns of that line, by their self-conscious interplay, bind their subjects ever more firmly to each other. As well, history furnished Shakespeare with one additional means by which the two characters are made to merge; that is, of course, the unforgettable fact that they have the same Christian name.

The degradation of honour and courage which Falstaff's presence offers the scene has often been discussed. One is reminded of Falstaff's capacity for sheer bestiality as he defiles the body lying near him; a capacity made more real, perhaps, by the use to which he subsequently puts the newly mangled corpse. As an ironic travesty, the gesture has an axiomatic dramatic function in keeping with the structure of parody running through the drama. However, less obvious – aside from the action's merely narrative purpose – is the reason for the action in relation, not to the scheme or structure of the drama but, precisely, to the Prince's killing of Hotspur.

A nation in a state of civil war is one in which law has failed to create or maintain order. And so it is beyond the law that the state must seek the means of stability. The means are often those of repression, which always carries the threat of resistance. Thus do the two opposing forces of tyranny and resistance to tyranny promise the fruition of actual conflict. Societies suffering repression can explode in violence which is artistically expressed as an image of the artist's political prejudice. As the violent riots of *Henry VI* are devoid of the seeds of social order, in *I Henry IV* the conflict and its hero are presented so as to emphasise a socially beneficial outcome. Here, the blood that is shed fulfils the requirements of blood rituals. It is, one might say, 'clean' blood resulting from what René Girard has called 'good' acts of violence.[15] That is, it is blood which has been shed for the larger advantage of the national welfare. And as we look back at the blood imagery related to the Hal / Hotspur conflict, it becomes clear that Hotspur's blood has been represented as that of the sacrificial creature whose death will redeem his world, and into whose life and person are concentrated the rage, anxiety, and fear of a threatened nation. His death, then, sometimes regarded as tragic, is also utterly necessary for the continuation of the nation. Dover Wilson regards it as a favourable feature of Hal's character that his 'epitaph on Hotspur contains not a word of triumph',[16] and perhaps he is right. But, for Shakespeare and his audience, more significant, perhaps, is the fact that Hotspur's greatness was very nearly sufficient unto his purposes: the world was almost overturned, and with it the reign of the regicide Henry IV. Hal's presence here naturally palliates the thought, since Hal is the successor to the throne of the tyrant and, just as surely, the golden hero of the drama.

At his death and because of it, Hotspur is transformed into a hero of tragic magnitude. Thus, when Falstaff rises and hacks at his corpse, he commits a direct assault upon the sanctity of the ritual that has just been performed. His act suddenly infuses the scene with uncleanness by an almost casual reversal of the ritual that has just passed. The return to life of Falstaff is no miracle, but a rather sour joke, made somewhat sourer by the attitude of shallow boasting which accompanies it. The return to prose, to a disordered, unrhythmic speech which breathes selfish relief and opportunism is a wicked riposte to Hal. But the physical attack on Hotspur's corpse is a *crime* against the ethos of heroism to which the prince and, in a dramatic sense, the nation have been committed. Falstaff's act is a negation and a degradation of the cleansing by blood. And yet the repeated exposure to violence can inure us to it. While we are indeed shocked by the callous treatment of Hotspur's corpse, the very brutality of that treatment and its very extensiveness gradually accustom us to the shocking fact that a slain hero is being dragged around like a side of beef. The corpse of Hotspur gradually becomes the focus not merely of Falstaff's opportunism, but of a grotesque, huge, successful joke – 'one of the best jokes in the whole drama'[17] upon whose point is balanced the question of ritual purification. Yet Falstaff's imitative act of violence rebounds upon himself: any doubts as to his locus in the moral scheme of the play are vividly resolved by his disruption of the cycle of the ritual. The emphatic terminus implied by Hal's parting words is crassly mocked by Falstaff rising up. The act of cutting Percy's thigh is represented as antithetical to Hal's death-fight with Percy: as the fight was a lucid example of the purifying violence seen only in drama and ritual, so the attack on the corpse affirmed the value of the rite by its implied but debased re-enactment of the encounter.

Hal, Hotspur, and Falstaff are, then, related through ritual, both in itself and as depicted through the dark glass of parody and travesty. Furthermore, it is through ritual that they are connected to their world in the play's intensest moments. To call Falstaff's impersonation of Hal's father in the tavern scene a parody is to diminish the force of a scene in which a youth enacts one of the deepest universal desires of man as he overthrows his tyrannical father. The scene of oath-taking, discussed earlier, is a conscious, deliberate, and calculated retraction of the desires enacted in the tavern. As such, it is either utterly false or it is the heroic conquest of reason and responsibility – that is, social pressure and expectation – over the urging of the unconscious mind – that is, individual nature. It is thus profitable to see the tavern ritual and its climatic, if soft-spoken, conclusion ('I do, I will' [II.iv.475]) as a ritual of exorcism by which Prince Hal, through the contrived dramatisation of his innermost promptings, rids himself of the demons of his deepest desires. As J. I. M. Stewart has argued with reference to the rejection of Falstaff: Hal, 'by a displacement common enough in the evolution of a ritual, kills Falstaff instead of killing the king, his father'.[18]

Hotspur, on the other hand, does not grow or change. From first to last his purpose is to gain glory and renown. Even at his death, it is to his honours that he refers as having been more dearly won of him than his life. His sheer consistency makes him an apt victim in the cruel drama of ritual sacrifice. A Hotspur who can go to his death proclaiming the value of a moral system which is by its nature exclusive of the vast world from which it derives, cannot be the hero who heals the world. His presence nearly always provides discordancy, charming and witty though it may be. He is the heart of the whirlwind that rages through the nation, and it is this heart that must be stilled for the sake of peace. In short, as with other tragic characters, it is Hotspur's death alone that can heal the world.

From Derek Cohen, *Shakespearean Motives* (London, 1988), pp. 22–35.

NOTES

[Derek Cohen's essay forms a chapter of his book *Shakespearean Motives*. The essay appeared originally under the title 'The Rites of Violence in *1 Henry IV*' in *Shakespeare Survey*, 38 (1985). Cohen draws on early anthropological studies such as James Frazer's *The Golden Bough* (of which the work here cited, *The Scapegoat*, forms the sixth volume) but also on more recent, poststructuralist anthropological work, such as that of René Girard. Quotations are from the Arden edition of *Henry IV, Part One*, ed. A. R. Humphreys (London, 1960). Ed.]

1. Northrop Frye, *Fools of Time* (Toronto, 1967), p. 4.

2. In *The Scapegoat* (London, 1913), James Frazer discusses the role and function of that human being upon whom the evils and sorrows of the society are concentrated and through the death of whom the society is released from its suffering. The process of Hotspur's death suggests that he is Hal's and the nation's scapegoat. Frazer remarks the many ceremonies in primitive and ancient societies whereby regeneration and purification were possible only after the killing of a human scapegoat or the death of a god (pp. 22–7, passim).

3. In describing dramatic climax, Fredson Bowers ('The Structure of *King Lear*', *Shakespeare Quarterly*, 31:1 [1980]) emphasises the conscious ethical decision of that moment in the drama which determines the inevitability of its outcome. He argues that 'the rising complications of the action culminate in a crucial decision by the protagonist, the nature of which constitutes the turning point of the play and will dictate the . . . catastrophe' (p. 8).

4. Lawrence Danson, *Tragic Alphabet* (New Haven and London, 1974), p. 21.

5. If the status of Hal as hero is to be acknowledged, we must recognise that it is owed in large measure to the sheer stage power of the soliloquy. Hal's presumption in addressing us directly has the effect of placing him uppermost: he goes beyond the audible reflection of, say, Falstaff on honour, to the point of taking us into his confidence, promising *us* a happy surprise, and then, here, realising that promise.

6. Virginia M. Carr, 'Once More into the Henriad: "Two-Eyed" View', *Journal of English and Germanic Philology*, 78:4 (1978), 535.

7. Carr's reference to the gradualism of the reintroduction of ceremonies which integrate their primitive substances is consistent with the prince's

so-called 'lysis' conversion, described by Sherman Hawkins as one which 'may include more than one crisis experience separated by periods of steady advance' ('The Structural Problem of *Henry IV*', *Shakespeare Quarterly*, 33:3 [Autumn, 1982], 296). I am suggesting that Hal's use of ritual in this scene is more significant than a single stage of development or an advance to his next strength: he is demonstrating, by his use of the language of ritual, his own actual control of a situation which by rights belongs to the monarch. King Henry's subjection to this control is signalised by the conviction of his acceptance of the vow.

8. René Girard, *Violence and the Sacred* (Baltimore, 1979), p. 37.

9. James L. Calderwood, '*I Henry IV*: Art's Gilded Lie', *English Literary Renaissance*, 3:1 (Winter, 1973), 137.

10. Maynard Mack, 'The Jacobean Shakespeare', *Jacobean Theatre*, ed. John Russell Brown and Bernard Hassis (New York, 1967), p. 13.

11. Norman Council, 'Prince Hal: Mirror of Success', *Shakespeare Studies*, VII (1974), 142–3.

12. Harold Jenkins, *The Structural Problem in Shakespeare's Henry the Fourth* (London, 1956), p. 9.

13. George Hibbard, *The Making of Shakespeare's Dramatic Poetry* (Toronto, 1981), p. 180.

14. Herbert Hartman, 'Prince Hal's Shewe of Zeale', *PMLA*, 46 (1931), 720.

15. Girard, *Violence and the Sacred*, p. 37.

16. J. Dover Wilson, *The Fortunes of Falstaff* (Cambridge, 1964), p. 67.

17. Ibid., p. 89.

18. J. I. M. Stewart, *Character and Motive in Shakespeare* (London, 1965), p. 138.

9

'Henry IV': Carnival and History

GRAHAM HOLDERNESS

It is a commonplace that the figure of Falstaff, or the 'world' that figure inhabits or creates, constitutes some kind of internal *opposition* to the ethical conventions, political priorities and structures of authority and power embodied in the sovereign hegemony of king, prince and court: the state. Falstaff is at the centre of a popular comic history, located within the deterministic framework of the chronicle-history play, which challenges and subverts the imperatives of necessitarian historiography; and it is important to stress that the chronicle-history frame is qualified and criticised, not simply by the free play of Shakespeare's 'wonderful' intelligence on the underlying issues, but by a confrontation of different dramatic discourses within the drama, a confrontation which brings into play genuinely historical tensions and contradictions, drawn both from Shakespeare's own time and from the reconstructed time of the historical past.

The kind of 'opposition' represented by Falstaff is often compared with the other oppositional tendencies which challenge the state in these plays: Falstaff's moral rebelliousness and illegality are seen as analogous to those forces of political subversion – the rebellion of the Percies and the Archbishop of York's conspiracy – which shake the stability of the Lancastrian dynasty. But though moral riotousness and political opposition are often arbitrarily connected by hostile propaganda, a state which ruthlessly suppresses the latter often finds space for the former – regarded perhaps as the legitimate exercise of freedom guaranteed to a despotic ruling class by the 'stability' of its government (e.g. the court of the Stuarts). It has been recognised that the revelry and satire of Falstaff constitute kinds of social practice which were afforded a legitimate space in medieval culture. . . .

In the Middle Ages, Bakhtin writes: 'a boundless world of humorous forms and manifestations opposed the official and serious tone of medieval ecclesiastical and feudal culture . . . the culture of folk carnival humour'. These forms were, according to Bakhtin's most illuminating emphasis, basically *popular* expressions of folk culture: though they were built into the formal structure of medieval culture, they contained and signified (like the Roman Saturnalia) a completely different conception of human society:

> All those forms of protocol and ritual based on laughter and consecrated by tradition existed in all the countries of medieval Europe; they were sharply distinct from the serious, official, ecclesiastical, feudal and political cult forms and ceremonials. They offered a completely different, non-official, extra-ecclesiastical and extra-political aspect of the world, of man, and of human relations; they built a second world in which all medieval people participated more or less, in which they lived during a given time of the year.[1]

Clearly the 'carnival' (Bakhtin's generic title for all saturnalian customs and practices) was a contradictory social institution: its whole *raison-d'être* was that of opposition to established authority; it rejected all official norms and conventions; inverted established hierarchies: flouted, satirised and parodied the rituals, institutions and personalities of power. And yet it was countenanced, permitted, even fostered by those very authorities. Only a very rigid, hierarchical and static society needs such organised release and limited, temporary liberation; only a very stable, confident society can afford to permit them. By the late sixteenth century matters were different: the continuities of pagan ritual and belief were being harshly attacked by the Puritans; the precarious religious settlement made any mockery of religious authority (even, later in Elizabeth's reign, of Catholicism)[2] impossible; and the various attempts to stabilise a rapidly changing social and class structure, continued under the Stuarts, made the image of the world turned upside-down particularly distasteful to established authority. The potency of these ideas can be measured by the fact that later, in the Civil War period, such comic inversions became the basis of serious, revolutionary social criticism. From the medieval rituals in which the text 'He hath put down the mighty from their seats, and exalted them of low degree' inaugurated a temporary inversion of social hierarchy, to the radical social theories of Winstanley and the Fifth Monarchy men, there is a definite though complex and contradictory historical continuity.³ . . . It should then be possible to analyse any example of carnival festivity or saturnalian custom, and any literary production flowing from these social forms, in terms of this contradiction: from the point of view of the people, carnival is an expression of the independent values, the humanism of popular culture, a fantasy of equality, freedom and abundance which challenges the social order; from the point of view of authority, carnival is a means of incorporating and controlling the energies and anti-authoritarian emotions aroused by carnival licence. This cultural contradiction, this confrontation of popular and authoritarian discourses, will prove a sound basis for defining the function of Falstaff. . . .

Bakhtin finds the central *image* of the carnival attitude is that of the *body*: the 'material bodily principle' which is always regarded as 'deeply positive'. It is a symbol for (or rather a direct imaginative expression of) 'the people, constantly growing and renewed'. As a conception of human nature this image of the people as a giant (gargantuan) collective body pre-dates the formation of a strictly-defined and differentiated atomised individual which, in Bakhtin's terms, is a development of the Renaissance. . . .

The dominant *style* of carnival discourse is the *grotesque*. The carnivalising imagination creates gargantuan images of huge bodies, enormous appetites, surrealistic fantasies of absurdly inflated physical properties.

Carnival is humorous and satirical, and its laughter always *materialises*: concretises the spiritual in the physical, the ideal in the material, the 'upper' strata of life and society into the 'lower'. Ideals, pretensions, elevated conceptions of human nature cannot survive the enormous assertions of human sensuality: the pride of physical life mocks and degrades everything which seeks to transcend or escape it. Hence this grotesque humour of the body provides a firm basis for satire (a word often historically confused with the half-human, half-bestial figure of the satyr).

While the 'bourgeois ego' limits human life to the birth and death of a differentiated individual, the grotesque bodily image of carnival is that of a perpetually unfinished process of change and renewal: 'The grotesque image reflects a phenomenon in transformation, an as yet unfinished metamorphosis, of death and birth, growth and becoming.'⁴ The grotesque body is therefore deeply ambivalent, since it contains both processes of creation and destruction, vitality and dissolution – a simultaneity of the antitheses of life glimpsed in one dimension: 'In this image we find both poles of transformation, the old and the new, the dying and the procreating, the beginning and the end of the metamorphosis.'[5]

The grotesque image is not sealed off from the outer world: it merges into its environment as if symbolising some unity of man and nature. Hence in carnival and carnivalesque literature there is a recurrent emphasis on the physical points of entry and exit (mouth, nose, genitals, anus) and on processes of reproduction and defecation – processes which guarantee the perpetuity of 'the ever unfinished, ever creating body'. Where classicism in art later represented the body as complete, self-sufficient, enclosed and perfect, with its relation to the outer world sealed off, the grotesque insisted on that relation by displaying and caricaturing the body in its external relations. . . .

Falstaff clearly performs the function, in *Henry IV Parts I and II*, of carnival. He constitutes a constant focus of opposition to the official and serious tone of authority and power: his discourse confronts and challenges those of king and state. His attitude to authority is always parodic and satirical: he mocks authority, flouts power, responds to the pressures of social duty and civic obligation by retreating into Bacchanalian revelry. His world is a world of ease, moral licence, appetite and desire; of humour and ridicule, theatricals and satire, of community, freedom and abundance; a world created by inverting the abstract society, the oppression and the hierarchy of the official world. In the tavern the fool reigns as sovereign; on the high road the thief is an honest man; while in the royal court the cares and duties of state frown on the frivolity and absurdity of saturnalian revelry. To this extent Falstaff can be located in that *popular* tradition of carnival and utopian comedy defined by Bakhtin. . . .

Falstaff *is* Bakhtin's 'material bodily principle' writ large: his enormous size and uncontrolled appetite characterise him as a collective rather than an individual being. His self-descriptions employ a grotesque style of caricature and exaggeration to create the monstrous image of a figure larger than life, bigger than any conceivable individual:

> Have you any levers to lift me up again, being down?
> (*1HIV*.II.ii.34)

I do here walk before thee like a sow that hath overwhelmed all her
litter but one.

(*IIHIV*.I.ii.10–11)

– and he frequently discourses in his own brand of grotesque fantasy,
which works by inflating the small into the enormous: his subsequent
narrative of the robbery (*IHIV*.II.iv.160–212) or his disquisition on
Bardolph's nose (*IHIV*.III.iii.23–49). The collective being is created
by foregrounding this concrete image of the material body, but also
by means linguistic and dramatic: Falstaff is not a coherent individual subject but a polyphonic clamour of discourses, a fluid coun-
terfeiter of dramatic impersonations.

Falstaff's satirical humour 'degrades' – i.e. translates the abstract
into the concrete, the spiritual into the physical: 'A plague of sighing
and grief! It blows a man up like a bladder!'(*IHIV*.II.iv.327–8). The
conventional physical effects of grief are inverted, producing fatness
rather than emaciation: the breath exhaled in sighs becomes the
gaseous inflation of an unsettled stomach. The Prince observes that
Falstaff's enormous sensual concreteness contains no space for non-
material entities: 'There's no room for faith, truth nor honesty in
this bosom of thine: it is all filled up with guts and midriff'
(*IHIV*.III.iii.152–3).

For Bakhtin the grotesque bodily image 'reflects a phenomenon in
transformation', contains the processes of both creation and dissolution. This deep ambivalence is utterly characteristic of Falstaff, who
seems to constitute a medium in which these antithetical processes
generate simultaneously. Physical sloth and inertia co-exist with
vivid vitality of imagination; age and youth are interchangeable.
During the Gad's Hill robbery Falstaff poses, under cover of dark-
ness, as a lithe young gallant mugging the elderly and obese bourgeoisie:

Ah, whoreson caterpillars, bacon-fed knaves, they hate us youth! . . .
No, ye fat chuffs, I would your store were here! On, bacons, on! What,
ye knaves! young men must live!

(*IHIV*.II.ii.81–2; 84–6)

and later to the Lord Chief Justice:

You that are old consider not the capacities of us that are young; you
do measure the heat of our livers with the bitterness of your galls; and
we that are in the vaward of our youth, I must confess, are wags too!

(*IIHIV*.I.ii.172–6)

To moralise these passages would give us a pitiable image of age masquerading as youth. In fact, they present the audacious paradoxes of carnival, in which death and life, age and youth co-exist in the same figure, held together in impossible simultaneity by the force, zest and gaiety of carnival humour, balanced but unillusioned, poised but explosively liberating. The Prince again acknowledges this as Falstaff's essential nature in seasonal metaphors: 'Farewell, the latter spring! Farewell, All-Hallown summer!'; which anticipates Bakhtin's: 'in this image we find both poles of transformation, the old and the new, the dying and the procreating, the beginning and the end of the metamorphosis.'[6]

Bakhtin's account of the demise of the carnival and the grotesque in literature as neo-classicism advanced, coincides precisely with the fate of Falstaff in criticism. The modern critical traditions derive from John Dover Wilson's *The Fortunes of Falstaff* (1943), a monument of ideological consolidation dating from that amazingly fertile period of Shakespeare reproduction, the Second World War. Dover Wilson argues that the later eighteenth century inaugurated a diversionary tendency of Falstaff criticism: where Dr Johnson had been able to hold, with neo-classical centrality, a 'balanced' view (which Dover Wilson attempts to reconstitute), romanticism, *via* the sentimentalism of Maurice Morgann and the republicanism of Hazlitt, introduced an 'imbalance' into the poised edifice of criticism, establishing as norms certain radical attitudes: disloyalty and distaste towards the Prince, unqualified admiration for Falstaff, a preference for comic opposition over conservative royalism, for instinct and desire over reason and self-control, for moral and political subversion over the preservation of 'order' in the state.[7] Dr Johnson, apparently, 'still lived in Shakespeare's world, a world which was held together, and could only be held together by authority based on and working through a carefully preserved gradation of rank. He was never tired of proclaiming the virtues of the Principle of Subordination . . .'[8] According to Dover Wilson, Johnson 'shared Shakespeare's political assumptions', which are embodied in Ulysses' speech on 'degree' in *Troilus and Cressida*; and was therefore able to understand Shakespeare where the romantics could not. Dover Wilson does not, however, claim to derive his critical authority from the same ground of sympathetic – because partisan – comprehension. In fact his position is identical to that of Tillyard, whose *Shakespeare's History Plays* belongs to the same historical moment, the same cultural intervention, as Dover Wilson's book on Falstaff: both share the apparently scholarly (but implicitly polemical) privileging of 'order', defined as a hierarchical state ruled by the 'Principle of Subordination'. Dover Wilson's cultural / ideological strategy is clear: to re-establish a pristine but disrupted 'order' in the criticism of *Henry IV*, in Shakespeare studies, and thence in the problematical society of war-time Britain. The political intention is obvious, but naturally unacknowledged; it is articulated instead as a *moral* reconstituting of the proper context for appreciating Falstaff:

> Shakespeare's audience enjoyed the fascination of Prince Hal's 'white-bearded Satan' for two whole plays, as perhaps no character on the world's stage had ever been enjoyed before. But they knew, from the beginning, that the reign of this marvellous Lord of Misrule must have an end, that Falstaff must be rejected by the Prodigal Prince, when the time for reformation came. And they no more thought of questioning or disapproving of that finale, than their ancestors would have thought of protesting against the vice being carried off to Hell at the end of the interlude.[9]

'Shakespeare's audience' here is a fictional construction invented merely to confirm the critic's own views. Yet Dover Wilson can confidently ascribe to that phantom a definitive moral perspective in which Falstaff plays a strictly temporary and limited role: an isolated space of pleasure circumscribed by the unshakeable certainties of moral truth. With even greater confidence Dover Wilson asserts his definition of the moral judgment Shakespeare's audience would have passed on Prince Hal's riotous youth:

> Vanity . . . was a cardinal iniquity in a young prince or nobleman of the sixteenth and seventeenth centuries; . . . this is the view that his father and his own conscience take of his mistreadings; and as the spectator would take it as well, we must regard it as the thesis to which Shakespeare addressed himself.[10]

In short, the play is being located within a moralistic framework developed by critics like Tillyard and Dover Wilson during the Second World War, a moralistic perspective entirely out of sympathy with the popular traditions of carnival comedy from which Falstaff developed. Once this structure was erected and consolidated, and the threat posed by Falstaff to bourgeois criticism deflected, it became possible to affirm a nostalgic and sentimental pleasure in what Falstaff had to offer. This balancing act, a strategic counterpointing of constraint and canonisation, is skilfully engineered in Dover Wilson's conclusion:

> Falstaff, for all his descent from a medieval devil, has become a kind of god in the mythology of modern man, a god who does for our imaginations very much what Bacchus or Silenus did for those of the ancients; and this because we find it extraordinarily exhilarating to contemplate a being free of all the conventions, codes and moral ties that control us as members of a human society, . . .
>
> Yet the English spirit has ever needed two wings for its flight, Order as well as Liberty . . . this balance which the play keeps between the bliss of freedom and the claims of the common weal has been disturbed by modern critics . . . I have endeavoured to do something to readjust the balance. In effect, it has meant trying to put Falstaff in his place . . . I offer no apologies for constraining the old boar to feed in the old frank . . .[11]

Dover Wilson, scholar, critic and public servant, has evidently inherited the world and the ideology of Prince Henry: there is an unbroken continuity of the 'English spirit' between himself and

> . . . English Henry, in whose person Shakespeare crowns *noblesse oblige*, generosity and magnanimity, respect for law, and the selfless devotion to duty which comprise the traditional ideals of our public service.

Falstaff can be afforded only a severely limited space in this scheme of things, which is evidently Dover Wilson's bizarre conception of an actual world, his view of the point where the play's ideology merges into a reality outside itself: but once his influence within it has been securely controlled by 'balanced' criticism, he can be safely distanced into myth, given the freedom of an unreal realm of 'imagination', and canonised as a quaint, lovable but innocuous minor divinity.

A measure of the powerfully influential character of this view on subsequent criticism of the *Henry IV* plays, is the extent to which C. L. Barber's study of saturnalian comedy depends upon it. Barber adopts the same image of the Prince as Tillyard and Dover Wilson:

> The play is centred in Prince Hal, developing in such a way as to exhibit in the prince an inclusive, sovereign nature fitted for kingship.[12]

Barber, like Tillyard and Dover Wilson, considers the play's central issue to be that of the Prince's position relative to 'misrule': will he prove noble or degenerate? will he learn to exercise strict control over saturnalian licence, or will his 'holiday' become his 'everyday'?

> The interregnum of a Lord of Misrule, delightful in its moment, might develop into the anarchic reign of a favourite dominating a dissolute King. Hal's secret, which he confides early to the audience, is that for him Falstaff is merely a pastime, to be dismissed in due course . . .

Even within Barber's extremely subtle and perceptive account can be discerned a gravitation towards the 'official', permissive view of saturnalian comedy rather than its popular, subversive view: misrule operates only in relation to rule, disorder cannot exist without order, a mock king derives his meaning from the real king and can have no independent status or validity – 'the dynamic relation of comedy to serious action is saturnalian rather than satiric . . . the misrule works, through the whole dramatic rhythm, to consolidate rule'.[13] Barber acknowledges, in a very interesting passage[14] that Falstaff represented some force potentially subversive: not the 'dependent holiday scepticism' which could be comfortably accommodated within a monolithic medieval society, but, in the much more diverse and rapidly changing society of Elizabethan England, a 'dangerously self-sufficient everyday scepticism' threatening to fracture the imposed perimeters, expand the allotted space, of licensed saturnalian revelry. He argues further that the rejection of Falstaff can only be accomplished by the employment of primitive magic in the hands of a king whose 'inclusive, sovereign nature' has been drastically reduced and narrowed. Yet Barber will not admit that Falstaff represents a power which the play can barely contain because the historical contradictions it brings into play by confronting popular and establishment discourses are so sharp and insoluble: to do so would break down the sustained effort to achieve and maintain 'balance'. Instead Barber sees the rejection as the inevitable, the only possible outcome of the play's interrogation or 'trial' of Falstaff:[15] 'The result of trial is to make us see perfectly the necessity for the rejection of Falstaff as a man, as a favourite of the king, as a leader of an interest at court.'

The editor of the New Arden Shakespeare texts of *Henry IV* is able to quote approvingly from both Dover Wilson and Barber, and to support the idea of the plays as a 'unified vision' with the names of New Critics Cleanth Brooks and Robert B. Heilman.[16] He writes, in the Tillyard tradition, of 'the great idea of England', quotes (with qualification but with overall approval) Dover Wilson's '*Henry IV* is

Shakespeare's vision of the "happy breed of men" that was his England', and endorses C. L. Barber's view that in saturnalian comedy misrule operates to consolidate rule.[17] There is a gestural recognition of Falstaff's comic opposition, but a correspondingly firm insistence that Shakespeare was not 'amoral' or 'infinitely tolerant':

> There is history here, as well as comedy – history which requires responsible action . . . [Shakespeare] upholds good government, in the macrocosm of the state, and the microcosm of man . . . his vision is of men living, however conflictingly, in a nation, a political-moral family.[18]

The rejection of Falstaff is 'necessary, well-prepared, and executed without undue severity'; 'Shakespeare *has* here achieved a balanced complexity of wisdom'.[19] . . .

The ultimate collision and sundering of the Prince and Falstaff, the famous 'rejection-scene' at the end of *Henry IV Part Two* is enacted by a final confrontation of patrician and plebian dramatic discourses, of ruling-class and popular cultures. The occasion is a national ritual of church and state, the coronation of the Prince as King Henry V. The King has already, in V.ii., articulated the ideology of national unity and social harmony which the coronation pageant is designed to celebrate: he has made peace with his brothers and the nobility, and assured the Lord Chief Justice that 'the great body of our state' (defined here, in the standard Elizabethan usage, as the joint power of king and nobility, 'prince and peers', not as the whole body of society) is safely and harmoniously reintegrated. The royal progress to Westminster Abbey, a formal ritual expressing political and ecclesiastical dignity and power, is, however, accompanied, or pursued, by a procession of a different kind: a grotesque antimasque which falls into a parodic and oppositional relation to the majesty and solemnity of the royal pageant:

> Trumpets sound, the King and his train pass over the stage: after them enter Falstaff, Shallow, Pistol, Bardolph, and the Page.

Falstaff's company attempts to transform the coronation into a carnival, in which the clown can speak with familiarity of the king as an equal – 'God save thee, my sweet boy!', and in which the subversive energies of saturnalian licence challenge the formality of patrician ritual with a comic flurry of intense dramatic activity:

> **Falstaff** (*to Shallow*) O, if I had had time to have made new
>   liveries, I would have bestowed the thousand pound I borrowed

of you. But 'tis no matter, this poor show doth better, this doth
infer the zeal I had to see him.

Shallow   It doth so.

Falstaff   It shows my earnestness of affection –

Shallow   It doth so.

Falstaff   My devotion –

Shallow   It doth, it doth, it doth.

Falstaff   As it were, to ride day and night, and not to deliberate,
not to remember, not to have patience to shift me –

Shallow   It is best, certain.

Falstaff   But to stand, stained with travel, and sweating with desire
to see him, thinking of nothing else, putting all affairs else in
oblivion, as if there were nothing else to be done but to see him

. . .

Pistol   My knight, I will inflame thy noble liver,
And make thee rage.
Thy Doll, and Helen of thy noble thoughts,
Is in base durance and contagious prison,
Hal'd thither
By most mechanical and dirty hand.
Rouse up Revenge from ebon den with fell Alecto's snake,
For Doll is in.

Falstaff dramatises himself in yet another role, that of the parasite or
flattering courtier: his speeches are not, as the sentimentalists held,
earnest protestations of personal affection, but self-conscious, im-
personal role-plays in which he constructs himself a character by self-
reflexive caricature. He is supported on the one hand by Shallow's
opportunistic encouragement, and on the other by Pistol's rhetorical
indignation. This parodic antimasque confronts the official ritual
with the dynamic energies of comic drama; with the flexibility and
dramatic freedom of the comic-history mode, in which characters
can act free of historical determination; with a *rapprochement* of
different styles – the naturalistic situation, for example, in which
Falstaff mingles with a crowd at a public event, is incongruously
juxtaposed with Pistol's incurable penchant for literary parody.
Dover Wilson's reaction to this conjuncture will give a fair indication
of its true quality: he imposes a rhetorical insistence on preserving
intact the solemnity of the coronation ritual, freeing its inviolable
sacredness from the threat of parody or subversion:

. . . at this moment, with the crown of England newly placed upon his
head, the chrism still glistening upon his forehead, and his spirit
uplifted by one of the most solemn acts of dedication and consecration

which the Christian Church has to offer, all his thoughts will be concentrated upon the great task to which he has been called, its duties and responsibilities.[20]

Meanwhile the Falstaff-action is condemned in a revealing phrase: V.iv., in which Doll is hauled to prison by most mechanical and dirty hand, is described as 'gruesome-grotesque', displaying 'the ugliest side of Eastcheap life'. Bakhtin defined the 'grotesque' as the characteristic style of carnival discourse: here the word has lost all positive meaning and is used as a term of moral opprobrium. There can be no room in this orthodox, rehabilitating criticism for a sympathetic view of the grotesque, of carnival, of comic opposition: those styles which exist to 'consecrate inventive freedom', to encourage the *rapprochement* of different discourses, to liberate from the prevailing point-of-view of the world, must have their functions severely limited, subordinated to the hegemony of moral order, political hierarchy and the oppressive uniformity of an official culture.

The Prince's speech of rejection (V.v.47) imposes on the situation silence, stillness and formality; and establishes a definite rupture between official and popular cultures. His accents are those of the city attacking the popular drama:

> How ill white hairs become a fool and jester!

Confronted by the miraculous and comic resurrection of Falstaff on the field of Shrewsbury (reminiscent of popular dramas such as the mummers' plays) at the end of *Henry IV Part One*, the Prince acknowledges the power invoked by that dramatic *tour-de-force*:

> . . . is it fantasy that plays upon our eyesight?
> (*IHIV*.V.iv.134)

On becoming king he renounces both the playful freedom of theatrical illusion and the generous humour of saturnalian liberty:

> Being awak'd, I do despise my dream . . .

It is, of course, an established fact that prior to Shakespeare's drama there existed a tradition of popular culture – a subculture, incorporated into yet intrinsically in tension with the official culture of the Tudor nation-state. This culture was democratic and utopian rather than hierarchical and pragmatic, imaginative and fantastic rather than realistic and historicist. It voiced some of the aspirations of sections of the common people – peasant, artisan, apprentice, lower bourgeoisie and clergy; and above all, it was, to some degree, *hostile* to the official culture which sanctioned it. In view of all this it is possible to detach the figure of Falstaff from the moralistic perspective into which the play fails to place him, and into which criticism since the early twentieth century has struggled to incorporate him, and to recognise as positive and liberating many aspects of the figure which seem, from the moralistic perspective, to be negative and oppressing. The important thing to recognise is that these dramas bring into play separate and incompatible visions of history; they identify the popular vision with the institution of drama itself; they celebrate the dialectical conflict of these contradictory cultural energies; and they articulate a profound regret at the final effect of closure which signals the impending victory of one dominant conception of 'history' over the complex plurality of Renaissance historiographical practices.

From Graham Holderness, *Shakespeare's History* (Dublin, 1985), pp. 79, 82–101. See also the revised edition, *Shakespeare Recycled: The Making of Historical Drama* (Hemel Hempstead, 1992), pp. 110–57.

NOTES

[Graham Holderness's historical-materialist essay is extracted from a chapter of his book on Shakespeare's history plays, originally published as *Shakespeare's History* (Dublin, 1985). Holderness draws on anthropological studies largely through the work of Mikhail Bakhtin, member of an important group of Russian linguistic and literary theoreticians working in the USSR from the 1920s onwards. Quotations are from A. R. Humphreys (ed.), *The Arden Shakespeare: Henry IV, Part One* (London, 1960), and *The Arden Shakespeare: Henry IV, Part Two* (London, 1960). Ed.]

1. Mikhail Bakhtin, *Rabelais and his World*, trans. Helen Iswolsky (Cambridge, Mass., 1968). This work was first published in the USSR in 1965, though written in 1940.

2. See C. L. Barber, *Shakespeare's Festive Comedy* (Princeton, 1959), pp. 50–1.

3. See A. L. Morton, *The English Utopia (London, 1978)*.

4. Bakhtin, *Rabelais*, p. 24.

5. Ibid., p. 24.

6. Ibid., p. 24.

7. J. Dover Wilson, *The Fortunes of Falstaff* (Cambridge, 1964), p. 5ff.

8. Ibid., p. 7.

9. Ibid., p. 22.

10. Ibid., p. 25.

11. Ibid., p. 128.

12. Barber, *Shakespeare's Festive Comedy*, p. 216.

13. Ibid., p. 226.

14. Ibid., pp. 213–14.

15. Ibid., p. 216.

16. A. R. Humphreys (ed.), *The Arden Shakespeare: Henry IV, Part One* (London, 1960), p. lvi.

17. Ibid., p. lvi.

18. Ibid., p. lvii.

19. A. R. Humphreys (ed.), *The Arden Shakespeare: Henry IV, Part Two* (London, 1960), p. lx–lxi.

20. Dover Wilson, *Fortunes of Falstaff*, p. 120.

10

'Henry V': Text and History

ANNABEL PATTERSON

For the fifth act in his history of the fifth Henry, Shakespeare suddenly required of his audience a shift in historical perspective. They are invited to imagine Henry's return, victorious from Agincourt, in terms of another anticipated return, presumably closer to their own immediate interest:

> now behold
> In the quick Forge and working-house of Thought,
> How London doth powre out her Citizens,
> The Maior and all his Brethren in best sort,
> Like to the Senatours of th'antique Rome,
> With the Plebeians swarming at their heeles,
> Goe forth and fetch their Conqu'ring Caesar in:
> As by a lower, but by loving likelyhood,
> Were now the Generall of our gracious Empresse,
> As in good time he may, from Ireland comming,
> Bringing Rebellion broached on his Sword,
> How many would the peacefull Citie quit,
> To welcome him?
>
> (*Folio*, TLN 2872–85)[1]

This Chorus, with its startling analogy between Elizabeth's most famous predecessor and her most notorious subject, Robert Devereux, second earl of Essex, currently in charge of the Irish campaign, demands that we juggle at least two meanings of 'history' as a category of thought: the fifteenth-century history that Shakespeare

165

took over from Holinshed and others and rewrote to his own speci-
fications, and the events in which he and his theatre were environ-
mentally situated in the late 1590s, and to some extent embroiled;
while its *content* – the nature of popular leadership and the numer-
ical signs of popularity ('How *many* would the peacefull Citie quit/
to welcome him?') – requires a still more athletic intellectual response. Or rather, in Shakespeare's own terminology, the required
activity is not so much athletic as artisanal, 'the quick Forge and
working-house of Thought' associating the right imagination not
with society's leaders but rather with that plebeian citizenry whose
very breach of their normal workaday behaviour is the sign of the
extraordinary. And the fact that this Chorus did *not* appear in the
only text of the play published in Shakespeare's lifetime raises still
another issue – the relationship between 'history', 'popularity' and
bibliography, or the story of how Shakespeare's playtexts were circulated in their own time and survived into ours. In the case of *Henry
V* the story of the text is inseparable from the political history that is
both its content and its context, as also from the thematics of the
popular, here defined not as protest or festival but as the relationship
of the many to the charismatic leader.*

More than almost any other play of Shakespeare's, and certainly
more than any other 'history', *Henry V* has generated accounts of
itself that agree, broadly speaking, on the play's thematics – popular
monarchy, national unity, militarist expansionism – but fall simply,
even crudely, on either side of the line that divides belief from
scepticism, idealism from cynicism, or, in contemporary parlance,
legitimation from subversion. The most extreme example of the
idealising view, the film directed by Sir Laurence Olivier, was pre-
miered in November 1944, in the context of the invasion of Nor-
mandy, and dedicated to the Commandos and Airborne Troops of
Great Britain, 'the spirit of whose ancestors it has been humbly
attempted to recapture'.[2] In the same year appeared E. M. W. Tillyard's
influential study of the history plays, closely followed, in 1947, by
Lily B. Campbell's, which to different degrees represented *Henry V*
as the climax (successful or unsuccessful) of Shakespeare's own
version of the Tudor myth, with Henry himself as Elizabeth's prototype.[3] As the nationalism of these projects was implicit, compared at
least to Oliver's production, so their power to suggest an orthodoxy
was greater.[4] Conversely, the age of nuclear deterrence and of ethic-
ally ambiguous geopolitical alliances has produced a criticism, both

in England and in the United States, that looks rather at the tensions and contradictions in the Elizabethan ideology of ideal ruler, unified state, and providential history.[5] . . .

The two surviving texts of *Henry V* point in different interpretive directions; the Folio can possibly sustain the hypothesis of ideological confusion or deliberate ambiguity; whereas the theses of Campbell and Tillyard could be better supported by *The Cronicle History of Henry the fifth*, the first Quarto version, which has long been ruled out of interpretative account by Shakespearean bibliographers, and placed in the evaluative category of the 'Bad Quartos', that is to say, beyond interpretive reach.[6] Though less textually unstable than *Hamlet* or *King Lear*, where the Quarto texts have strong claims to authorial cachet, *Henry V* therefore presents a unique challenge to the new textual studies, since its publication history is ineluctably connected to the major critical disagreements over the play's meaning and cultural function.

For the first Quarto version is not only shorter than the Folio but tonally different from it. Among the most striking absences in the Quarto are all five Choruses and the final Epilogue; hence, in the fifth Chorus, the non-appearance of the allusion to Essex's anticipated return from Ireland, which Gary Taylor has called 'the only explicit, extra-dramatic, incontestable reference to a contemporary event anywhere in the canon';[7] and with no epilogue, there is no final let-down, no admission that the legendary victory at Agincourt accomplished nothing, since in the following reign the regents for Henry VI 'lost France, and made his England bleed' (TLN 3379). These last lines, which subsume the heroic moment in the recursive patterns of history, were also excised from the Olivier production, which otherwise retained most of the Choruses,[8] and even in 1623 the Folio arrangement of the English histories by chronology of reign rather than of composition submerges the sceptical effect and makes Henry the centre of the historical sweep through the fifteenth century rather than the last, inconclusive statement of the second tetralogy.

Also missing from the Quarto is Act I, scene i, where the bishops cynically discuss how they are to motivate the war and distract the House of Commons from their plan to reclaim ecclesiastical property; the Hostess's claim in II.i. that Falstaff is dying because 'The King has killed his heart'; almost all of the Harfleur episode, including the famous 'Once more unto the breach' speech by Henry, and most of his threats of violence upon the besieged citizens; much of

the material in the scene before the battle of Agincourt, especially
Henry's closing soliloquy on the hardships of kingship; several scenes
in the French camp; all of Burgundy's speech on the damages suffered by France in the war; and much of the wooing scene between
Kate and Henry. There is, however, nothing in the stage-historical
records to refute the Quarto's claim that it represents the play as it
was 'sundry times' acted by the Chamberlain's Company.[9] We simply do not know, in fact, what the performative version of *Henry V*
was like; the Quarto may very well be closer than the Folio to what
the London audiences actually saw on the stage at the absolute turn
of the century.

The interest of the 1600 text has long been obscured by the theory
of the Bad Quartos, a conception that took its authority from the
piracy theory first circulated by the editors of the 1623 Folio, who
referred to 'stolne, and surreptitious copies, maimed, and deformed
by the frauds and stealthes of injurious impostors that exposed them'
(A3r). And the piracy theory was in turn supported by that of
memorial reconstruction, or dictation from memory by one or more
actors complicit with a piratical printer.[10] These theories, rich in
moral opprobrium, easily merged with subjective accounts of the
quality of the differences observed, with the Folio versions of the
plays being designated as 'artistically' superior. But this entire hypothesis is now in question. A more sceptical view is emerging of the
claims made by John Heminge and Henry Condell in promoting their
own edition; the theory of memorial reconstruction is under attack;
and Peter Blayney, in rejecting the notion of piracy, draws our
attention to Humphrey Moseley's own advertisement for the
Beaumont and Fletcher Folio of 1647, where, in the course of ex-
plaining why he has taken the trouble to acquire authorial manuscripts, Mosely witnesses to an entirely reputable method of
transmitting abridged playtexts to potential publishers:

> When these Comedies and Tragedies were presented on the Stage, the
> Actours omitted some Scenes and Passages (with the Author's consent)
> as occasion led them; and when private friends desir'd a Copy, they
> then (and justly too) transcribed what they Acted.[11]

The parentheses here, 'with the author's consent' and 'justly too',
speak to a theatrical practice of communal ownership of acting
versions, and the open, legitimate exchange, commercial or otherwise, of transcriptions made by the actors of those versions.[12]

Memorial reconstruction may still be needed to explain those parts of a Quarto text (fewer than has been claimed) which are patently so garbled as to resist explanation by this new sociology of the theatre. But we can now understand a feature of Quarto texts that memorial reconstruction could not account for – the omission of whole scenes or large blocks of material. In the case of *Henry V*, the omitted materials are so bulky and so crucial that other hypotheses have gradually emerged. The Arden edition admits at least three, each implying intention – the aesthetic ('cut for compression'), the political ('cut . . . possibly for censorship') and the socioeconomic ('cut . . . for a reduced cast on tour in the provinces').[13] These suggestions, if not incompatible, derive from quite different critical assumptions and agendas; and poised uncertainly between them is the inference that the style of the Quarto version is more popular, in the sense of being lower and more *common* than the Folio. As John Walter put it for the Arden edition, 'Generally there is a lowering of pitch, a substitution of cliché and common currency of daily speech for the more heightened style of the Folio.'

This notion was first proposed by Alfred Hart in 1942, in support of his own version of the Bad Quarto theory. For him the Quartos were memorial reconstructions of previous abridgements of the plays prepared by Shakespeare's own company in accordance with theatrical experience. The excisions, Hart thought, were often theatrically intelligent but linguistically impoverished. The professional abridger 'knew his audience loved an interesting story, packed with plenty of action and told in simple language, and rid the play of similes, amplificatory passages, platitudes, philosophic reflections, repetition, classical commonplaces, and literary ornament.'[14] But even the best of Bad Quartos (and *Henry V* is one of the best) reveal reportorial incompetence incompatible with the work of 'an educated man':

> Most of the [divergent] passages share certain characteristics in common – little elevation of thought, a certain coarseness verging on vulgarity, almost complete lack of fancy or imagination, dull, pedestrian and irregular verse, poor and overworked vocabulary, frequent errors in grammar and syntax, and a primitive type of sentence-construction. King, queen, cardinal, duchess, peer, soldier, lover, courtier, artisan, peasant, servant and child all speak alike . . . Essentially each of these and many other speeches exhibit all the marks of garrulous illiteracy . . .
>
> (p. 104)

From the newly self-conscious posture that a critic in the 1980s is privileged to adopt, one can see how deeply Hart's view of the Bad Quartos has collated the moralism of his predecessors in the field of bibliography with a class consciousness that distinguishes the 'educated' text (one that endorses social hierarchies) from the 'illiterate' reproduction that blurs them.

Hart's theory of the text was split – not only between contradictory notions of good theatre and good writing, but also between his wished-for separation of Shakespeare from Badness and the knowledge that within the theatrical practice of the Chamberlain's Men such separation was unlikely. Hart actually imagined a scene in which Shakespeare, having previously, 'on fire with passion and emotions . . . filled *Hamlet* with 1600 lines of long speeches', later heard them read aloud. He would then, Hart felt, 'have shaken his head in critical disapproval and accepted the decision of his fellows to declaim less than a half of these speeches on the stage' (p. 168). In this scenario, Shakespeare collaborates in the act of abridgment at least to the point of authorising major cuts; and the notion of Shakespeare's 'critical disapproval' of his own longer first draft runs counter to Hart's own critical disapproval of the Bad Quartos in general.

Hart's confusions mark the transition from a Romantic aesthetics of genius to a modern sociology of the theatre. The notion that censorship was one motive for the Quarto's reductions has different origins. In 1928, Evelyn May Albright argued that the Folio 'represents the text of a play intended for use on a special occasion at the Globe before an audience of statesmen and courtiers at the critical moment preceding the return of Essex from Ireland in the autumn of 1599.'[15] She saw the Folio as being broadly supportive of Essex and his policies, whereas the Quarto, intended for publication, was 'shorn of the most significant personal and political references' (p. 753). She thus keyed the play not into the history of printing, but into political history, specifically the history of Essex's rebellion, whose connection to Shakespeare's company has long been established. I refer to the special production on 5 February 1601, the eve of the earl of Essex's rebellion, of 'the play . . . of Kyng Harry the iiijth, and of the kylling of Kyng Richard the second played by the L. Chamberlen's players'.[16] And while Albright's thesis of *another* special performance (of *Henry V* itself) is incapable of proof, that notorious production of *Richard II* is certainly part of the story of why and how the later play came into existence. . . .

We need to resituate both Quarto and Folio in their larger, mutual relationship to persons, events and cultural practices; and among those practices were the writing and rewriting of history, and the surveillance of those who attempted it. Historiography, in the sixteenth and early seventeenth century, was no academic discipline but a matter of public interest, both in the sense that the material of English history was popular material for the emergent national theatre, and because (for a set of reasons which included this same popular appeal) the government regarded English historical materials as subject to its own control. . . .

For underlying the official scrutiny of historiography, which included, of course, the possibility of commissioning histories or inducing historians to serve the agendas of particular monarchs, was the concern that the public appetite for knowledge of the past should be satisfied only by such *versions* of history, official history, that the government could itself regard with complacence.

But Shakespeare could have seen from the beginning of his career how difficult it was to maintain the uplifting tone that official history demanded. True, in 1548 the title page of Hall's *Chronicle* had been able to read the wars of the Roses as an essay on 'union', and the dynastic struggles between different stems of Edward III's family tree as culminating naturally in Henry VIII, 'the indubitable flower and very heir of the said lineage.'[17] In 1580, Stow's *Chronicles*, dedicated to the earl of Leicester, offered history to the 'gentle Reader' as a 'discouragement of unnaturall subjects from wicked treasons, pernitious rebellions, and damnable doctrines'.[18] In accordance with this programme, pre-Tudor history was interpreted on Stow's ornamental frontispiece as a design in which Elizabeth replaced Henry as dynastic flower, placed symmetrically above the stem of Richard II, the stem that went nowhere. We are beginning to see that such designs were deliberately imposed on more complex and intractable materials.[19] And when Shakespeare turned (for all plays subsequent to *Henry VI, Part II*) to the 1587 Holinshed, the most obvious lesson offered by the English chronicles was that they continually invoked their own incapacity for closure. History did not stop where one would like it to; worse, it would continue when the Tudor dynasty, for want of a lineal descendant from Elizabeth, would itself be cut off like the stem descending from Richard. This fact alone is sharply registered by Shakespeare in the Folio epilogue to *Henry V*, where the choric effort to delineate the reign an epic success succumbs to history's incompleteness:

> *Thus farre*, with rough, and all-unable pen,
> Our bending Author hath pursu'd the story . . .
>   (TLN 3368–9)

But it was not only in its lost capacity for closure that English history exuded anxiety. The 1587 edition of Holinshed, which continued the story through Elizabeth's reign to the end of 1586, is a calendar of woes. It foregrounds natural disasters, local crimes and their punishment, instances of treason and their punishment, leading for their climax to the Babington Plot and the hideous execution of the conspirators, whose complicity with Mary Queen of Scots leads to *her* trial and condemnation. The supplement thus reveals a design, if not a desire, for a downbeat ending, a dying fall. . . .

Elizabethan historians, then, might have certain difficulties in controlling their material. But there was one phase of pre-Tudor history that, as Sir John Hayward discovered, was a particularly dangerous one for the historian to explore, especially if, as Hayward also discovered, he keyed his version of it into current affairs. By dedicating his *History of Henry IV* to the earl of Essex, Hayward indicated, intentionally or unintentionally, a connection between the popular local hero that Essex had become and the Lancastrian usurper who made himself king at the expense of Richard II. There seems little doubt that Hayward's difficulties were caused by widespread acceptance of this analogy, and exacerbated two years later when, on the eve of Essex's rebellion, his steward Gilly Merrick arranged for that special performance of 'the play . . . of Kyng Harry the iiijth'. Whether or not that play was *written* by Shakespeare, a question that now seems undecidable, the most important point for our purposes is that the performance was *connected* by contemporaries to Hayward's *History*, and the two were assumed to have had similar subversive motives. William Camden, himself a historian of repute, wrote in his *Annals*:

> Merrick was accused . . . that he had . . . procured an old out-worne play of the tragicall deposing of King Richard the second, to be acted upon the public stage before the Conspirators; which the lawyers interpreted to be done by him, as if they would now behold that acted upon the stage, which was the next day to be acted in deposing the Queene. And *the like censure given upon a Booke of the same argument,* set forth a little before by Hayward a learned man, and dedicated to the Earle of Essex, as if it had beene written as an example and incitement to the deposing of the Queene; an unfortunate thing to the

author, who was punished by long imprisonment for his untimely setting forth thereof, and for these words in his preface to the Earle: *Great thou art in hope, greater in the expectation of future time.* (italics added)[20]

In Camden's view, it is far from always or certainly the case that history, as Stow had claimed in 1580, serves to discourage 'unnaturall subjects from wicked treasons, pernitious rebellions, and damnable doctrines'. Sometimes it encouraged them.

The Quarto text of *Henry V* came out between 4 and 14 August 1600. It therefore fell smack into the middle of the Hayward/Essex crisis, to which Shakespeare's own company was connected, at least on the night of 7 February 1601. We might argue indefinitely whether they acted in ignorance of the play's topical significance (an unlikely possibility); their release after questioning by the Privy Council probably reflected the government's wish for as few martyrs as possible. But a decision to print the Quarto, or to let it be printed, could not possibly have been unwary, given the Bishops' Order in June 1599, restating the restrictions on historical publication, and probably in part an official response to Hayward's indiscretion. The Quarto was, moreover, registered less than a month after Hayward's imprisonment in July 1600, which in turn followed closely upon the preliminary examination of Essex at York House in June 1600. But the *Cronicle History* that made it to the Stationer (past the temporary 'stay') was, in fact, a Lancastrian history that would pass the closest inspection. It had nothing to do with deposition, and very little with rebellion. Rather it presented an *almost* unproblematic view of a highly popular monarch whose most obvious modern analogy was Elizabeth herself.

In a benign political semantics, 'popularity' replaces 'obedience'. Elizabeth had had great success in working the cultural signs of popularity, through the myth of the Virgin queen, the progresses, the Accession Day celebrations, and the symbolic icons. But as even Roy Strong's chronology of these icons reveals,[21] the older she grew, and the greater grew the public anxiety about the succession, the more welcome to her were symbolic portraits and emblems of unqualified power and vitality. Yet the eyes and ears on her mantle in the 'Rainbow' portrait (dated 1602 by Strong, in the aftermath of the Essex rebellion) were a none-too-subtle reminder that the myth needed the support of public surveillance, that the cultural forms of late Elizabethanism took the form they did because the queen and her ministers were watching. And if the Quarto *Henry V* could be read as presenting an idealised, figurative, historically displaced portrait of her, and one that was, by regendering, consistent with her own heroic rhetoric at Tilbury, it could only improve the credit of the Chamberlain's Men, who, the Quarto asserted, had 'sundry times' been loyally staging this story.

The Folio text, however, was a very different matter, since it spoke directly, at least in the fifth Chorus, to Elizabeth's last and most dangerous challenge by a rival allure. Precisely at the moment of *Henry V*'s composition, in fact, she was locked into a competition for public visibility and popular sympathy with Essex, who had the charismatic advantages of youth, personal attractiveness, great physical height, a list of military successes at Rouen, Cadiz, and the Azores, and above all his masculinity. . . . On 28 September 1599, with the Irish campaign a shambles, Essex made his unauthorised return to England, and in forty-eight hours was committed to custody. By late November he was facing charges of misgovernment of the campaign. 'Libels' in his support were circulated in London.[22] On 29 December preachers at Paul's Cross prayed for Essex by name, and attacked the government.

This evidence, taken together with the furor over Hayward's *History*, indicates that from February 1599 to February 1601 England witnessed a struggle not only for the popular imagination but also, obviously, for control of the media by which that imagination was stimulated. And during the summer of 1599, while Essex was in Ireland with the results of his campaign as yet unknown, Shakespeare, we know, was at work on a version of *Henry V* that included the Choruses. If the earlier Choruses are written in the mood of chivalric celebration and enthusiasm (being 'on fire') that *The Fair Maid of the West* associated with Essex's earlier campaigns:

> Now all the Youth of England are on fire,
> And silken Dalliance in the Wardrobe lyes:
> Now thrive the Armorers, and Honors thought
> Reignes solely in the breast of every man.
> They sell the Pasture now, to buy the Horse;
> . . .
> For now sits Expectation in the Ayre,
>
> (TLN 463–70)

the fifth Chorus pinpoints the Elizabethan moment of 'Expectation' more exactly, and explicitly connects it to the theme of popularity that the *Henry IV* plays had inaugurated. By a strenuous act of the visual imagination which must substitute for the deficiencies of dramatic representation, the reader/audience is invited to 'behold' the analogy with which we began:

How London doth powre out her Citizens,
The Maior and all his Brethren in best sort,
Like to the Senatours of th'antique Rome,
With the Plebeians swarming at their heeles,
Goe forth and fetch their Conqu'ring Caesar in:
As by a lower, but by loving likelyhood,
Were now the Generall of our gracious Empresse,
As in good time he may, from Ireland comming,
Bringing Rebellion broached on his Sword,
How many would the peacefull Citie quit,
To welcome him? much more, and much more cause,
Did they this Harry.

(TLN 2872–85)

Almost every term in this extraordinary passage bristles with innuendo and intellectual challenge. In the leisure provided by the 'Forge and working-house of Thought', however quick, as distinct from the instant reception that staged drama imposes, these ambiguities can be unfolded. Not the least of them is Shakespeare's invocation of an artisanal metaphor for thought itself; but the governing peculiarity is that he should have chosen to insert so tendentious a passage into a play already, by virtue of its historical subject, generically suspect. Nor was it only that he had chosen to make a connection with Elizabeth's intransigent favourite only weeks after Hayward's *History* had been called in for doing the same thing. In thematising the *popular* and its role in earlier historical events (both Roman and English) Shakespeare made visible what the story of Hayward's *History* only reveals if one follows its details, that much of the anxiety it generated in official circles was connected to *its* popularity, its unusually wide circulation and distribution. Hayward, as much as Essex, had courted the public and succeeded. In the examination of Wolfe, the printer of Hayward's *History*, it was part of his defence that he yielded to popular demand for a second edition:

The people calling for it exceedingly . . . 1,500 of these books being almost finished in the Whitsun holidays of 1599, were taken by the wardens of the stationers, and delivered to the Bishop of London . . . The people having divers times since called to procure the continuation

of the history by the same author . . . Since the last edition was
supposed, a great number have been for it.[23]

. . . These official concerns with numbers, invaluable for establishing
the degree to which the entire crisis was a matter of informed public
concern, and for providing statistical content to the then-still-living
metaphor of publication, contribute a powerful gloss on Shakespeare's own emphasis on 'how *many*' would have flocked to welcome Essex back from Ireland, an emphasis, however, that the Folio
text is prepared to leave, by means of a question mark, indeterm-
inate.[24] . . .

Yet even within these self-imposed controls, the language is provocative. The city may be peaceful, but the welcoming crowd 'quits'
that stable environment for the liminal territory of Blackheath. The
analogy between Essex and Henry is preceded, moreover, by that
between fifteenth-century England and 'antique Rome', an analogy
that points to a major structural difference between them, since
'conquering Caesar', by definition Julius, was still the military agent
of a republic (however pushing at those limits), as distinct from the
imperial model established by Octavian and repeated by 'our gracious Empresse'. The very presence of the plebeians, 'swarming' at
the heels of the senators, reminds that empress of the popular 'many'
to whom she herself had deliberately appealed and on whose labour,
as in the beehive metaphor invoked by Henry's Archbishop, the
welfare of the hive depends. But the barely invoked beehive metaphor here has a more alarming connotation. Swarming, bees notoriously desert the hive under the leadership of another monarch.[25] . . .
As Jonathan Dollimore and Alan Sinfield have argued, the legend of
Henry's reign was 'a powerful Elizabethan fantasy simply because it
represented a single source of power in the state,' the fusion of
monarch and military hero in a single popular archetype.[26] The
allusion to Essex destabilises that fantasy, along with that other
Elizabethan myth propagated at Tilbury, that the queen herself could
play both roles. The Archbishop's metaphor of the beehive accomplished the same feat; but the suppressed metaphor of the swarm
works rather to distinguish general and empress, by signifying their
competition for popular support and approval. . . .

In 1600, then, the fifth Chorus was so ambiguous that Shakespeare's company, warned by the fate of Hayward's *History*, could
not have risked giving it the publicity of print, where its textual
instabilities would be fully open to inspection. It brought down with

it, perhaps, the rest of the Choruses, including those whose message might well have enhanced the simpler patriotism of the Quarto text as a whole. What Shakespeare intended by creating this dangerous instability in the first place is another question altogether. . . . Had he imagined a warning to Elizabeth, which would imply that the warning was capable of reaching her? Very unlikely. Or rather, had he planned an encoded incitement to Essex, intended for private performance before some audience of 'malcontents'? Even more unlikely, given that we know which play was actually performed on the eve of the rebellion. Or was the Folio version a well meant but ill-advised attempt at mediation, with the public stage conceived as the liminal territory where the playwright and actors took no sides, creating 'loving likelihoods' in the national interest? The representational slipperiness, then, by which Henry could configure *both* Elizabeth and Essex, at the end of a play whose protagonist was, if peerless, certainly not flawless, would not be a sign of Shakespeare's disinterestedness. Rather, it would contribute to an argument for a pragmatic reconciliation between general and empress, pragmatic in the sense that 'history', by refusing to settle their rivalry, provided no basis for decisively altering the current allocations of power and lines of authority. . . .

The Folio version of *Henry V*, then, produces at the level of consciousness what the earlier plays in both tetralogies merely produced – an image of the nation state as an ideal that survives the continuous struggle for power of competing aristocrats. What the Folio text does *not* produce, however, is the idealised model of national unity that some of Shakespeare's later readers have thought they found there. Where that model is actually found is in Archbishop Chichele's beehive speech, in the Folio firmly qualified by our prior recognition that the Archbishop is cynical, self-serving, and elitist.[27]

In contrast to organicist political theory that was manifestly coated with rhetorical honey, the subdued voice of 'our bending author' offers, penultimately, only the sexual and dynastic version of union, granting a festive and erotic colour to France's and Katherine's capitulation, providing we take the story 'thus far' and no further. And while the image of 'antique Rome' with its crowds of swarming plebeians anticipates *Coriolanus*, the play in which Shakespeare would a decade later re-examine the political structure through the lens of classical republicanism, in *Henry V* this inquiry is sporadic. The Folio text remains committed, though not without moments of distaste, to the system of government endorsed by centuries of English, rather than Roman history, and willing to entertain, though not without framing it as extreme imaginative effort ('Work, work, your thoughts'), a commitment to ideas of national greatness and agreement. What happened after the turn of the century was, and produced, another kind of story.

From Annabel Patterson, *Shakespeare and the Popular Voice* (Oxford, 1989), pp. 71–88.

NOTES

[Annabel Patterson's essay is taken from a chapter of her book on Shakespeare and popular culture. (The original chapter title is 'Back by Popular Demand: The Two Versions of *Henry V*'.) The book extends and sophisticates a long-running debate over the relationship between Shakespeare's drama and concepts of popular culture. For editions used as sources of quotation, see note 1 below. Ed.]

1. In this chapter, where the history of the play-text and the divergences between Quarto and Folio are at the centre of the argument, references are to the Norton facsimile, *First Folio of Shakespeare*, prepared by Charlton Hinman (New York, 1968); and from the Quarto text in *Shakespeare's Plays in Quarto*, ed. Michael Allen and Kenneth Muir (Berkeley and Los Angeles, 1981).

2. See *Film Scripts One*, ed. George P. Garrett, O. B. Hardison, Jr., and Jane R. Gelfman (New York, 1971), p. 40. But compare also Dover Wilson (ed.), *Henry V* (Cambridge, 1947), p. viii: 'Happening to witness a performance by Frank Benson and his company at Stratford in August or September 1914, I discovered for the first time what it was all about. The epic drama of Agincourt matched the temper of the moment, when Rupert Brooke was writing "The Soldier" and the Kaiser was said to be scoffing at our "contemptible little army" which had just crossed the Channel, so exactly that it might have been written expressly for it' (p. viii).

3. Lily B. Campbell, *Shakespeare's 'Histories': Mirrors of Elizabethan Policy* (San Marino, 1947, repr. London, 1964), pp. 255–305; E. M. W. Tillyard, *Shakespeare's History Plays* (New York, 1944, repr. 1947), pp. 304–14. Tillyard took a less sanguine view of *Henry V* than Campbell, regarding it as a routine and formulaic performance without the energies invested in the two parts of *Henry IV*.

4. For a larger analysis and critique of the 'theme of England', as promoted

by Tillyard and by Olivier's production, see Graham Holderness, *Shakespeare's History* (Dublin and New York, 1985), pp. 18–26, 184–200.

5. See, for instance, Stephen Greenblatt, 'Invisible Bullets', in *Shakespearean Negotiations: The Circulation of Social Energy in Renaissance England* (London, Berkeley and Los Angeles, 1988), pp. 21–65; Jonathan Dollimore and Alan Sinfield, 'History and Ideology: the instance of *Henry V*', in *Alternative Shakespeares*, ed. John Drakakis (London, 1985), pp. 206–27; and Larry S. Champion, '"What Prerogatives Meanes": Perspective and Political Ideology in *The Famous Victories of Henry V*', *South Atlantic Review*, 53 (1988), 1–19, which provides an account of Shakespeare's most important source as 'either a glorification of monarchy or as an attack on its corruption, egocentricity, and militaristic monomania' (p. 14), depending on the spectator's own position. Earlier sceptical readings were primarily characterological in focus, including even that of Gerald Gould, who in the immediate aftermath of World War I revolted against 'the more hideous "Prussianisms" with which Shakespeare has endowed his Henry'. See 'A New Reading of *Henry V*', *English Review* (1919), 42.

6. All references are to the editions cited in note 1.

7. Gary Taylor (ed.), *Henry V* (Oxford, 1984), p. 7 (italics added).

8. See *Film Scripts One*, p. 134: the film's final words are as follows:

> Small time: but in that small, most greatly lived
> This star of England: Fortune made his
> sword: and for his sake
> In your fair minds let this acceptance take.

9. It is sometimes assumed that the Folio text, though not deriving from a promptbook, represents an acting version, and that, on the basis of Choric references to staging, especially to the 'wooden O' of the fifth Chorus, it was designed for the Globe theatre built in 1599; but it is equally assumed in other instances (such as *Hamlet*) that the Folio text was sometimes or always abridged in performance.

10. See A. W. Pollard, *Shakespeare's Folios and Quartos: A Study in the Bibliography of Shakespeare's Plays, 1594–1685* (London, 1909); W. W. Greg (ed.), *The Merry Wives of Windsor* (Oxford, 1910); his theory was refined in *Two Elizabethan Stage Abridgements* (Oxford, 1923).

11. Peter Blayney, 'Shakespeare's Fight', referring to Francis Beaumont and John Fletcher, *Comedies and Tragedies* (London, 1647), Sig. A2r.

12. Since Mosely did not in fact base his edition on these theatrical transcriptions, but rather, as he insists, on authorial manuscripts, he himself had nothing to gain by establishing the social legitimacy of the practices here described.

13. J. H. Walter (ed.), *King Henry V* (Cambridge, Mass., 1954), p. xxxv.

14. Alfred Hart, *Stolne and Surreptitious Copies: A Comparative Study of Shakespeare's Bad Quartos* (Melbourne, 1942), p. 130.

15. Evelyn May Albright, 'The Folio version of *Henry V* in relation to Shakespeare's Times', *PMLA*, 42 (1982), 722–56. This contributed to a long and intemperate argument between herself and Ray Heffner, who preferred to separate Shakespeare from politics. On Albright's side, see 'Shakespeare's *Richard II* and the Essex conspiracy', *PMLA*, 42 (1927), 686–720; and 'Shakespeare's *Richard II*, Hayward's *History of Henry IV* and the Essex conspiracy', *PMLA*, 46 (1931), 694–719; for Heffner's rebuttal, see 'Shakespeare, Hayward and Essex', *PMLA*, 45 (1930), 754–80, an essay which nevertheless contains invaluable information about Hayward's involvement with Essex.

16. See the confession of Sir Gilly Merrick, Essex's steward, on 5 March 1601, *Calendar of State Papers Domestic, 1598–1601*, vol. 278, art. 78, p. 575.

17. Edward Hall, *The Union of the two noble and illustrate famelies of Lancastre and York . . . proceeding to the reign of the high and prudent prince King Henry the Eighth, the indubitable flower and very heir of the said lineages* (London, 1548).

18. John Stow, *The Chronicles of England, from Brute unto this present yeare of Christ, 1580* (London, 1580), iiiir.

19. For reactions against Tillyard's over-emphasis on providentialist history as the only historiography available, see H. A. Kelly, *Divine Providence in the England of Shakespeare's Histories* (Princeton, 1957); Graham Holderness, *Shakespeare's History* (New York, 1985), pp. 14–39.

20. William Camden, *The Historie of the Princesse Elizabeth*, tr. R. Norton, 4 parts (London, 1630), 4, pp. 192–33. Compare also John Chamberlain, whose letters during 1599 kept Dudley Carleton informed of every stage of Essex's affairs. On 1 March 1599, Chamberlain remarked, 'The erle of Essex is crased, but whether more in body or minde is doubtfull', and, some sentences later, reported on the scandal over Hayward's *History*: 'Here hath ben much descanting about yt, why such a story shold come out at this time, and manye exceptions taken, especially to the epistle . . . dedicated to the erle of Essex'. *Letters of John Chamberlain*, ed. Norman McLure, 2 vols (Philadelphia, 1939), 1, pp. 69–70. In both Camden's view and Chamberlain's, it was the *timing* or 'untimely' aspect of Hayward's book, in the context of the greater scandal that Essex was creating, that rendered it subject to the conspiracy theory.

21. See Roy Strong, *The Cult of Elizabeth: Elizabethan Portraiture and Pageantry* (London, 1977), pp. 46–55.

22. *Historical Manuscripts Commission, Penshurst*, ed. C. L. Kingsford, 2, pp. 132, 146, 169.

23. Calendar of State Papers Domestic, 1598–1601, vol. 28, art. 278, pp. 450–1. Cited by Heffner, 'Shakespeare, Hayward and Essex', p. 761.

24. Compare Albright, 'The Folio version', p. 734, on the connection between this stress on numbers and the figures later cited in testimony about the rebellion.

25. The classic text here was Virgil, *Georgics*, 4, pp. 67–87, a passage traditionally supposed to have figuratively described the struggle for power between Octavian and Antony.

26. Jonathan Dollimore and Alan Sinfield, 'History and Ideology: the instance of *Henry V*', in *Alternative Shakespeares*, ed. John Drakakis (London, 1985), p. 220 ['History and Ideology: *Henry V*', in this volume, p. 191 – Ed.]. Their reading of the play, however, hews the neo-Marxist critical line that literature can only critique ideology unknowingly.

27. That the beehive speech survived in the Quarto, while the cynical negotiations of the first scene disappear, is further testimony to the relation between abridgment and a simpler form of patriotism. As a set piece, whose objective is to present the organicist theory of a united commonwealth, the beehive speech, with one salient exception, would have looked impeccable. The exception appears at the two lines wherein Shakespeare admitted the humanitarian aspect of that legislation from which, in Holinshed's account, the bishops were so eager to distract the king. The parliament of 1414 had proposed a bill to the effect that 'the temporal lands devoutly given, and disordinately spent by religious and other spiritual persons' should be appropriated by Henry to provide not only for national defence but for relief of the poor. Their presence in the sociopolitical system is registered in the Folio account of the hive, where the monarch surveys 'the poor Mechanick porters, crowding in / Their heavy burthens at his narrow gate' (ll. 347–8). In a speech otherwise reported in the Quarto with exceptional fidelity, these two lines significantly disappear.

11

History and Ideology: 'Henry V'

JONATHAN DOLLIMORE and ALAN SINFIELD

Theories of the ultimate unity of both history and the human subject derive from a western philosophical tradition where, moreover, they have usually implied each other: the universal being seen as manifested through individual essences which in turn presuppose universals. Often unawares, idealist literary criticism has worked within or in the shadow of this tradition, as can be seen for example in its insistence that the universal truths of great literature are embodied in coherent and consistent 'characters'.[1]

The alternative to this is not to become fixated on its negation – universal chaos and subjective fragmentation – but rather to understand history and the human subject in terms of social and political process. Crucial for such an understanding is a materialist account of ideology.

Ideology is composed of those beliefs, practices and institutions which work to legitimate the social order – especially by the process of representing sectional or class interests as universal ones.[2] This process presupposes that there are others, subordinate classes, who far from sharing the interests of the dominant class are in fact being exploited by that class. This is one reason why the dominant tend not only to 'speak for' subordinate classes but actively to repress them as well. This repression operates coercively but also ideologically (the two are in practice inseparable). So for example at the same time that the Elizabethan ruling fraction claimed to lead and speak for all, it persecuted those who did not fit in, even blaming them for the social instability which originated in its own policies. This is an instance of a process of displacement crucial then (and since) in the formation of dominant identities – class, cultural, racial and sexual.

Ideology is not just a set of ideas, it is material practice, woven into the fabric of everyday life. At the same time, the dominant ideology is realised specifically through the institutions of education, the family, the law, religion, journalism and culture. In the Elizabethan state all these institutions worked to achieve ideological unity – not always successfully, for conflicts and contradictions remained visible at all levels, even within the dominant class fraction and its institutions. The theatre was monitored closely by the state – both companies and plays had to be licensed – and yet its institutional position was complex. On the one hand, it was sometimes summoned to perform at Court and as such may seem a direct extension of royal power;[3] on the other hand, it was the mode of cultural production in which market forces were strongest, and as such it was especially exposed to the influence of subordinate and emergent classes. We should not, therefore, expect any straightforward relationship between plays and ideology: on the contrary, it is even likely that the topics which engaged writers and audiences alike were those where ideology was under strain. We will take as an instance for study *Henry V*, and it will appear that even in this play, which is often assumed to be the one where Shakespeare is closest to state propaganda, the construction of ideology is complex – even as it consolidates, it betrays inherent instability.

The principal strategy of ideology is to legitimate inequality and exploitation by representing the social order which perpetuates these things as immutable and unalterable – as decreed by God or simply natural. Since the Elizabethan period the ideological appeal to God has tended to give way to the equally powerful appeal to the natural. But in the earlier period both were crucial: the laws of degree and order inferred from nature were further construed as having been put there by God. One religious vision represented ultimate reality in terms of unity and stasis: human endeavour, governed by the laws of change and occupying the material domain, is ever thwarted in its aspiration, ever haunted by its loss of an absolute which can only be regained in transcendence, the move through death to eternal rest, to an ultimate unity inseparable from a full stasis, 'when no more *Change* shall be' and 'all shall rest eternally' (Spenser, *The Faerie Queene*, VII, ii). This metaphysical vision has its political uses, especially when aiding the process of subjection by encouraging renunciation of the material world and a disregard of its social aspects such that oppression is experienced as a fate rather than an alterable condition. Protestantism tended to encourage engagement in the world rather than withdrawal from it; most of the *The Faerie Queene* is about the urgent questing of knights and ladies. The theological underpinning of this activist religion was the doctrine of callings: 'God bestows his gifts upon us . . . that they might be employed in his service and to his glory, and that in this life.'[4] This doctrine legitimated the expansive assertiveness of a social order which was bringing much of Britain under centralised control, colonising parts of the New World and trading vigorously with most of the Old, and which was to experience revolutionary changes. At the same time, acquiescence in an unjust social order (like that encouraged by a fatalistic metaphysic of stasis) seemed to be effected, though less securely, by an insistence that 'whatsoever any man enterpriseth or doth, either in word or deed, he must do it by virtue of his calling, and he must keep himself within the compass, limits or precincts thereof'.[5] This ideology was none the less metaphysical.

Such an activist ideology is obviously appropriate for the legitimation of warfare, and so we find it offered by the Archbishop of Canterbury in *Henry V* – as the Earl of Essex set off for Ireland in 1599 Lancelot Andrewes assured the Queen in a sermon that it was 'a war sanctified'.[6] In the honeybees speech human endeavour is not denigrated but harnessed in an imaginary unity quite different from that afforded by stasis: 'So may a thousand actions, once afoot, / End in one purpose' (I.ii.211–12). Like so many political ideologies, this one shares something essential with the overtly religious metaphysic it appears to replace, namely a teleological explanation of its own image of legitimate power – that is, an explanation which is justified through the assertion that such power derives from an inherent natural and human order encoded by God. Thus the 'one purpose' derives from an order rooted in 'a rule in nature' (I.ii.188), itself a manifestation of 'heavenly' creation. God's regulative structuring of the universe. What this inherent structure guarantees above all is, predictably, obedience:

> Therefore doth heaven divide
> The state of man in divers functions,
> Setting endeavour in continual motion;
> To which is fixed, as an aim or butt,
> Obedience.
>
> (I.ii.183–7)

And what in turn underpins obedience is the idea of one's job or calling – in effect one's bee-like *function* – as following naturally from a God-given identity: soldiers,

> armed in their stings,
> Make boot upon the summer's velvet buds;
> Which pillage they with merry march bring home
> To the tent-royal of their emperor.
>   (I.ii.193–6)

The activist ideology thus displaces the emphasis on stasis yet remains thoroughly metaphysical none the less. More generally: in this period, perhaps more than any since, we can see a secular appropriation of theological categories to the extent that it may be argued that Reformation theology actually contributed to secularisation;[7] nevertheless, it was an appropriation which depended upon continuities, the most important of which, in ideological legitimation, is this appeal to teleology.

Not only the justification of the war but, more specifically, the heroic representation of Henry, works in such terms. His is a power rooted in nature – blood, lineage and breeding: 'The blood and courage that renowned them / Runs in your veins' (I.ii.118–19) – but also deriving ultimately from God's law as it is encoded in nature and, by extension, society: France belongs to him 'by gift of heaven, / By law of nature and of nations' (II.iv.79–80). Conversely the French king's power is construed in terms of 'borrow'd glories', 'custom' and 'mettle . . . bred out' (II.iv.79, 83; III.v.29). With this theory of legitimate versus illegitimate power the responsibility for aggression is displaced onto its victims. Thus does war find its rationale, injustice its justification.

There are two levels of disturbance in the state and the ideology which legitimates it: contradiction and conflict.[8] Contradiction is the more fundamental, in the sense of being intrinsic to the social process as a whole – when for example the dominant order negates what it needs or, more generally, in perpetuating itself produces also its own negation. Thus, for example, in the seventeenth century monarchy legitimates itself in terms of religious attitudes which themselves come to afford a justification for opposition to monarchy. We shall be observing contradiction mainly as it manifests itself in the attempts of ideology to contain it. Conflict occurs between opposed interests, either as a state of disequilibrium or as active struggle; it occurs along the structural fault lines produced by contradictions.

Ideology has always been challenged, not least by the exploited themselves, who have resisted its oppressive construction of them and its mystification of their disadvantaged social position. One concern of a materialist criticism is with the history of such resistance, with the attempt to recover the voices and cultures of the repressed and marginalised in history and writing. Moreover, ideology is destabilised not only from below, but by antagonisms within and among the dominant class or class fraction (high, as opposed to popular, literature will often manifest this kind of destabilisation). Whereas idealist literary criticism has tended to emphasise the transcendence of conflict and contradiction, materialist criticism seeks to stay with them, wanting to understand them better.

Ideologies which represent society as a spurious unity must of necessity also efface conflict and contradiction. How successful they are in achieving this depends on a range of complex and interrelated factors, only a few of which we have space to identify here. One such will be the relative strength of emergent, subordinate and oppositional elements within society.[9] The endless process of contest and negotiation between these elements and the dominant culture is often overlooked in the use of some structuralist perspectives within cultural analysis.

One other factor which militates against the success of ideological misrepresentation involves a contradiction fundamental to ideology itself (and this will prove specially relevant to *Henry V*): the more ideology (necessarily) engages with the conflict and contradiction which it is its *raison d'être* to occlude, the more it becomes susceptible to incorporating them within itself. It faces the contradictory situation whereby to silence dissent one must give it a voice, to misrepresent it one must first present it.

These factors make for an inconsistency and indeterminacy in the representation of ideological harmony in writing: the divergencies have to be included if the insistence on unity is to have any purchase, yet at the same time their inclusion invites sceptical interrogation of the ideological appearance of unity, of the effacements of actual conflict. There may be no way of resolving whether one, or which one, of these tendencies (unity versus divergencies) overrides the other in a particular play, but in a sense it does not matter: there is here an indeterminacy which alerts us to the complex but always significant process of theatrical representation and, through that, of political and social process.

*

It is easy for us to assume, reading *Henry V*, that foreign war was a straightforward ground upon which to establish and celebrate national unity. In one sense this is so and it is the basic concern of the play. But in practice foreign war was the site of competing interests, material and ideological, and the assumption that the nation must unite against a common foe was shot through with conflict and contradiction. This was equally true for the hegemonic class fraction, though it was they who needed, urgently, to deny divisions and insist that everyone's purpose was the same. Queen Elizabeth feared foreign war because it was risky and expensive and threatened to disturb the fragile balance on which her power was founded. Members of the Privy Council favoured it – in some cases because it would strengthen their faction (puritans continually urged military support for continental protestants), in other cases because it would enhance their personal, military and hence political power. The Church resented the fact that it was expected to help finance foreign wars; but in 1588 Archbishop Whitgift encouraged his colleagues to contribute generously towards resistance to the Armada on the grounds – just as in *Henry V* – that it would head off criticism of the Church's wealth.[10]

For the lower orders, war meant increased taxation, which caused both hardship and resentment, as Francis Bacon testified in Parliament in 1593.[11] On the other hand war profited some people, though in ways which hardly inspired national unity. Some officers took money in return for discharging mustered men and enlisting others instead – Essex complained in Star Chamber in 1596 that 'the liege and free people of this realm are sold like cattle in a market'.[12] In 1589 Sir John Smith overheard two gentlemen joking that the recent military expedition against Spain 'would be worth unto one of them above a thousand marks and to the other above £400 . . . by the death of so many of their tenants that died in the journey: that the new fines for other lives would be worth that or more'.[13] War, in these aspects, must have tended to discredit ideas of shared national purpose. Indeed, there are a number of reports of mutinous individuals asserting that poor people would do better under the King of Spain.[14] This desperate inversion, whereby the demonised other of state propaganda was perceived as preferable, indicates the difficulty people have in envisaging alternatives to the existing power structure.

In fact, *Henry V* is only in one sense 'about' national unity: its obsessive preoccupation is insurrection. The King is faced with actual or threatened insurrection from almost every quarter: the Church, 'treacherous' fractions within the ruling class, slanderous subjects, and soldiers who undermine the war effort, either by exploiting it or by sceptically interrogating the King's motives. All these areas of possible resistance in the play had their counterparts in Elizabethan England and the play seems, in one aspect, committed to the aesthetic colonisation of such elements in Elizabethan culture; systematically, antagonism is reworked as subordination or supportive alignment. It is not so much that these antagonisms are openly defeated but rather that they are represented as inherently submissive. Thus the Irish, Welsh and Scottish soldiers manifest not their countries' centrifugal relationship to England but an ideal subservience of margin to centre. Others in the play are seen to renounce resistance in favour of submission. Perhaps the most interesting instance of this is the full and public repentance of the traitors, Cambridge, Grey and Scroop. Personal confession becomes simultaneously a public acknowledgement of the rightness of that which was challenged. It is of course one of the most authoritative ideological legitimations available to the powerful: to be sincerely validated by former opponents – especially when their confessional self-abasement is in excess of what might be expected from the terms of their defeat.

Nevertheless, we should not assume inevitable success for such strategies of containment; otherwise how could there have been Catholic recusants, the Essex rebellion, enclosure riots? *Henry V* belongs to a period in which the ideological dimension of authority – that which helps effect the internalisation rather than simply the coercion of obedience – is recognised as imperative and yet, by that self-same recognition, rendered vulnerable to demystification. For example, the very thought that the actual purpose of the war might be to distract from troubles at home would tend to undermine the purposed effect. The thought is voiced twice in *II Henry IV*: it is part of the advice given to Hal by his father (IV.v.212–15) and John of Lancaster envisages it in the final speech. It is suppressed in *Henry V* – yet it twice surfaces obliquely (II.i.90–2; IV.i.228–9).

At the height of his own programme of self-legitimation Henry 'privately' declares his awareness of the ideological role of 'ceremony' (IV.i.242–5). In the same soliloquy Henry speaks his fear of deceptive obedience – masking actual antagonism. It is a problem of rule which the play represses and resolves and yet reintroduces here in a half-rationalised form, as the 'hard condition! / Twin-born with greatness' is presented initially as the sheer burden of responsibility carried by the ruler, the loneliness of office, but then as a particular kind of fear. As the soliloquy develops its sub-text comes to the fore, and it is the same sub-text as that in the confrontation with Bates and Williams: the possibility, the danger of subjects who disobey. What really torments Henry is the inability to ensure obedience. His 'greatness' is 'subject to the breath / Of every fool', 'instead of homage sweet' he experiences 'poison'd flattery', and although he can coerce the beggar's knee he cannot fully control it (IV.i.240–1, 256–7). Not surprisingly, he has bad dreams. The implication is that subjects are to be envied not because, as Henry suggests, they are more happy in fearing than (like him) being feared, but almost the reverse: because as subjects they cannot suffer the king's fear of being disobeyed and opposed. Henry indicates a paradox of power only to misrecognise its force by mystifying both kingship and subjection. His problem is structural, since the same ceremonies or role-playing which constitute kingship are the means by which real antagonisms can masquerade as obedience – 'poison'd flattery'. Hence, perhaps, the slippage at the end of this speech from relatively cool analysis of the situation of the labouring person (referred to initially as 'private men', lines 243–4) into an attack on him or her as 'wretched slave . . . vacant mind . . . like a lackey' (274–9), and finally 'slave' of 'gross brain' (287–8).

The play circles obsessively around the inseparable issues of unity and division, inclusion and exclusion. Before Agincourt the idea of idle and implicitly disaffected people at home is raised (IV.iii.16–18), but this is converted into a pretext for the King to insist upon his army as a 'band of brothers' (IV.iii.60). Conversely, unity of purpose may be alleged and then undercut. The Act III Chorus asks:

> who is he, whose chin is but enrich'd
> With one appearing hair, that will not follow
> These cull'd and choice-drawn cavaliers to France?
> (ll. 22–4)

But within fifty lines Nym, the Boy and Pistol are wishing they were in London.

However, the threat of disunity did not involve only the common people. That the king and the aristocracy have more interest in foreign wars and in the area of 'England' produced by them than do the common people is easy enough for us to see now. But such a straightforward polarisation does not yield an adequate account of the divergent discourses which inform *Henry V*; on the contrary, it accepts uncritically a principal proposition of Elizabethan state ideology, namely that the ruling class was coherent and unified in its purposes, a proposition necessary to the idea that the state could be relied upon to secure the peace of all its subjects. Evidence to the contrary was dangerous, helping to provoke the thought that most violence stemmed from the imposition of 'order' rather than its lack. In practice, however, power was not coherently distributed. The Elizabethan state was in transition from a feudal to a bourgeois structure, and this had entailed and was to entail considerable violent disruption.[15] Whilst the aristocracy helped to sponsor the ideology of the monarch's supreme authority, it actually retained considerable power itself and the power of the crown probably decreased during Elizabeth's reign.[16] Elizabeth could maintain her position only through political adroitness, patronage and force – and all these, the latter especially, could be exercised only by and through the aristocracy itself. Elizabeth could oppose the Earl of Leicester if supported by Burghley, or vice versa, but she could not for long oppose them both. After the death of Leicester in 1589 the power struggle was not so symmetrical. The rise of the youthful, charismatic and militarily impressive Earl of Essex introduced a new element: he rivalled the Queen herself, as Burghley and Leicester never did. The more service, especially military, Essex performed, the more he established a rival power base, and Elizabeth did not care for it.[17] The Irish expedition was make or break for both; Essex would be away from court and vulnerable to schemes against him, but were he to return with spectacular success he would be unstoppable. In the event he was not successful, and thus found himself pushed into a corner where he could see no alternative but direct revolt. The exuberance of *Henry V* leads most commentators to link it with the early stages of the Irish expedition when the successful return could be anticipated; the Chorus of Act V (ll. 29–35) actually compared Henry's return to England with it and there are indeed parallels between Henry and Essex. Both left dangers at home when they went to war, besieged Rouen, sacked foreign towns, were taken to represent a revival of chivalry and national purpose; Essex was already associated with Bolingbroke.[18] The crucial difference of course is that Essex is not the monarch. That is why Henry must be welcomed 'much more, and much more cause'. Henry is both general and ruler, and therefore the structural problem of the over-mighty subject – the repeated theme of other plays – does not present itself.

The existence of such a profound structural flaw at the centre of state power affords a cardinal exemplification of why the representation of ideological containment so often proves complex and ambiguous. The pyramid of the Tudor Myth was under strain at its very apex, for the legitimate ruler was not the most powerful person – the same issue promotes the action of *Henry VI*, *Macbeth* and many other plays. *Henry V* was a powerful Elizabethan fantasy simply because it represented a single source of power in the state. Nothing is allowed to compete with the authority of the King. The noblemen are so lacking in distinctive qualities that they are commonly re-organised or cut in production. And the point where the issue might have presented itself – the plot of Cambridge, Scroop and Grey – is hardly allowed its actual historical significance. Holinshed makes it plain that Cambridge's purpose in conspiring against Henry was to exalt to the crown Edmund Mortimer and after that himself and his family; that he did not confess this because he did not want to incriminate Mortimer and cut off this possibility; that Cambridge's son was to claim the crown in the time of Henry VI and that this Yorkist claim was eventually successful.[19] Cambridge makes only an oblique reference to this structural fault in the state (II.ii.155–7). The main impression we receive is that the conspirators were motivated by greed and incomprehensible evil – according to Henry, like 'Another fall of man' (l. 142). Such arbitrary and general 'human' failings obscure the kind of instability in the ruling fraction to which the concurrent career of Essex bore witness.

That the idea of a single source of power in the state was, if not a fantasy, a rare and precarious achievement is admitted in the Epilogue. The infant Henry VI succeeded, 'Whose state so many had the managing, / That they lost France and made his England bleed' (ll. 11–12). Many managers disperse power and unity falls apart.

The aristocracy is the most briskly handled of the various agents of disruption. Whether this is because it was the least or the most problematic is a fascinating question, but one upon which we can only speculate. *Henry V* far more readily admits of problems in the role of the Church, though the main effect of this is again to concentrate power, now spiritual as well as secular, upon the King. The Archbishop's readiness to use the claim to France to protect the Church's interests tends to discredit him and the Church, but this allows the King to appropriate their spiritual authority. Thus power which, in actuality, was distributed unevenly across an unstable fraction of the hegemonic class is drawn into the person of the monarch; he becomes its sole source of expression, the site and guarantee of ideological unity. This is a crucial effect of a process already identified, namely a complex, secular appropriation of the religious metaphysics in the legitimation of war:

> his wildness, mortified in him,
> Seem'd to die too; yea, at that very moment,
> Consideration like an angel came,
> And whipp'd th'offending Adam out of him,
>
> (I.i.26–9)

The language is that of the Prayer Book service of Baptism: Henry takes over from the Church sacramental imagery which seems to transcend all worldly authority. Thus he is protected at once from any imputation of irreligion which might seem to arise from a preparedness to seize Church property, and he becomes the representative of the personal piety which adhered only doubtfully to the bishops. In him contradictions are resolved or transcended. This presumably is why the clerics are not needed after Act I. From the beginning and increasingly, Henry's appeals to God, culminating in the insistence that 'God fought for us' (IV.viii.122), enact the priestly role as Andrews in his sermon on the Essex expedition identified it. He observed that in successful Old Testament wars 'a captain and a Prophet sorted together':[20] the two roles are drawn into the single figure of Henry V.

On the eve of Agincourt Henry gives spiritual counsel to his soldiers:

> Every subject's duty is the king's; but every subject's soul is his own. Therefore should every soldier in the wars do as every sick man in his bed, wash every mote out of his conscience; and dying so, death is to him advantage; or not dying, the time was blessedly lost wherein such preparation was gained.
>
> (IV.i.182–9)

It is the high point of Henry's priestly function, the point at which the legitimation which religion could afford to the state is most fully incorporated into a single ideological effect. Yet Henry is defensive and troubled by the exchange and Williams is not satisfied. What has happened, surely, is that the concentration of ideological power upon Henry seems to amount also to concentration of responsibility:

> Upon the king! let us our lives, our souls,
> Our debts, our careful wives,
> Our children, and our sins lay on the king!
>
> (IV.i.236–8)

In the play the drive for ideological coherence has systematically displaced the roles of Church and aristocracy and nothing seems to stand between the king and the souls of his subjects who are to die in battle.

The issue is handled in two main ways by Henry. First, he reduces it to the question of soldiers who have committed serious crimes, for which Henry can then refuse responsibility; initial questions about widows and orphans (IV.i.141–3) slip out of sight. Second, the distinction between him and his subjects is effaced by his insistence that 'the king is but a man' (IV.i.101–2) and that he himself gains nothing, indeed loses from the power structure:

> O ceremony, show me but thy worth!
> What is thy soul of adoration?
> Art thou aught else but place, degree, and form,
> Creating awe and fear in other men?
> Wherein thou art less happy, being fear'd,
> Than they in fearing.
>
> (IV.i.250–5)

Here the king himself is collapsed, syntactically, into the mere shows of ceremony: 'thou' in the third line quoted refers to 'ceremony', in the fifth to Henry, and he slips from one to the other without the customary formal signals.[21] The effect, if we credit it, is to leave 'place, degree, and form', 'awe and fear' standing without the apparent support of human agency: Henry engrosses in himself the ideological coherence of the state and then, asked to take responsibility for the likely defeat of Agincourt, claims to be an effect of the structure which he seemed to guarantee.

The Act II Chorus wants to proclaim unity: 'honour's thought / Reigns solely in the breast of every man' – but is rapidly obliged to admit treachery: 'O England! . . . Were all thy children kind and natural!' (ll. 3–4, 16, 19). The following scene is not however about Cambridge, Scroop and Grey, but Nym, Bardolph and Pistol. This disputatious faction proves much more difficult to incorporate than the rebel nobility. Increasingly, since *II Henry IV*, sympathy for these characters has been withdrawn; from this point on there seems to be nothing positive about them. It is here that Fluellen enters, offering an alternative to Falstaff among the lesser gentry and an issue – the control of England over the British Isles – easier to cope with. Fluellen may be funny, old-fashioned and pedantic, but he is totally committed to the King and his purposes, as the King recognises (IV.i.83–4). The low characters are condemned not only to death but to exclusion from national unity; it is as if they have had their chance and squandered it. Gower describes Pistol as 'a gull, a fool, a rogue, that now and then goes to the wars to grace himself at his return into London under the form of a soldier' (III.vi.68–70) and Bardolph endorses the identification:

> Well, bawd I'll turn,
> And something lean to cut-purse of quick hand.
> To England will I steal, and there I'll steal:
> And patches will I get unto these cudgell'd scars,
> And swear I got them in the Gallia wars.
>   (V.i.89–93)

This group, disbanded soldiers, was a persistent danger and worry in Elizabethan society; William Hunt suggests that 'embittered veterans and deserters brought back from the Low Countries the incendiary myth of an army of avengers'.[22] Two proclamations were issued in 1589 against 'the great outrages that have been, and are daily committed by soldiers, mariners and others that pretend to have served as soldiers, upon her Highness' good and loving subjects'; martial law was instigated to hang offenders.[23] The Elizabethan state was prepared to exclude from its tender care such persons, perhaps exemplifying the principle whereby dominant groups identify themselves by excluding or expelling others; not only are the virtues necessary for membership identified by contrast with the vices of the excluded, but, often, the vices of the dominant are displaced onto the excluded. That Pistol has this degree of significance is suggested by the play's reluctance to let him go. He is made to discredit himself once more at Agincourt (IV.iv) and in his final confrontation with Fluellen he is clumsily humiliated (V.i).

Despite the thorough dismissal of Bardolph, Nym and Pistol, *Henry V* does not leave the issue of lower-class disaffection. If those characters must be abandoned because unworthy or incapable of being incorporated into the unified nation, yet others must be introduced who will prove more tractable.

The issue of the English domination of Wales, Scotland and Ireland appears in the play to be more containable, though over the centuries it may have caused more suffering and injustice than the subjection of the lower classes. The scene of the four captains (III.iii) seems to effect an effortless incorporation, one in which, as Philip Edwards has pointed out, the Irish Macmorris is even made to protest that he does not belong to a distinct nation.[24] The English captain, of course, is more sensible than the others. Most attention is given to Fluellen – Wales must have seemed the most tractable issue, for it had been annexed in 1536 and the English church and legal system had been imposed; Henry V and the Tudors could indeed claim to be Welsh. The jokes about the way Fluellen pronounces the English language are, apparently, for the Elizabethan audience and many since, an adequate way of handling the repression of the Welsh language and culture; the annexation of 1536 permitted only English speakers to hold administrative office in Wales.[25]

Ireland was the great problem – the one Essex was supposed to resolve. The population was overwhelmingly Catholic and liable to support a continental invader, and resistance to English rule proved irrepressible, despite or more probably because of the many atrocities committed against the people – such as the slaughter of all the six hundred inhabitants of Rathlin Island by John Norris and Francis Drake in 1575. The assumption that the Irish were a barbarous and inferior people was so ingrained in Elizabethan England that it seemed only a natural duty to subdue them and destroy their culture.[26] Indeed, at one level their ideological containment was continuous with the handling of the disaffected lower-class outgroup (a proclamation of 1594 dealt together with vagabonds who begged 'upon pretense of service in the wars without relief' and 'men of Ireland that have these late years unnaturally served as rebels against her majesty's forces beyond the seas').[27] But much more was at stake in the persistent Irish challenge to the power of the Elizabethan state, and it should be related to the most strenuous challenge to the English unity in *Henry V*: like Philip Edwards, we see the attempt to conquer France and the union in peace at the end of the play as a representation of the attempt to conquer Ireland and the hoped-for unity of Britain.[28] The play offers a displaced, imaginary resolution of one of the state's most intractable problems.

Indeed, the play is fascinating precisely to the extent that it is implicated in and can be read to disclose both the struggles of its own historical moment and their ideological representation. To see the play in such terms is not at all to conclude that it is merely a deluded and mystifying ideological fantasy. We observed that the King finally has difficulty, on the eve of Agincourt, in sustaining the responsibility which seems to belong with the ideological power which he has engrossed to himself: thus the fantasy of establishing ideological unity in the sole figure of the monarch arrives at an impasse which it can handle only with difficulty. As we have argued, strategies of containment presuppose centrifugal tendencies, and how far any particular instance carries conviction cannot be resolved by literary criticism. If we attend to the play's different levels of signification rather than its implied containments, it becomes apparent that the question of conviction is finally a question about the diverse conditions of reception. How far the King's argument is to be credited is a standard question for conventional criticism, but a materialist analysis takes several steps back and reads real historical conflict in and through his ambiguities. Relative to such conflict, the question of Henry's integrity becomes less interesting.

   If *Henry V* represents the fantasy of a successful Irish campaign it also offers, from the very perspective of that project, a disquietingly excessive evocation of suffering and violence:

> If not, why, in a moment look to see
> The blind and bloody soldier with foul hand
> Defile the locks of your shrill-shrieking daughters;
> Your fathers taken by the silver beards,
> And their most reverend heads dash'd to the walls;
> Your naked infants spitted upon pikes,
> Whiles the mad mothers with their howls confus'd
> Do break the clouds, as did the wives of Jewry
> At Herod's bloody-hunting slaughtermen.
>   (III.iii.33–41)

This reversal of Henry's special claim to Christian imagery – now he is Herod against the Innocents – is not actualised in the play (contrary to the sources, in which Harfleur is sacked), but its rhetoric is powerful and at Agincourt the prisoners are killed (IV.vi.37). Here and elsewhere, the play dwells upon imagery of slaughter to a degree which disrupts the harmonious unity towards which ideology strives. So it was with Ireland: even those who, like the poet Edmund Spenser, defended torture and murder expressed compunction at the effects of English policy:

> they were brought to such wretchedness, as that any stony heart would have rued the same. Out of every corner of the woods and glens

they came creeping forth upon their hands, for their legs would not bear them. . . . They did eat of the dead carions . . .[29]

The human cost of imperial ambition protruded through even its ideological justifications, and the government felt obliged to proclaim that its intention was not 'an utter extirpation and rooting out of that nation'.[30] The claim of the state to be the necessary agent of peace and justice was manifestly contradicted. Ireland was, and remains, its bad conscience.

Henry V can be read to reveal not only the strategies of power but also the anxieties informing both them and their ideological representation. In the Elizabethan theatre to foreground and even to promote such representations was not to foreclose on their interrogation. We might conclude from this that Shakespeare was indeed wonderfully impartial on the question of politics; alternatively, we might conclude that the ideology which saturates his texts, and their location in history, are the most interesting things about them.

From John Drakakis (ed.), *Alternative Shakespeares* (London, 1985), pp. 210–27.

NOTES

[Jonathan Dollimore and Alan Sinfield's essay is a slightly cut version of their 'History and Ideology: the instance of *Henry V*', in *Alternative Shakespeares*, an important collection of radical essays on Shakespeare. It is included here as an example of the kind of politically engaged and theoretical approach characterising the 'cultural materialism' which they contributed very largely to establishing in Britain, especially through their edited anthology *Political Shakespeare* (Manchester, 1985). Ed.]

1. Here we are primarily concerned to offer a critique of the ideology which falsely unifies history; for a similar and fuller critique of subjectivity, see Jonathan Dollimore, *Radical Tragedy: Religion, Ideology and Power in the Drama of Shakespeare and his Contemporaries* (Brighton and Chicago, 1984), esp. chapters 1, 10 and 16.

2. A materialist criticism will be concerned with aspects of ideology additional to those dealt with here and our emphasis on ideology as legitimation, though crucial, should not be taken as an exhaustive definition of the concept. For a fuller discussion of ideology in the period, see Dollimore, *Radical Tragedy*, esp. chapters 1 and 16; and, more generally, Janet Wolff, *The Social Production of Art* (London, 1981).

3. See Stephen Orgel, 'Making Greatness Familiar', in Stephen Greenblatt, *The Power of Forms in the English Renaissance* (Oklahoma, 1982).

4. William Perkins, *Works*, ed. Ian Breward (Abingdon, 1970), p. 150. See Alan Sinfield, *Literature in Protestant England, 1560–1660* (London and Totowa, NJ, 1983), pp. 37–8, 134–5.

5. Perkins, *Works*, p. 449.

6. Lancelot Andrewes, *Works*, 11 vols (Oxford, 1841), 1, p. 325.

7. See Sinfield, *Literature in Protestant England, 1560–1660*, chapter 7.

8. This distinction derives from (but also differs from) Anthony Giddens, *A Contemporary Critique of Historical Materialism*, vol. 1 (London, 1981), pp. 231–7.

9. See Raymond Williams, *Marxism and Literature* (London, 1977), pp. 121–7.

10. John Strype, *The Life and Acts of John Whitgift*, vol. 1 (London, 1822), pp. 524–6. See further, Felicity Heal, *Of Prelates and Princes* (Cambridge, 1980).

11. J. E. Neale, *Elizabeth I and her Parliaments, 1584–1601* (London, 1957), pp. 309–10.

12. Lucy De Bruyn, *Mob Rule and Riots* (London, 1981), p. 36.

13. William Hunt, *The Puritan Movement* (Cambridge, Mass. and London, 1983), p. 33.

14. Ibid., pp. 60–1.

15. Perry Anderson, *Lineages of the Absolutist State* (London, 1974), pp. 16–59, 113–42.

16. W. T. MacCaffrey, 'England, the Crown and the New Aristocracy, 1540–1600', *Past and Present*, 30, 52–64.

17. G. B. Harrison, *The Life and Death of Robert Devereux, Earl of Essex* (London, 1937), p. 102 and chapters 9–12.

18. Ibid., pp. 214–15.

19. Geoffrey Bullough, *Narrative and Dramatic Sources of Shakespeare*, vol. 4 (London, 1966), p. 386.

20. Andrewes, *Works*, 1, p. 326.

21. See Gary Taylor's note on IV.i.250–5 in his edition of *Henry V* (London, 1982).

22. Hunt, *The Puritan Movement*, p. 60; see for an instance p. 50; and also De Bruyn, *Mob Rule and Riots*, pp. 26–62.

23. De Bruyn, *Mob Rule and Riots*, p. 62.

24. Philip Edwards, *Threshold of a Nation* (Cambridge, 1979), pp. 75–8, referring to *Henry V*, III.ii.125–7. Edwards shows how an Irish captain who had been in Essex's army made a similar protest.

25. David Williams, *A History of Modern Wales*, 2nd edition (London 1977), chapter 3.

26. David Beers Quinn, *The Elizabethans and the Irish* (Ithaca, NY, 1966), chapters 4, 5 and 7. See also Edwards, *Threshold of a Nation*.

27. Paul L. Hughes and James F. Larkin, *Tudor Royal Proclamations*, 3 vols (New Haven, 1969), pp. 134–5.

28. Edward, *Threshold of a Nation*, pp. 74–86.

29. Edmund Spenser, *A View of the Present State of Ireland* (Oxford, 1970), p. 104.

30. Hughes and Larkin, *Tudor Royal Proclamations*, 3, p. 201.

Further Reading

A full range of current theoretical approaches to Shakespeare can be sampled in a number of useful critical anthologies: *Shakespeare and the Question of Theory*, ed. Patricia Parker and Geoffrey Hartman (New York and London: Methuen, 1985); *Political Shakespeare*, ed. Jonathan Dollimore and Alan Sinfield (Manchester: Manchester University Press, 1985); *Alternative Shakespeares*, ed. John Drakakis (London: Methuen, 1985); *Shakespeare Reproduced*, ed. Jean E. Howard and Marion F. O'Connor (London: Methuen, 1987); *The Shakespeare Myth*, ed. Graham Holderness (Manchester: Manchester University Press, 1988).

Additional suggestions for further reading are given below, essay by essay.

1

Various permutations of the 'Tillyard orthodoxy' established in E. M. W. Tillyard, *The Elizabethan World Picture* (London: Chatto & Windus, 1943), and *Shakespeare's History Plays* (London: Chatto & Windus, 1944) can be found exemplified in G. Wilson Knight, *The Olive and the Sword* (London: Oxford University Press, 1944); Lily B. Campbell, *Shakespeare's Histories: Mirrors of Elizabethan Policy* (San Marino: Huntingdon Library, 1947); D. A. Traversi, *Shakespeare from 'Richard II' to 'Henry V'* (London: Hollis & Carter, 1957); M. M. Reese, *The Cease of Majesty: A Study of Shakespeare's History Plays* (London: Edward Arnold, 1961); and J. Dover Wilson, *The Fortunes of Falstaff* (Cambridge: Cambridge University Press, 1964). Well before the advent of more self-consciously theoretical, political and poststructuralist critical methodologies, this orthodoxy was questioned across a broad range of literary and historical positions (including that of Robert Ornstein): see for example Irving Ribner, *The English History Play in the Age of Shakespeare* (Princeton, NJ: Princeton University Press, 1957); A. P. Rossiter, *Angel with Horns and other Shakespeare Lectures*, ed. Graham Storey (London: Longmans Green, 1961); Wilbur Sanders, *The Dramatist and the Received Idea: Studies in the Plays of Marlowe and Shakespeare* (Cambridge: Cambridge University Press, 1968); Moody E. Prior, *The Drama of Power* (Evanston, Illinois: Northwestern University Press, 1973). An extensive theoretical discussion of the place of Tillyard's work in intellectual history can be found in Hugh Grady, *The Modernist Shakespeare* (Oxford: Clarendon Press, 1991). Studies of sources and historiographical contexts which also entail a critique of the Tillyard position include Henry Ansagar Kelly, *Divine Providence in the England of Shakespeare's Histories* (Cambridge, Mass.: Harvard University Press, 1970); Peter Saccio, *Shakespeare's English Kings: History, Chronicle and Drama* (New York, 1977); and Graham Holderness, *Shakespeare Recycled: The Making of History* (Hemel Hempstead: Harvester-Wheatsheaf, 1991).

2

Leonard Tennenhouse's work can be read alongside Stephen Greenblatt's essay on the second tetralogy, 'Invisible Bullets', in *Shakespearean Negotiations: The Circulation of Social Energy in Renaissance England* (London: Oxford University Press, 1988). Greenblatt also discusses New Historicism in his 'Introduction' to *Learning to Curse: Essays in Early Modern Culture* (London: Routledge, 1990), pp. 1–15. For other basic New Historicist texts see Louis Adrian Montrose, 'Renaissance Literary Studies and the Subject of History', *English Literary Renaissance*, 16 (1986), 5–12, and 'Of Gentlemen and Shepherds: the Politics of Elizabethan Pastoral Form', *English Literary History*, 50:3 (1983), 415–59; Jonathan Goldberg, *James I and the Politics of Literature: Jonson, Shakespeare, Donne and their Contemporaries* (Baltimore: Johns Hopkins University Press, 1983), and 'Shakespearean Inscriptions: the Voicing of Power', in *Shakespeare and the Question of Theory*, ed. Patricia Parker and Geoffrey Hartman (New York and London: Methuen, 1985); Stephen Orgel, *The Illusion of Power: political theatre in the English Renaissance* (Berkeley: University of California Press, 1975).

3

There is within contemporary feminist criticism both variety and diversity of critical approaches. The methodology employed by Linda Bamber and others has been criticised for 'essentialism' by Kathleen McKluskie in 'The Patriarchal Bard: feminist criticism and Shakespeare (*King Lear* and *Measure for Measure*)', in *Political Shakespeare*, ed. Jonathan Dollimore and Alan Sinfield (Manchester: Manchester University Press, 1985). Ann Thompson discusses this controversy in '"The warrant of womanhood": Shakespeare and feminist criticism', in *The Shakespeare Myth*, ed. Graham Holderness (Manchester: Manchester University Press, 1988). 'Positive' feminist readings of Shakespeare include Irene Dash, *Wooing, Wedding and Power* (New York: Columbia University Press, 1981), and Marianne Novy, *Love's Argument: Gender Relations in Shakespeare* (Chapel Hill, Indiana and London: University of North Carolina Press, 1984). More 'negative' readings include Peter Erickson, *Patriarchal Structures in Shakespeare's Drama* (Berkeley: University of California Press, 1985), and Kathleen McKluskie, *Renaissance Dramatists* (Hemel Hempstead: Harvester-Wheatsheaf, 1989). Feminist work which insists on the interpenetration of feminist theory and historical studies can be found in Juliet Dusinberre, *Shakespeare and the Nature of Women* (London: Macmillan, 1975); Lisa Jardine, *Still Harping on Daughters: Women and Drama in the Age of Shakespeare* (Brighton: Harvester-Wheatsheaf, 1983); Catherine Belsey, *The Subject of Tragedy: Identity and Difference in Renaissance Drama* (London: Methuen, 1985); *The Matter of Difference: Materialist Feminist Criticism of Shakespeare*, ed. Valerie Wayne (Hemel Hempstead: Harvester-Wheatsheaf, 1991). A useful general introduction to feminist theory and criticism is Toril Moi, *Sexual / Textual Politics: Feminist Literary Theory* (London: Methuen, 1985).

4

The synthesis of feminism and psychoanalysis represented by Coppélia Kahn can also be found in Jacqueline Rose, 'Sexuality in the Reading of Shakespeare', in *Alternative Shakespeares*, ed. John Drakakis (London: Methuen, 1985); and Joel Fineman, 'The Turn of the Shrew', in *Shakespeare and the Question of Theory*, ed. Patricia Parker and Geoffrey Hartman (New York and London: Methuen, 1985). Other examples, together with a range of feminist approaches, can be found in *The Woman's Part: Feminist Criticism of Shakespeare*, ed. C. R. S. Lenz, G. Greene and C. T. Neely (Urbana, Ill.: University of Illinois Press, 1980). A general anthology of psychoanalytic approaches can be found in *Representing Shakespeare: New Psychoanalytic Essays*, ed. Coppélia Kahn and Murray M. Schwarz (Baltimore: Johns Hopkins University Press, 1980).

5

The theoretical background to Robert Knapp's essay, in which 'poststructuralist' methods move closer to the principles of 'deconstruction', is to be found in such works as Paul de Man, *Blindness and Insight: Essays in the Rhetoric of Contemporary Criticism* (New York and London: Oxford University Press, 1971). This type of work points towards the influence of Jacques Derrida: see his *Of Grammatology*, trans. G. C. Spivak (Baltimore: Johns Hopkins University Press, 1976). Christopher Norris's *Deconstruction: Theory and Practice* (London: Methuen, 1982) is a useful introduction. There are few 'pure' examples of deconstructionist criticism: texts which display a strong influence include Jonathan Goldberg, *Voice Terminal Echo: Postmodernism and English Renaissance Texts* (New York and London: Methuen, 1986); and for a notable British example, see Malcolm Evans, *Signifying Nothing: Truth's True Contents in Shakespeare*, 2nd edition (Hemel Hempstead: Harvester-Wheatsheaf, 1989).

6

The volume from which Catherine Belsey's essay is taken, *Uses of History: Marxism, Postmodernism and the Renaissance*, ed. Francis Barker, Peter Hulme and Margaret Iverson (Manchester: Manchester University Press, 1991) contains a range of theoretical discussions about post-modernism.

The basic theoretical text is J.-F. Lyotard, *The Postmodern Condition: a Report on Knowledge*, trans. Geoff Bennington and Brian Massumi (Manchester: Manchester University Press, 1984). Important interventions into the debates between Marxism and post-modernism include Frederic Jameson, 'Postmodernism, or the Cultural Logic of Late Capitalism', *New Left Review*, 146 (1984), 53–92, and 'Postmodernism and Consumer Society', in *Postmodern Culture*, ed. Hal Foster (London: Pluto Press, 1985); and Terry Eagleton, 'Capitalism, Modernism and Postmodernism', *New Left Review*, 152 (1985), 60–73. For Marxism see Raymond Williams, *Marxism and Literature* (London: Oxford University Press, 1977).

7

For readings of Shakespeare with comparable approaches to language, see Terence Hawkes, *Shakespeare's Talking Animals* (London: Methuen, 1977); Joseph A. Porter, *The Drama of Speech Acts: Shakespeare's Lancastrian Tetralogy* (Berkeley: University of California Press, 1979). Harry J. Berger, Jr writes on the second tetralogy with a linguistic approach comparable with Calderwood's, in 'Psychoanalysing the Shakespeare Text', in *Shakespeare and the Question of Theory*, ed. Patricia Parker and Geoffrey Hartman (New York and London: Methuen, 1985). Such approaches were founded by Ferdinand de Saussure, *Course in General Linguistics*, trans. Wade Baskin (London, 1974). See also Terence Hawkes, *Structuralism and Semiotics* (London: Methuen, 1977) for an introduction to Saussure's work and influence.

8

The anthropological approach to Shakespeare is best exemplified by C. L. Barber, *Shakespeare's Festive Comedy: A Study of Dramatic Form and its Relation to Social Custom* (Princeton: Princeton University Press, 1959). See also his 'The Family in Shakespeare's development: tragedy and sacredness', in *Representing Shakespeare: New Psychoanalytic Essays*, ed. Coppélia Kahn and Murray M. Schwarz (Baltimore: Johns Hopkins University Press, 1980). An important text in this area is René Girard, *Violence and the Sacred* (Baltimore: Johns Hopkins University Press, 1979). For a view of the relations between drama and ritual very different from Cohen's, see Graham Holderness, 'Endgames', in Graham Holderness, Nick Potter and John Turner, *Shakespeare: Out of Court* (London: Macmillan, 1990), pp. 236–48.

9

For other discussions of carnival see Michael D. Bristol, *Carnival and Theatre: Plebian Culture and the Structure of Authority in Renaissance England* (London: Methuen, 1985), and Peter Stallybrass and Allon White, *The Politics and Poetics of Transgression* (London: Methuen, 1990). The basic theoretical text is Mikhail Bakhtin, *Rabelais and his World*, trans. Helen Iswolsky (Cambridge, Mass.: CIT Press, 1968).

10

Annabel Patterson's concern with the 'popular' in Shakespeare can be paralleled in Robert Weimann, *Shakespeare and the Popular Tradition in the Theatre*, trans. Robert Schwarz (Baltimore: Johns Hopkins University Press, 1978), and Kiernan Ryan, *Shakespeare* (Hemel Hempstead: Harvester-Wheatsheaf, 1989). The Quarto texts are currently available only in facsimile or variorum editions, or in the collection *Shakespeare's Plays in Quarto*, ed. Michael Allen and Kenneth Muir (Berkeley and Los Angeles: University of California Press, 1981). Harvester-Wheatsheaf will be publishing, under the series title *Shakespearean Originals*, new single editions of some Quarto texts, including *The Cronicle Historie of Henry the fift*, ed. Graham Holderness and Bryan Loughrey (Hemel Hempstead, 1992).

11

For other studies in ideology from analogous positions, see Jonathan Dollimore, *Radical Tragedy: Religion, Ideology and Power in the Drama of Shakespeare and his Contemporaries* (Brighton: Harvester-Wheatsheaf, 1984); Francis Barker, *The Tremulous Private Body: Essays in Subjection* (London: Methuen, 1984); and Catherine Belsey, *The Subject of Tragedy: Identity and Difference in Renaissance Drama* (London: Methuen, 1985).

Notes on Contributors

Linda Bamber is Associate Professor at Tufts University, and author of *Comic Women, Tragic Men: Gender and Genre in Shakespeare* (1982).

Catherine Belsey is Professor of English in the University of Wales. She is author of *Critical Practice* (1980), *The Subject of Tragedy: Identity and Difference in Renaissance Drama* (1985), *John Milton: Language, Gender, Power* (1988); and co-editor (with Jane Moore) of *The Feminist Reader: Essays in Gender and the Politics of Literary Criticism* (1989).

James L. Calderwood is Professor of English and Comparative Literature and Associate Dean of Humanities at the University of California, Irvine. He has published various books on Shakespeare, including *Metadrama in Shakespeare's 'Henriad'* (1979), *If It Were Done* (1986) and *Shakespeare and the Denial of Death* (1989).

Derek Cohen is Associate Professor, York University. He is author of *Shakespearean Motives* (1988), and co-editor (with Deborah Heller) of *Jewish Presences in English Literature* (1990).

Jonathan Dollimore is Reader in the School of English and American Studies, University of Sussex. He is author of *Radical Tragedy: Religion, Ideology and Power in the Drama of Shakespeare and his Contemporaries* (1984), and *Sexual Dissidence: Augustine to Wilde, Freud to Foucault* (1991); and co-editor (with Alan Sinfield) of *Political Shakespeare: New Essays in Cultural Materialism* (1985).

Graham Holderness is Professor of Humanities at Hatfield Polytechnic. His published books include *D. H. Lawrence: History, Ideology and Fiction* (1982), *Shakespeare's History* (1985), *Shakespeare in Performance: 'The Taming of the Shrew'* (1989) and *Shakespeare Recycled: The Making of Historical Drama* (1992); (as co-author) *Shakespeare: The Play of History* (1988) and *Shakespeare: Out of Court* (1990) (with John Turner and Nick Potter); and (as editor) *The Shakespeare Myth* (1988) and *The Politics of Theatre and Drama* (1991).

Coppélia Kahn is Professor of English at Brown University, author of *Man's Estate: Masculine Identity in Shakespeare* (1981), and co-editor (with Peter Erickson) of *Shakespeare's 'Rough Magic': Renaissance Essays in Honour of C. L. Barber* (1985).

Robert S. Knapp is Professor at Reed College, and author of *Shakespeare: The Theater and the Book* (1989).

Robert Ornstein is Oviatt Professor Emeritus at Case Western Reserve University. He has published many editions, essays, articles and critical books on Renaissance drama, including *The Moral Vision of Jacobean Tragedy* (1960), *A Kingdom for a Stage: The Achievement of Shakespeare's History Plays* (1972), and *Shakespeare's Comedies: From Romance Farce to Romantic Mystery* (1986).

Annabel Patterson is Professor of Literature and English at Duke University. She is author of *Hermogenes and the Renaissance* (1970), *Marvell and the Civic Crown* (1978), *Censorship and Interpretation* (1984), *Pastoral and Ideology* (1987), *Shakespeare and the Popular Voice* (1989) and *Fables of Power* (1991).

Alan Sinfield is Professor in the School of Cultural and Community Studies at the University of Sussex. He is author of *Literature in Protestant England 1560–1660* (1983), *Society and Literature 1945–70* (1983), and *Literature, Politics and Culture in Postwar Britain* (1989); and co-editor (with Jonathan Dollimore) of *Political Shakespeare: New Essays in Cultural Materialism* (1985).

Leonard Tennenhouse is Visiting Professor at the University of Minnesota. He is author of *Power on Display: The Politics of Shakespeare's Genres* (1986); editor of *The Practice of Psychoanalytic Criticism* (1976); co-editor (with Nancy Armstrong) of *The Violence of Representation: Studies in Literature and the History of Sexuality* (1989), and *The Ideology of Conduct: Essays on Literature and the History of Sexuality*; and has published numerous articles on Renaissance literature and critical theory.

Index